THE FATHERS
OF THE CHURCH

A NEW TRANSLATION

VOLUME 73

THE FATHERS
OF THE CHURCH

A NEW TRANSLATION

SAINT JOHN CHRYSOSTOM

APOLOGIST

Translated by

MARGARET A. SCHATKIN

PAUL W. HARKINS

THE CATHOLIC UNIVERSITY OF AMERICA PRESS
Washington, D.C.

Nihil obstat:
REVEREND HERMIGILD DRESSLER, O.F.M.
Censor Deputatus

Imprimatur:
REV. MSGR. JOHN F. DONOGHUE
Vicar General for the Archdiocese of Washington

October 31, 1983

The *nihil obstat* and *imprimatur* are official declarations that a book or pamphlet is free of doctrinal or moral error. No implication is contained therein that those who have granted the *nihil obstat* and the *imprimatur* agree with content opinions, or statements expressed.

LIBRARY OF CONGRESS CATALOGING IN PUBLICATION DATA

John Chrysostom, Saint, d. 407.
Apologist.

(Fathers of the church)
Translation of: Logos eis ton makarion Babylan, kai kata Ioulianou kai pros Hellēnas, and, Pros Hellēnas apodeixis hoti Theos estin ho Christos.
Bibliography: p.
Includes indexes.
Contents: Discourse on blessed Babylas, and against the Greeks—Demonstration against the pagans that Christ is God.
1. Jesus Christ—Divinity. 2. Apologetics—Early church, ca. 30-600. 3. Babylas, of Antioch, Saint.
I. John Chrysostom, Saint, d. 407. Pros Hellēnas apodeixis hoti Theos estin ho Christos. English. 1985. II. Title. III. Series.
BR60.F3J63   270 s   [239'.3]   84-21416
[BR65.C45]
ISBN 0-8132-0073-2

TO THE REVEREND DOCTOR
RUDOLPH E. ARBESMANN, O.S.A.
(1895–1982)

Professor Emeritus
Fordham University

CONTENTS

PREFACE

In March 1972 Doctor Margaret Schatkin offered to the late Doctor Bernard Peebles, then Editor of *The Fathers of the Church* series, her translation of Saint John Chrysostom's *Discourse on Blessed Babylas and Against the Greeks* for publication in FOTC. Already on hand were Doctor Paul Harkins's translations of two other works of Chrysostom: *Discourses Against Judaizing Christians* and *A Demonstration Against the Pagans that Christ is God,* originally intended by Harkins for a single volume.

Doctor Peebles decided that the *Discourses* alone would adequately constitute one volume and that the *Demonstration* could be suitably joined with Schatkin's work in a separate volume. After Doctor Peebles's untimely death, the Reverend Hermigild Dressler, O.F.M., Ph.D., succeeded him as the Editorial Director of the series. Through his efforts the *Discourses Against Judaizing Christians* (FOTC 68) appeared in 1979. During this time Harkins and Schatkin continued their work on these treatises by Chrysostom. Harkins revised his translation of the *Demonstration* while Father Dressler edited another work by Chrysostom translated by Harkins: St. John Chrysostom, *On the Incomprehensible Nature of God* (FOTC 72). Schatkin presented her critical edition of the Greek text of the *Discourse on Blessed Babylas and Against the Greeks* for publication in *Sources chrétiennes* with a French translation to be prepared by Cécile Blanc et al. After submitting her typescript of the critical edition of the Greek text to *Sources chrétiennes,* Schatkin further revised her English translation and wrote completely new notes for the present volume.

It would be appropriate to speak briefly about the format of this volume. Both translations were submitted along with a select bibliography, a list of abbreviations, an introduction, a general index, and an index of Holy Scripture. No attempt was made to consolidate the select bibliographies, the lists of abbreviations, or the indices because it was felt that each work should stand as an independent unit. When it proved necessary, however, the editorial department of *The Fathers of the Church* edited the material in such a manner that clarity would hopefully prevail. For example, even though two lists of abbreviations are to be found in this volume, only one abbreviation is used for a work cited by both translators.

We wish to extend our gratitude to the late Doctor Bernard Peebles, the Reverend Hermigild Dressler, O.F.M., Ph.D., and Doctor John Dillon, whose original conception, and subsequent encouragement, and editorial skills combined to bring this book to completion.

ACKNOWLEDGMENTS

We are grateful to the following for permission to reproduce copyrighted material:

Baker Book House, Grand Rapids, Michigan, for *The Proof of the Gospel Being the Demonstratio Evangelica of Eusebius of Caesarea*, translated by W. J. Ferrar, reprinted 1982. *Preparation for the Gospel: Eusebius*, translated by E.H. Gifford, reprinted 1981.

Cambridge University Press, Cambridge for *D. Iunii Iuvenalis Saturae XIV: Fourteen Satires of Juvenal*, ed. J.D. Duff 1898; reprinted 1962. *Origen: Contra Celsum* translated with an introduction and notes by H. Chadwick 1953; reprinted 1979.

The Daughters of Saint Paul, Boston and Doctor T. Halton, Washington for *In Praise of Saint Paul by Saint John Chrysostom* translated by T. Halton, 1963.

William B. Eerdmans Publishing Company, Grand Rapids, Michigan for *The Ante-Nicene Fathers: Translations of the Writings of the Fathers Down to A.D. 325*, edited by A. Roberts and J. Donaldson (new impression ed. A. Coxe). *A Select Library of the Nicene and Post-Nicene Fathers of the Christian Church*, edited by Ph. Schaff. *A Select Library of Nicene and Post-Nicene Fathers of the Christian Church: Second Series*, ed. Ph. Schaff and H. Wace. All reprinted 1978.

Methuen and Company, London for E. Gibbon, *The History of the Decline and Fall of the Roman Empire*, edited in seven volumes with an introduction, notes, appendices, and index by J.B. Bury, 10th ed., 1935.

The Oxford University Press, Oxford for *Eusebii Pamphili Chronici canones: latine uertit, adauxit, ad sua tempora produxit S. Eusebius Hieronymus*, edited by J.K. Fotheringham 1923. *Didascalia Apostolorum: The Syriac Version Translated and Accom-*

panied by the Verona Latin Fragments by R.H. Connolly 1929, reprinted 1969. *The Oxford English Dictionary,* edited by J.A.H. Murray et al. 1933.

The Reverend L. Mounteer, S.J., Bronx, New York for *Saint Augustine: The City of God Books 1–7* translated by D.B. Zema and G.G. Walsh, FOTC 8 1950.

DISCOURSE ON BLESSED BABYLAS AND AGAINST THE GREEKS

*([Tou makariōtatou Iōannou arkhiepiskopou
Konstantinoupoleōs tou Khrusostomou]
tou autou logos eis ton
makarion Babulan kai kata Hellēnōn)*

Translated by

MARGARET A. SCHATKIN

Boston College

Chestnut Hill, Massachusetts

CONTENTS

SELECT BIBLIOGRAPHY

Texts and Translations of the Discourse on Blessed Babylas and Against the Greeks (see below, *Introduction*, Secs. 82–83)
Duc, Fronton du (Fronto Ducaeus). *S. Johannis Chrysostomi opera omnia.* 12 vols. Paris 1609–33.
Savile, Henry. *S. Johannis Chrysostomi opera omnia.* 8 vols. Eton 1612.
Montfaucon, Bernard de. *S. Johannis Chrysostomi opera omnia.* 13 vols. Paris 1718–38 and Venice 1734–41. 2nd ed. by T. Fix. Paris 1834–39. Reprint of 2nd edition by J.-P. Migne. PG 47–64, Paris 1862. PG 50.533–72 is the text of *Bab.*
Jeannin, M. et al. *Oeuvres complètes.* 11 vols. Bar-le-Duc 1863–67. Reprint ed. Arras 1887–88.
Schatkin, Margaret A. "Critical Edition of, and Introduction to St. John Chrysostom's *De Sancto Babyla contra Iulianum et Gentiles.*" Edited for Ph.D. dissertation, Fordham University, 1967. Revised with French translation by Cécile Blanc et al. and to appear in SC.

Other Texts and Translations
The Ante-Nicene Fathers: Translations of the Writings of the Fathers Down to A.D. 325. Ed. A. Roberts and J. Donaldson. Edinburgh 24 vols. 1866–72. New impression ed. A. Coxe. 8 vols. Buffalo 1884–86. Reprint ed. Grand Rapids, Michigan 1978.
Augustine, St. *Saint Augustine: The City of God: Books 1–7.* Trans. D. Zema and G. Walsh. FOTC 8. New York 1950.
Chronicon paschale ad exemplar vaticanum recensuit Ludovicus Dindorfus. Bonn 1832. This text is reprinted in PG 92.69–1028.
Corpus Paroemiographorum Graecorum. Ed. E.L. von Leutsch and F.G. Schneidewin et al. 2 vols. with supplement. Göttingen etc. 1839–51 etc. Reprint ed. Hildesheim 1958.
Didascalia Apostolorum: The Syriac Version Translated and Accompanied by the Verona Latin Fragments. Ed. R.H. Connolly. Oxford 1929. Reprint ed. Oxford 1969.
Didascalia et Constitutiones Apostolorum I. Ed. F.X. Funk. Paderborn 1905.
Ephraem, Saint. *Adversus Iulianum hymni 4.* Trans. G. Bickell. *Zeitschrift für katholische Theologie* 2 (1878): 335–56.
Eusebius of Caesarea. *Against Hierocles.* In *Philostratus, The Life of Apollonius of Tyana.* Trans. F.C. Conybeare. Loeb Classical Library. 2 vols. Cambridge, Mass., 1960. 2:484–605.
———— *The Ecclesiastical History and the Martyrs of Palestine.* Trans. H.J. Lawlor and J.E.L. Oulton. 2 vols. London 1954.
———— *Eusebius Werke* Vol. 2: *Die Kirchengeschichte.* Ed. E. Schwartz. *Die Lateinische Übersetzung des Rufinus.* Ed. T. Mommsen. Part 2: *Die Bücher VI Bis X; Über Märtyrer in Palästina.* GCS 9.2. Leipzig 1908.

5

6 ST. JOHN CHRYSOSTOM

_____ *Eusebii Pamphili Chronici canones latine uertit, adauxit, ad sua tempora produxit S. Eusebius Hieronymus.* Ed. J.K. Fotheringham. London 1923.
_____ *Preparation for the Gospel.* Trans. E.H. Gifford. 2 vols. Oxford 1903. Reprint ed. Grand Rapids, Michigan 1981.
_____ *The Proof of the Gospel.* Trans. W.J. Ferrar. New York 1920. Reprint ed. 2 vols. in 1. Grand Rapids, Michigan 1981.
Jerome, Saint. *Hieronymus und Gennadius: De viris inlustribus.* Ed. C. Bernoulli. Freiburg im Breisgau and Leipzig 1895.
John Chrysostom, Saint. *De sacerdotio of St. John Chrysostom.* Ed. J.A. Nairn. Cambridge 1906.
_____ *Commentary on Saint John the Apostle and Evangelist.* Trans. Sr. Thomas Aquinas Goggin. FOTC 33 and 41. New York 1957, 1960.
_____ *In Praise of Saint Paul.* Trans. T. Halton. Boston 1963.
_____ *St. John Chrysostom: Discourses Against Judaizing Christians.* Trans. P.W. Harkins. FOTC 68. Washington, D.C. 1979.
_____ *St. John Chrysostom: On the Incomprehensible Nature of God.* Trans. P.W. Harkins. FOTC 72. Washington, D.C. 1984.
_____ *Lettre d'exil à Olympias et à tous les fidèles (Quod nemo laeditur).* Ed. and trans. A.-M. Malingrey. SC 103. Paris 1964.
_____ McKendrick, N.G. *"Quod Christus sit Deus of John Chrysostom."* Edited for Ph.D. dissertation, Fordham University, 1966.
Julian. *Oeuvres complètes.* Vol. 1, Part 2: *Lettres et fragments.* Ed. J. Bidez. Paris 1960.
_____ *Oeuvres complètes.* Vol. 2, Part 1: *Discours de Julien Empereur: A Thémistius, Contre Héracleios le cynique, Sur la mère de dieux, Contre les cyniques ignorants.* Ed. G. Rochefort. Paris 1963.
_____ *Oeuvres complètes.* Vol. 2, Part 2: *Discours de Julien Empereur: Les Césars, Sur Hélios-Roi, Le misopogon.* Ed. C. Lacombrade. Paris 1964.
_____ *Librorum Contra Christianos quae supersunt.* Ed. C. Neumann. Leipzig 1880.
Juvenal. *D. Iunii Iuvenalis Saturae XIV: Fourteen Satires of Juvenal.* Ed. J.D. Duff. Cambridge 1898. Reprint ed. Cambridge 1962.
Lactantius. *De la mort des persécuteurs.* Ed. and trans. J. Moreau. SC 39. Paris 1954.
_____ *Lactantius: The Divine Institutes, Books 1–7.* Trans. Sr. Mary Francis McDonald. FOTC 49. Washington, D.C. 1964.
Lauchert, F. *Die Kanones der wichtigsten altkirchlichen Concilien nebst den apostolischen Kanones.* Freiburg im Breisgau and Leipzig 1896.
Libanius. *Opera.* Ed. R. Foerster. 12 vols. Leipzig 1903–27. Reprint ed. Hildesheim 1963.
Minucius Felix. *Octavius.* Trans. G. W. Clarke. ACW 39. New York 1974.
_____ *Tertullian: Apologetical Works; Minucius Felix: Octavius.* Trans. R. Arbesmann et al. FOTC 10. New York 1950.
Origen. *Contra Celsum.* Ed. and trans. H. Chadwick. Cambridge 1953. Reprint ed. Cambridge 1979.
_____ *Origenes Werke* Vol. 1: *Die Schrift vom Martyrium; Buch I–IV Gegen Celsus.* Ed. P. Koetschau. GCS 2. Leipzig 1899.
_____ *Origenes Werke* Vol. 2: *Buch V–VIII Gegen Celsus; Die Schrift vom Gebet.* Ed. P. Koetschau. GCS 3. Leipzig 1899.
Otto, J.C.Th. *Corpus apologetarum Christianorum saeculi secundi.* 9 vols. Jena

1847–72. Volumes 1–5 containing the works of Justin Martyr were republished (3rd ed.) at Jena 1876–81.

Porphyry. *Porphyrii philosophi Platonici opuscula.* Ed. A. Nauck. 2nd ed. Leipzig 1886.

———— Porphyrius, *"Gegen die Christen," 15 Bücher: Zeugnisse, Fragmente und Referate.* Ed. A. von Harnack. In *Abhandlungen der königlichen preussischen Akademie der Wissenschaften, philosophisch-historische Klasse,* no. 1. Berlin 1916.

Scriptores Historiae Augustae. Ed. E. Hohl. Editio stereotypa editionis prioris 1927 cum addendis ad vol. 1 et 2. Leipzig 1927. Reprint ed. Leipzig 1955.

A Select Library of Nicene and Post Nicene Fathers. Ed. Ph. Schaff. 14 vols. New York 1887–93. Reprint ed. Grand Rapids, Michigan 1978. *Second Series.* Ed. Ph. Schaff and H. Wace. 14 vols. New York 1890–1900. Reprint ed. Grand Rapids, Michigan 1978.

Sulpicius Severus. *Niceta of Remesiana: Writings; Sulpicius Severus: Writings; Vincent of Lerins: Commonitories.* Trans. B. Peebles et al. FOTC 7. New York 1949.

Tertullian. *Tertulliani De anima.* Ed. J.H. Waszink. Amsterdam 1947.

Theodoret of Cyrrhus. *Theodoret: Kirchengeschichte.* Eds. L. Parmentier and F. Scheidweiler. 2nd ed. GCS 44. Berlin 1954.

Other Works

Albert, P. S. *Jean Chrysostome considéré comme orateur populaire.* Paris 1858.

Amann, É. "Pénitence-sacrement." *Dictionnaire de théologie catholique.* Eds. A. Vacant, E. Mangenot, É. Amann. 16 vols. Paris 1931–72. 12,1(1933): 748–845.

Arbesmann, R., ed. *Aurelius Augustinus, Die Sorge für die Toten.* Würzburg 1975.

Asmus, R. "Die Invektiven des Gregorius von Nazianz im Licht der Werke des Kaisers Julian." *Zeitschrift für Kirchengeschichte* 31 (1910): 325–67.

Baur, C. *John Chrysostom and His Time.* Trans. M. Gonzaga. 2 vols. Westminster Maryland 1959–60.

———— "Wann ist der hl. Chrysostomus geboren?" *Zeitschrift für katholische Theologie* 52 (1928): 401–6.

Benzinger, I. "Daphne." *Paulys Real-Encyclopädie der classischen Altertumswissenschaft.* Ed. G. Wissowa (1901): 2136–38.

Bidez, J. *Vie de Porphyre: Le philosophe néo–platonicien.* Gent and Leipzig 1913. Reprint ed. Hildesheim 1964.

Bidez, J. and Cumont F. *Les Mages hellénisés: Zoroastre, Ostanès et Hystaspe d'après la tradition grecque.* 2 vols. Paris 1938.

Bouché-Leclercq, A. *Histoire de la divination dans l'antiquité.* 4 vols. Paris 1979–82.

Bowersock, G.W. *Julian the Apostate.* Cambridge, Massachusetts 1978.

Brightman, F.E. and Hammond, C.E., eds. *Liturgies Eastern and Western.* Volume I: Eastern Liturgies. Oxford 1896. Reprint ed. Oxford 1965.

Brinkerhoff, D. *A Collection of Sculpture in Classical and Early Christian Antioch.* New York 1970.

Brown, P. *The Cult of the Saints: Its Rise and Function in Latin Christianity.* Chicago 1981.

———— "The Rise and Function of the Holy Man in Late Antiquity." In *Society and the Holy in Late Antiquity.* Berkeley 1982. Pp. 103–52.

Canivet, P. *Histoire d'une entreprise apologétique au ve siècle.* Paris 1957.

Capelle, W. and Marrou, H.I. "Diatribe." *Reallexikon für Antike und Christentum.* Ed. Th. Klauser. 12 vols. to date. Stuttgart 1950–. 3(1957): 990–1009.

Carter, R.E. "Saint John Chrysostom's Rhetorical Use of the Socratic Distinction Between Kingship and Tyranny." *Traditio* 14 (1958): 367–71.

Christ, W. von. *Geschichte der griechischen Literatur.* 6th ed. Ed. W. Schmid and O. Stählin. Vol. 2, Pt. 2: *Die nachklassische Periode der griechischen Literatur von 100 bis 530 nach Christus.* Munich 1961.

Coleman-Norton, P.R. "St. Chrysostom and the Greek Philosophers." *Classical Philology* 25 (1930): 305–17.

Cumont, F. *Oriental Religions in Roman Paganism.* Chicago 1911. Reprint ed. New York 1956.

D'Alton, J.F. *Selections from St. John Chrysostom.* London 1940.

Delehaye, H. "Les deux saints Babylas." *Analecta Bollandiana* 19 (1900): 5–8.

———— *Les origines du culte des martyrs.* 2nd ed. Subsidia hagiographica, no. 20. Brussels 1933.

———— *Les passions des martyrs et les genres littéraires.* 2nd ed. Subsidia hagiographica, no. 138. Brussels 1966.

———— "Les premiers *libelli miraculorum.*" *Analecta Bollandiana* 29 (1910): 427–34.

———— "Les recueils antiques de miracles des saints." *Analecta Bollandiana* 43 (1925): 5–85.

Downey, G. *Antioch in the Age of Theodosius the Great.* Norman, Oklahoma 1962.

———— *A History of Antioch in Syria from Seleucus to the Arab Conquest.* Princeton 1961.

———— "Philanthropia in Religion and Statecraft in the Fourth Century after Christ." *Historia* 4 (1955): 199–208.

———— "The Shrines of St. Babylas at Antioch and Daphne." In *Antioch on–the–Orontes 2: The Excavations 1933–1936.* Ed. R. Stillwell. Princeton 1938. Pp. 45–48.

Durant, W. *The Life of Greece: The Story of Civilization* 2. New York 1939.

Dutoit, E. *Le thème de l'adynaton dans la poésie antique.* Paris 1936.

Elser, Dr. "Der hl. Chrysostomus und die Philosophie." *Theologische Quartalschrift* 76 (1894): 550–76.

Ely, F.H. "On *prēnēs genomenos* in Acts 1:18." *Journal of Theological Studies* 13 (1912): 278–85, 415.

Erasmus, D. *Opus Epistolarum Des. Erasmi Roterodami,* vol. 7: *1527–1528.* Ed. P.S. Allen. Oxford 1928.

Festugière, A.J. *Antioche païenne et chrétienne: Libanius, Chrysostome et les moines de Syrie.* Paris 1959.

Gallagher, E.V. *Divine Man or Magician? Celsus and Origen on Jesus.* SBL Dissertation Series. Chico, California 1982.

Gallay, P. *Langue et style de saint Grégoire de Nazianze.* Paris 1933.

Geffcken, J. "Kaiser Julianus und die Streitschriften seiner Gegner." *Neue Jahrbücher für das klassische Altertum* 21 (1908): 161–95.

———— *Zwei griechische Apologeten.* Leipzig 1907.

Gelzer, H. *Sextus Julius Africanus und die byzantinische Chronographie.* Leipzig 1885.

Gibbon, E. *The History of the Decline and Fall of the Roman Empire.* Ed. J.B. Bury. Vol. 2. London 1935.

Giordani, I. *The Social Message of the Early Fathers.* Patterson, New Jersey 1944. Reprint ed. Boston 1977.

Grabar, A. *Martyrium: Recherches sur le culte des reliques et l'art chrétien antique.* 2 vols. Paris 1946.

Grant, R.M. *The Earliest Lives of Jesus.* London 1961.

Greene, W.C. *Moira: Fate, Good and Evil in Greek Thought.* Cambridge, Massachusetts 1944. Reprint ed. New York 1963.

Haddad, G. *Aspects of Social Life in Antioch in the Hellenistic-Roman Period.* Ph.D. dissertation. University of Chicago 1949.

Haight, E.H. *Apuleius and his Influence.* New York 1927.

Halkin, F. *Inédits byzantins d'Ochrida, Candie et Moscou.* Subsidia hagiographica, no. 38. Brussels 1963.

Harnack, A. . *Die Zeit des Ignatius und die Chronologie der antiochenischen Bischöfe bis Tyrannus.* Leipzig 1898.

————— *Geschichte der altchristlichen Literatur bis Eusebius.* 2nd ed. 2,1. Leipzig 1893–1901. Reprint ed. Leipzig 1958.

————— *The Mission and Expansion of Christianity in the First Three Centuries.* Trans. J. Moffatt. London and New York 1908. Reprint ed. New York 1962.

Jackson, A. *Zoroaster: The Prophet of Ancient Iran.* New York 1898.

Jaeger, W. *Paideia: The Ideals of Greek Culture.* 2nd ed. Trans. G. Highet. 3 vols. Oxford 1965.

————— "Tyrtaeus on True Arete." In *Five Essays.* Trans. A.M. Fiske. Montreal 1966. Pp. 103–42.

Jedin, H. and Dolan, J., eds. *Handbook of Church History* (vols. 2–10 are entitled *History of the Church*). 10 vols. New York 1965–81. Vol. 1 (1965): K. Baus. *From the Apostolic Community to Constantine* with a General Introduction to Church History by H. Jedin. Vol. 2 (1980): K. Baus, H.–G. Beck, E. Ewig, H.J. Vogt. *The Imperial Church from Constantine to the Early Middle Ages.* Trans. A. Biggs.

Jordan, H. *Geschichte der altchristlichen Literatur.* Leipzig 1911.

Kaufmann-Bühler, D. "Eusebeia." *Reallexikon für Antike und Christentum.* Ed. Th. Klauser. 12 vols. to date. Stuttgart 1950– . 6(1966): 1043–47.

Kekelidze, K. *Monumenta hagiographica Georgica. Pars Prima: Keimena.* Tiflis (Tbilisi, U.S.S.R.) 1918. (This work is in Georgian.)

King, P. *American Archaeology in the Mideast.* Philadelphia 1983.

Kusch, H. "Diogenes von Sinope." *Reallexikon für Antike und Christentum.* Ed. Th. Klauser. 12 vols. to date. Stuttgart 1950–. 3(1957): 1063–75.

Laistner, M.L.W. *The Greater Roman Historians.* Berkeley 1947. Reprint ed. Berkeley 1966.

Lassus, J. "L'église cruciforme: Antioche-Kaoussié 12–F." In *Antioch on-the-Orontes* 2: *The Excavations 1933–1936.* Ed. R. Stillwell, Princeton 1938. Pp. 5–44.

————— *Sanctuaires chrétiens de Syrie.* Paris 1947.

Laurin, J.-R. *Orientations maîtresses des apologistes chrétiens de 270 à 361.* Analecta Gregoriana 61. Rome 1954.

Leduc Fr. "L'eschatologie, une préoccupation centrale de saint Jean Chrysostome." *Proche–orient chrétien* 29 (1969): 109–34.

Lenain de Tillemont, L.S. *Histoire des empereurs et des autres princes qui ont regné durant les six premiers siècles de l'Église.* (6 vols.) Vol. 3. Venice 1732.

———— *Mémoires pour servir à l'histoire ecclésiastique des six premiers siècles.* (16 vols.) Vol. 11. Venice 1732.

Levenson, D.B. *A Source and Tradition Critical Study of the Stories of Julian's Attempt to Rebuild the Jerusalem Temple.* Ph.D. dissertation. Harvard University 1980.

Livingstone, R.W. *The Greek Genius and Its Meaning to Us.* London 1915.

Lucius, E. *Die Anfänge des Heiligenkults in der christlichen Kirche.* Tübingen 1904.

Maas, P. "Zu den Beziehungen zwischen Kirchenvätern und Sophisten." *Sitzungsberichte der preussischen Akademie der Wissenschaften, Phil.-hist. Klasse.* Berlin 1912. 2:1123–26.

Malingrey, A.-M. "Les délais de la justice divine chez Plutarque et dans la littérature judéo–chrétienne." *Actes du VIIIe Congrès de l'Association G. Budé.* Paris 1969. Pp. 542–50.

Malley, W.J. *Hellenism and Christianity: The Conflict between Hellenic and Christian Wisdom in the Contra Galilaeos of Julian the Apostate and the Contra Julianum of St. Cyril of Alexandria.* Analecta Gregoriana 210. Rome 1978.

Marrou, H.I. *A History of Education in Antiquity.* Trans. G. Lamb. New York 1964.

Merlin, P. "Dissertation sur ce que rapporte Saint Chrysostome du Martyre de Saint Babylas, contre la censure injurieuse que fait M. Bayle de la Narration du Saint Docteur." In *Mémoires de Trévoux.* Juin 1737. Pp. 1051–76.

Moffatt, J. "Great Attacks on Christianity, 2: Porphyry, *Against Christians.*" *The Expository Times* 43 (1931): 72–78.

Naegele, A. "Chrysostomus und Libanios." In *Chrysostomika.* Rome 1908. Pp. 81–142.

Natorp, P. "Diogenes (44)." *Paulys Real–Encyclopädie der classischen Altertumswissenschaft.* Ed. G. Wissoma (1903): 765–73.

Neander, A. *Der heilige Johannes Chrysostomus.* 2 vols. Berlin 1848.

———— *The Life of St. Chrysostom.* Trans. J.C. Stapleton. London 1845.

Olmstead, A.T. "The Mid-Third Century of the Christian Era." *Classical Philology* 37 (1942): 241–62, 398–420.

O'Meara, J.J. *Porphyry's Philosophy from Oracles in Augustine.* Paris 1959.

Papadopoulos-Kerameus, A. *Sullogē palaistinēs kai suriakēs hagiologias* I. Pravoslavnyj Palestinskij Sbornik XIX.3(57). Petropolis (Leningrad) 1907.

Parke, H. and Wormell, D. *The Delphic Oracle.* 2 vols. Oxford 1956.

Peeters, P. "La passion de S. Basile d'Épiphanie." *Analecta Bollandiana* 48 (1930): 302–23.

Peters, F.E. *The Harvest of Hellenism.* New York 1970.

Petit, P. *Libanius et la vie municipale à Antioche au IVe siècle après J.–C.* Paris 1955.

———— "Recherches sur la publication et la diffusion des discours de Libanius." *Historia* 5 (1956): 479–509.

Pfister, F. *Der Reliquienkult im Altertum.* 2 vols. Giessen 1909–12.

Puniet, P. de. "Catéchuménat." *Dictionnaire d'archéologie chrétienne et de liturgie.* Eds. F. Cabrol and H. Leclercq. 15 vols. Paris 1924–53. 2,2(1924): 2579–2621.

Quasten, J. *Patrology* 3: *The Golden Age of Greek Patristic Literature from the Council of Nicaea to the Council of Chalcedon.* Utrecht 1960.

Rand, E.K. *The Building of Eternal Rome.* Cambridge, Massachusetts, 1943. Reprint ed. New York 1972.

Rentinck, P. *La cura pastorale in Antiochia nel IV secolo.* Rome 1970.

Rose, H.J. *A Handbook of Greek Mythology.* New York 1959.

Rostovtzeff, M. *The Social and Economic History of the Hellenistic World.* 3 vols. Oxford 1941.

Rush, A.C. *Death and Burial in Christian Antiquity.* The Catholic University of America Studies in Christian Antiquity 1. Washington, D.C. 1941.

Sandmel, S. *Philo of Alexandria: An Introduction.* New York 1979.

Schaff, Ph. *History of the Christian Church.* 3rd. ed. 3 vols. New York 1904–10. Reprint ed. Grand Rapids, Michigan 1964.

Schatkin, M. "The Authenticity of St. John Chrysostom's *De sancto Babyla, contra Iulianum et gentiles.*" In *Kyriakon: Festschrift Johannes Quasten.* Ed. P. Granfield and J.A. Jungmann. Münster Westf. 1970. 1: 479–89. (In certain details corrected and amplified by the present work.)

Schultze, V. *Altchristliche Städte und Landschaften* 3: *Antiocheia.* Gütersloh 1930.

Seitz, A. *Die Apologie des Christentums bei den Griechen des IV. und V. Jahrhunderts in historisch-systematischer Darstellung.* Würzburg 1895.

Sievers, G. *Das Leben des Libanius.* Berlin 1868.

Simonetti, M. "Sulla struttura dei panegirici di S. Giovanni Crisostomo." In *Rendiconti del R. Istituto Lombardo di scienze e lettere: Classe di lettere e scienze morali e storiche* 86 (1953): 159–80.

Soffray, M. *Recherches sur la syntaxe de saint Jean Chrysostome d'après les Homélies sur les statues.* Paris 1939.

Stelzenberger, J. *Die Beziehungen der frühchristlichen Sittenlehre zur Ethik der Stoa.* Munich 1933.

Straub, J. "Die Himmelfahrt des Julianus Apostata." *Gymnasium* 69 (1962): 310–26.

TeSelle, E. *Augustine's Strategy as an Apologist.* Villanova, Pennsylvania 1974.

Vandenberghe, B.H. *John of the Golden Mouth.* London 1958.

Volkmann, R. *Rhetorik der Griechen und Römer.* Handbuch der klassischen Altertumswissenschaft 2,3. Munich 1901.

Warburton, W. *Julian, or a Discourse concerning the earthquake and fiery eruption which defeated that emperor's attempt to rebuild the temple at Jerusalem, in which the reality of a divine interposition is shown, the objections to it answered, and the nature of that evidence which demands the assent of every reasonable man to a miraculous fact is considered and explained.* 2nd ed., with additions. London 1751.

Warfield, B. *Counterfeit Miracles.* New York 1918. Reprint ed. London 1972.

Whale, J.S. "Great Attacks on Christianity: Celsus." *The Expository Times* 42 (1930): 119–24.

Wright, W. "An Ancient Syrian Martyrology." *Journal of Sacred Literature* 8 (1865–66): 45–56, 423–32.

York, J.M. "The Image of Philip the Arab." *Historia* 21 (1972): 320–32.

Žitnik, M. "*Theos philanthrōpos* bei Johannes Chrysostomus." *Orientalia Christiana Periodica* 41 (1975): 76–118.

ABBREVIATIONS

I. *Texts*

Abbreviations of classical texts are taken from the *Oxford Classical Dictionary*, ed. N.G.L. Hammond and H.H. Scullard, 2nd ed., Oxford 1970. Abbreviations and editions of Greek patristic texts are from *A Patristic Greek Lexicon*, ed. G.W.H. Lampe, Oxford 1961, to which reference is made for additional data. Abbreviations of Latin patristic texts are from A. Blaise, *Dictionnaire latin-français des auteurs chrétiens*, Turnhout 1962.

List of select abbreviations:

A. WORKS OF CHRYSOSTOM

Bab.	*Discourse on Blessed Babylas and against the Greeks*
Pan. Bab. 1	*Homily on the Holy Martyr, Saint Babylas* (trans. T.P. Brandram, NPNF 9 (1889) 141–43)
Jud. 1-8	*Discourses against Judaizing Christians* (trans. P. Harkins, FOTC 68)
Jud. et gent.	*Demonstratio contra Iudaeos et gentiles quod Christus sit deus* (= *Demonstration against the Pagans that Christ is God*) This is translated in the second part of this volume.

B. WORKS OF OTHER CHURCH FATHERS

Cels.	Origen, *Contra Celsum*
Chron. Pasch.	*Chronicon Paschale*
Const. App.	*Constitutiones Apostolorum*
D.e.	Eusebius, *Demonstratio evangelica*
H.e.	*Historia ecclesiastica*
Hierocl.	Eusebius, *Contra Hieroclem*
Inc.	Athanasius, *De incarnatione*
P.e.	Eusebius, *Praeparatio evangelica*

II. *Modern Works*

AB	*Analecta Bollandiana.* Brussels 1882–.
ANF	Ante-Nicene Fathers. Reprint Eerdmans.
ACW	*Ancient Christian Writers.* Westminster, Md. and London (later Ramsey, N.J.) 1946–.
AASS	*Acta Sanctorum.* Ed. The Bollandists. Antwerp and Brussels 1643–.
BHG	Halkin, F. *Bibliotheca hagiographica graeca.* 3rd ed. 3 vols. Subsidia hagiographica, no. 8a. Brussels 1957. *Bibliotheca*

13

	hagiographica graeca auctarium. Subsidia hagiographica, no. 47. Brussels 1969.
BHL	*Bibliotheca hagiographica latina antiquae et mediae aetatis.* Ed. The Bollandists. 2 vols. Brussels 1898–1901. *Bibliotheca hagiographica latina antiquae et mediae aetatis supplementi editio altera auctior.* Subsidia hagiographica, no. 12. Brussels 1911.
CMH	*The Cambridge Medieval History.* Planned by J.B. Bury and H.M. Gwatkin et al. Cambridge and New York 1911–36.
CSEL	*Corpus scriptorum ecclesiasticorum latinorum.* Vienna 1866–.
FOTC	*The Fathers of the Church.* New York and Washington 1947–.
GCS	*Die griechischen christlichen Schriftsteller der ersten Jahrhunderte.* Leipzig and Berlin 1897–.
NPNF	Nicene and Post Nicene Fathers. Reprint Eerdmans.
OCD	*The Oxford Classical Dictionary.* 2nd ed. Oxford 1970.
OED	J.A.H. Murray et al., eds. *The Oxford English Dictionary.* Oxford 1933.
PG	Migne, J.P., ed. *Patrologiae cursus completus: Series graeca.* 161 vols. Paris 1857–66.
PGL	*A Patristic Greek Lexicon.* Ed. G.W.H. Lampe. Oxford 1961.
PL	Migne, J.P., ed. *Patrologiae cursus completus: Series latina.* 221 vols. Paris 1844–55.
RACh	*Reallexikon für Antike und Christentum.* Ed. Th. Klauser. Stuttgart 1950–.
RE	Pauly, A., Wissowa, G., Kroll, W. *Realencyclopädie der classischen Altertumswissenschaft.* Stuttgart 1894–.
SC	*Sources chrétiennes.* Paris 1942–.
SHA	Hohl, E., ed. *Scriptores Historiae Augustae.* Leipzig 1927; Reprint Leipzig 1955.
SVF	*Stoicorum Veterum Fragmenta.* Collected by H.F. von Arnim. 4 vols. Leipzig 1903–24. Reprint Stuttgart 1964.

INTRODUCTION

DATE

The Discourse on Blessed Babylas and against the Greeks was probably written between 363 and 379–80. The date of composition must be after 363 because the peace treaty made with Persia upon the death of emperor Julian is mentioned (Bab. 123). In all likelihood the discourse was composed before 379–80 because it contains no reference to the martyr's shrine (martyrium) built for Babylas across the Orontes river near Antioch. This shrine, constructed under the supervision of Meletius, bishop of Antioch, was completed in 379–80.[1] Chrysostom does not mention the new martyrium or Meletius's intention to build it (cf. Bab. 126). He states, on the contrary, that as he wrote, the relics of Babylas were back in their original resting place, namely, the Christian cemetery of Antioch outside the Daphne gate (Bab. 126; cf. Bab. 90, 91, 93). Therefore the discourse was evidently composed before Meletius had undertaken to build the new shrine for Babylas.

(2) It is possible that Meletius encouraged Chrysostom to write this discourse in praise of martyr Babylas and his relics. Chrysostom was the spiritual son of Meletius.[2] As a result of the edict of toleration issued by Gratian in 378, Meletius had

---

[1] The date is arrived at by Glanville Downey, "The Shrines of St. Babylas at Antioch and Daphne," in Antioch on-the-Orontes 2: The Excavations 1933–1936, ed. Richard Stillwell (Princeton 1938) 47. This martyrium, which contained the remains of Babylas and later the body of Meletius, has been identified with a cruciform church excavated opposite the city of Antioch in 1935. See Jean Lassus, "L'église cruciforme: Antioche-Kaoussié 12–F," in Antioch on-the-Orontes 2, 5–44.

[2] Palladius, V. Chrys. 5. See. P.R. Coleman-Norton, Palladii Dialogus de vita sancti Johannis Chrysostomi, edited with revised text (Cambridge, Massachusetts 1928) 28. (Hereinafter Coleman-Norton, Palladii Dialogus.) A. Neander, Der heilige Johannes Chrysostomus (Berlin, 1848) 1: 18–22.

returned to Antioch after a six year exile under the Arian
emperor Valens. He was then recognized as the rightful
bishop of Antioch (379).[3] Meletius was devoted to the martyrs, and personally directed the construction of a shrine for
Babylas, as Chrysostom attests.[4] It might be at this time, as
part of the spiritual rebuilding of his church, that Meletius
suggested to Chrysostom the composition of a discourse on
Babylas to justify veneration of the great Antiochene martyr.

(3) All this suggests 378 as the probable year in which the
discourse was composed. This date is supported by Chrysostom's statement at Bab. 117 that it is the twentieth year since
the burning of the temple at Daphne. According to Ammianus Marcellinus, the fire occurred on 22 October 362
(Hist. 22.13.1). Accordingly, it would seem that Chrysostom
was writing in the year 382, if the number is taken literally. It
was, however, Chrysostom's usual practice to round off numbers and exaggerate (or reduce) them for rhetorical effect.[5]
In the present instance, as the context suggests, the number is
probably exaggerated. Hence the year 378 may be given as
the approximate time of composition.

OCCASION, PURPOSE, AND BACKGROUND

(4) The following circumstances were influential in the
composition of the discourse on Babylas. Taken as a whole,
these factors attest that the discourse was not simply a schol-

---

[3] Downey, "The Shrines of St. Babylas," 47. Possibly Chrysostom also returned to the city at this time (378), after having spent six years as a hermit in
the mountainous environs of Antioch during the persecution of Valens. Two
years later he was ordained a deacon by Meletius (380?). Palladius, V. Chrys. 5
(Coleman-Norton, Palladii Dialogus 28).

[4] Pan. Bab. 1.3 (PG 50.533 f.). The veneration of martyrs was a foremost
expression of Christian piety in fourth-century Antioch. See Pietro Rentinck,
La cura pastorale in Antiochia nel IV secolo (Roma 1970) 127–43. Chrysostom's
passionate fondness for martyr Babylas is characteristic.

[5] Chrysostom Baur, "Wann ist der hl. Chrysostomus geboren?," Zeitschrift
für katholische Theologie 52 (1928): 404 n. 5. Add to the examples given by
Baur: Bab. 85. Vid. 2.90 ff. (SC 138: 120 f.). Jud. 6.2 (PG 48.905). Hom. 9.2 in 1
Cor. (PG 61.77).

arly exercise but responded to certain issues and conflicts of the day.

The Pagan Reaction I: Porphyry, Hierocles

Porphyry. (5) The Neoplatonic philosopher Porphyry (233–305) undertook the twofold task of revitalizing paganism and impugning Christianity. Refutation of Porphyry, whom Augustine calls "the most learned of the philosophers, though the bitterest enemy of the Christians" (*Civ.* 19.22), occupied Christian apologists throughout the fourth and fifth centuries.[6] It would be almost inconceivable that Chrysostom would have been unaffected by these debates.

(6) In his early work, *Philosophy from Oracles*, Porphyry seems to have tried to give to paganism a system of revelation based upon oracles analogous to the scriptures of Jews and Christians.[7] Chrysostom's discourse on Babylas seems to respond to Porphyry's treatise on oracles in a general way. For example, Chrysostom shows that Christ is superior to the pagan oracles; specifically, he shows that Christ's prediction in Jn 14.12, referred to as an "oracle" *(chrēsmos),*[8] has been fulfilled in history. By contrast the oracular god Apollo is shown to be ignorant and helpless, because he could not defend his own temple and statue from fire. In *Bab.* 73 ff. Chrysostom narrates how the oracle of Apollo at Daphne was silenced and overpowered by the relics of Babylas. This constitutes a polemic against pagan oracles.[9] It is probable that Chrysostom used Eusebius, *P.e.* 4–5 as a source for his

---

[6] Including Arnobius, Eusebius, Augustine, and Theodoret. John J. O'Meara, *Porphyry's Philosophy from Oracles in Augustine* (Paris 1959) 2 and passim.

[7] Anton Seitz, *Die Apologie des Christentums bei den Griechen des IV. und V. Jahrhunderts in historisch-systematischer Darstellung* (Würzburg 1895) 4.

[8] *Bab.* 9. The designation of the scriptures as *oracula* in the last six books of *The City of God* is owing to the influence of Porphyry, according to O'Meara, *Porphyry's Philosophy* 63.

[9] Cf. *Bab.* 127: "(Babylas) exposed the nonsense of divination, shattered its mask, and displayed all its hypocrisy laid bare, having silenced and defeated by main force the one (Apollo) who seemed to be its master."

polemic.[10] Chrysostom and Eusebius have the same understanding of divination in the Greek oracles. Both believe that those revered as gods at the sites of the Greek oracles are really evil demons, who hide their own ignorance and impotence by deceiving humanity.[11]

(7) Porphyry's fifteen books *Against Christians* were "the most extensive and scholarly work composed against Christianity in antiquity."[12] The voluminous work was excerpted twice around the year 300, for use by pagans in their struggle against the church. Hierocles apparently plagiarized it for his *Philalēthēs*.[13] An "unknown" made an epitome in two books, which was probably quoted by Macarius Magnes.[14] The emperor Julian possibly depended on it for his treatise against Christians. Libanius also seems to have read the work.[15] Although Constantine may have suppressed the work before the council of Nicea, nevertheless copies must have been preserved, because emperors Theodosius II and Valentinian III had to repeat the order to destroy the books in 448.[16]

(8) The earliest literary response on the part of the Christians came from Methodius, perhaps during the lifetime of Porphyry. The twenty-five books of Eusebius against Porphyry which followed were probably written before the aforementioned decree of Constantine. When emperor Julian renewed the literary battle against Christianity, Apollinarius of Laodicea wrote a refutation of Porphyry's anti-Christian work in thirty books.[17] Gregory of Nazianzus says

---

[10] In these books Eusebius quoted extensively from Porphyry, *Philosophy from Oracles*. For specific parallels between P.e. and *Bab.* see below, *Bab.* 80, 88 with notes.

[11] This was the traditional Christian view. J.H. Waszink, ed., *Tertulliani De anima* (Amsterdam 1947) 498.

[12] Adolf von Harnack, *Porphyrius Gegen die Christen 15 Bücher: Zeugnisse, Fragmente und Referate*, Abhandlungen der königlich preussischen Akademie der Wissenschaften, Jahrgang 1916, Philosophisch-historische Klasse, 1 (Berlin 1916) 3.

[13] Ibid. 29.

[14] Ibid. 27. See *econtra* T.D. Barnes, "Porphyry *Against the Christians:* Date and the Attribution of Fragments," *The Journal of Theological Studies* 24 (1973): 424–42.

[15] Ibid. 32 and 7 n.2.   [16] Ibid. 5.

[17] Ibid. 6. According to Philostorgius, the refutation of Apollinarius surpassed those of Eusebius and Methodius (H.e. 8.14; J. Bidez, ed., *Philostorgius*

that his two orations against Julian were written in retaliation for "the lies of Porphyry" and the *Misopogon* of Julian (*Or.* 5.41; PG 35.717). Chrysostom's teacher, Diodore of Tarsus, wrote a work entitled *Contra Porphyrium, de animalibus et sacrificiis.* This work, however, was apparently not directed towards Porphyry's *Against Christians* but towards his *De abstinentia.*[18]

(9) In his treatise against Christians Porphyry systematically attacked the scriptures: their mutual contradictions and their relation to the church.[19] The first book of *Against Christians* contained an assault on the credibility of the apostles and evangelists. Porphyry attributed the successful entrance of Christianity into the world to egregious deceit.[20] He labeled Christ and the apostles frauds, their miracles fictions,[21] and their writings lies and deceit. The actual text of Porphyry does not survive but Eusebius seemingly reproduces the argument of Porphyry in D.e. 3.4–5. For example, D.e. 3.4.38 contains the following suppositional accusation against the apostles:

> Let them exalt their teacher with lying words, and spare no falsity: let them record in fictitious narrative his miracles and works of wonder, so that they may gain admiration and felicitation for being the pupils of such a master.[22]

Throughout chapters four and five of D.e. 3 the words *pseudesthai, plattesthai,* and *planasthai* are repeated. The creed

---

Kirchengeschichte, GCS 21[1913]: 115). Philostorgius also wrote against Porphyry (H.e. 10.10; J. Bidez, ed. *Philostorgius Kirchengeschichte,* GCS 21 [1913]: 130)—an indication of the continuing influence of Porphyry's work, at least into the first third of the fifth century.

[18] Harnack, *Porphyrius* 35.   [19] Ibid. 11.

[20] Seitz, *Die Apologie* 251.

[21] The accusation that Christ's miracles are fictions *(plasmata)* seems already to have been made by Celsus (*Cels.* 2.13 ff., 48). Cf. R.M. Grant, *The Earliest Lives of Jesus* (London 1961) 70 ff., 123. Porphyry also employed the term *plasma* in his literary criticism of Homer (*De antro nympharum* 4; A. Nauck, ed., *Porphyrii philosophi Platonici opuscula,* 2nd ed. [Leipzig 1886]) 57f.

[22] I.A. Heikel, *Eusebius Werke VI: Die Demonstratio evangelica,* GCS 23 (1913): 117; *The Proof of the Gospel,* trans. W.J. Ferrar (New York 1920; reprint ed., 2 vols. in 1, Grand Rapids, Michigan 1981), p. 128. This quotation and the one directly below from Ferrar's translation are reprinted with the kind permission of Baker Book House.

of the apostles is suppositionally formulated as: "Perhaps truth is the same thing as evil, and falsehood must then be the opposite of evil" (D.e. 3.4.58).[23] Eusebius undertook to vindicate Christianity from the charge of deceit in D.e.3.3–5 (= *Theophany* 5.21 ff.). Here he demonstrates that deception is inconsistent with the elevated character of Christ's teachings (chap. 3) and with his divine works, which are evidence of his divinity (chap. 4.21–29). Deceit is also illogical and historically improbable (chap. 4.32–5).

(10) The discourse on Babylas seems to be a partial response to the accusation that the success of Christianity is based upon the fraud and deceit of the apostles. Chrysostom says that the victory of Christianity is not owing to the apostles but to the power of Christ: "The cause was not these fishermen's words and miracles, but the words and miracles of Christ's power, which was working in them" (*Bab.* 16).[24] The miracles of the apostles are not fiction but truth, and can never be disproved by any adversary: "Light will never be darkness so long as it is light; neither will the truth of the facts asserted by us ever be refuted: for they are the truth, and there is nothing stronger than this" (*Bab.* 21).[25] The thesis that divine power is the source of Christian victory over paganism is illustrated by the history of Babylas, who in life exhibited courage as a bishop and whose remains possess divine power (*Bab.* 109). As a bishop Babylas defended his church against an evil emperor (*Bab.* 30–33); after death, his relics produced sobriety at Daphne and silenced the oracle of Apollo located there (*Bab.* 67 ff.). The discourse on Babylas is so constructed as to prove from contemporary history that the New Testament record is trustworthy (*Bab.* 22). The heroism of Babylas as a bishop proves the existence of *parrhēsia* (courage) among

---

[23] Heikel, *Demonstratio evangelica*, GCS 23 (1913): 121; Ferrar, trans. *Proof of the Gospel* 133.

[24] The power of Christ manifested in the church is the theme of Chrysostom's other apologetic treatise, *Jud. et. gent.*, which is translated in this volume.

[25] Similarly, in *Jud. et gent.* 11 Chrysostom shows that the Old Testament prophecies are not fictions (PG 48.828; N.G. McKendrick, "*Quod Christus sit Deus* of John Chrysostom," edited for Ph.D. dissertation [Fordham University 1966] 101).

the apostles.[26] The contemporary miracles, associated with the relics of Babylas, prove the reality of apostolic miracles.[27]

(11) In addition to this argument based on contemporary miracles, [28] which determines the structure of the discourse, Chrysostom uses several traditional pragmatic proofs in the prologue. Already with Eusebius the pragmatic proof was the most powerful argument in favor of Christianity.[29] In *Bab.* Chrysostom marshals three such empirical proofs to show that the apostolic preaching is not a fiction. His first argument is drawn from the geographical spread of the Christian religion in his own time:

> In our world there is no land, no nation, no city, where these miracles are not celebrated, which if fiction would never have attracted notice (*Bab.* 10).

His second argument refers to the indestructibility of the gospel:

> Our doctrine, which you say is fiction, has been assailed by tyrants, kings, orators of invincible eloquence, as well as by

---

[26]*Bab.* 50: "(Babylas) bridled the impudence of those who say that our religion is boasting and fiction, for he manifested by his actions the probability that men of such character existed in the past, when the prominence of miracles gave them even greater authority."

[27]*Bab.* 22: "Everyone who is not insane and mindless will acknowledge that events of the past, which we know of by hearsay, are no less credible than present events which we observe. However, in order to win total victory, I wish to mention a miraculous event that occurred in our generation." *Bab.* 73: "If, therefore, one doubts the works accomplished by the apostles, let him consider the present events and desist from his impudence forever." *Bab.* 75: "I shall proceed to the proof itself, after which it will not be possible even for the most impudent to contradict either the ancient miracles, the power of the martyr, or the weakness of the demon." The relation between biblical and contemporary miracles is described by Chrysostom in his authentic homily on Romanus thus: "The later (miracles) are more miraculous than the earlier. In fact, the ones preceded so that the others might not be disbelieved. The ones accustomed our mind in advance so that the others might not disturb us. The others occurred so that the invisible (miracles) of the past might be believed on account of the manifest recent ones (*Pan. Rom.* 1.4; PG 50.612).

[28]The use of contemporary miracles as an apologetic device to prove biblical miracles is found earlier in Eusebius, H.e. 10.4.6, 9, 29, 33.

[29]On the pragmatic proof being a most powerful argument in favor of Christianity see Eusebius, P.e. 1.3.5–11 (GCS 43,1: 11–13).

philosophers, sorcerers, magicians, and demons, and "their tongues against them are made weak" . . . (*Bab.* 11).[30]

His third argument concerns the humble status of the apostles, to whom such invention would be foreign:

One of those who did this, Paul, was a tent maker; another, Peter, was a fisherman. It would never have occurred to people so ordinary and humble to invent such a thing, except if someone is prepared to say that they were raving lunatics. That they were not lunatics is clear from what they accomplished when they spoke, and from those who are still persuaded by them even now (*Bab.* 16).

Here Chrysostom may have in mind the accusation of Porphyry that the apostles were ignorant men.[31]

[30] Chrysostom usually argues in this way for the invincibility of the church. E.g., *Hom.* 4.2. *in Is.* 6:1: "Let Greeks and Jews hear our accomplishments and the preeminence of the church. How many made war upon the church, but never conquered her? How many tyrants? How many generals? How many emperors? Augustus, Tiberius, Gaius, Claudius, Nero, men distinguished by eloquence and power, made war upon her while she was still young but did not root her out. Thus the assailants have been silenced and forgotten and the object of their attack transcends heaven" (PG 56.121).

[31] Harnack, *Porphyrius*, p. 28. Cf. Lactantius, *Inst.* 5.3.1 (CSEL 19.406), trans. M-F. McDonald, *Lactantius: The Divine Institutes Books I–VIII*, FOTC 49 (Washington 1964) 333: "The desire of pretending and cleverness, then, were missing from these writers because they were untrained." Chrysostom, *Hom.* 3.4 *in* 1 *Cor.* (PG 61.27f. trans. H. Cornish and J. Medley with T.W. Chambers in 1889 in vol. 12 of *A Select Library of Nicene and Post-Nicene Fathers*, ed. Ph. Schaff, 14 vols. [New York 1887–93; reprint ed. Grand Rapids, Michigan: William B. Eerdmans Publishing Company 1978] 14. Permission has been granted by William B. Eerdmans Publishing Company to reprint material from *A Select Library of Nicene and Post–Nicene Fathers* [hereinafter NPNF]. Subsequent translations in this series will give the translator's name, NPNF volume, date of publication by Schaff, and page[s].): "Wherefore, lest we fall into the same error, and be laughed to scorn, arguing thus with Greeks, whenever we have a controversy with them; let us charge the Apostles with want of learning; for this same charge is praise. And when they say that the Apostles were rude, let us follow up the remark and say that they were also untaught and unlettered, and poor, and vile, and stupid, and obscure. It is not a slander on the Apostles to say so, but it is even a glory that, being such, they should have outshone the whole world. For these untrained, and rude, and illiterate men, as completely vanquished the wise, and powerful, and the tyrants, and those who flourished in wealth and glory and all outward good things, as though they had not been men at all: from whence it is manifest that great is the power of the Cross; and that these things were done by no human strength."

In addition Chrysostom turns the accusation of deceit
against the pagans (retortion):

> Tell me why it is that the great Zoroaster and Zamolxis are
> unknown to most people except for a few? Because all that
> was said about them was fiction (*Bab.* 10).

He also accuses the pagan teachers of lying (*Bab.* 2-3).[32]

(12) Is Chrysostom replying to the accusations made by
Porphyry in book one of *Against Christians?* It is not impossible that the church father had access to the text of Porphyry,
even though it apparently had been suppressed by Constantine.[33] In fact, Chrysostom actually alludes to anti-Christian
writings and says that whatever remains of them is preserved
in the Christian community.[34] Moreover there is evidence that
he may have possessed a copy of Porphyry's treatise. In *Hom.*
17.3–4 *in Jo.* he refutes the charge that the miracles of Christ
are inventions. At the end of the discussion he mentions two
anti-Christian treatises:

> We should like, if you enjoyed a great deal of leisure, to
> bring before all of you the book of a certain foul pagan
> philosopher written against us, and also that of that other
> older one, in order, in this way at least, to arouse you and
> draw you out of your excessive apathy.[35]

It has been suggested that the earlier writing is that of Celsus
and the other that of Porphyry (or Plotinus or Julian).[36]

---

[32] Possibly the anti-pagan may have been the original form of the accusation. Philo, for example, considered the Greek myths "inventions" (see Ioannes Leisegang, *Indices ad Philonis Alexandrini opera,* s.v. *plasma*). Emperor Julian admits that pagans fabricated myths about their gods (*Librorum contra
Christianos quae supersunt,* ed. C. Neumann [Leipzig 1880] 167). In this vein
Chrysostom writes that the devil "invented the myth" about Daphne (*Bab.*
69).

[33] Harnack, *Porphyrius* 31. Above, note 16.

[34] *Bab.* 11: "If anything at all is found preserved, one finds it being preserved by Christians."

[35] Chrysostom, *Hom. in Jo.* 17.4 (PG 59.113), trans. T. Goggin, *St. John
Chrysostom: Commentary on St. John the Apostle and Evangelist: Homilies 1–47,*
FOTC 33 (Washington 1957) 171–72.

[36] Dr. Elser, "Der hl. Chrysostomus und die Philosophie," *Theologische Quartalschrift* 76 (1894): 566.

Hierocles. (13) Probably before the outbreak of the great persecution under Diocletian (303), Sossianus Hierocles, prefect of Egypt, wrote the anti-Christian pamphlet, *Philalēthēs,* which may have depended largely upon Porphyry. Eusebius, in a youthful work, wrote a partial refutation of Hierocles entitled *Against the Life of Apollonius of Tyana written by Philostratus, occasioned by the parallel drawn by Hierocles between him and Christ,* usually known as *Against Hierocles.*[37] In this work Eusebius stated that Hierocles was the only anti-Christian writer to compare Christ with Apollonius of Tyana (*Hierocl.* 1). According to W. Christ, however, Porphyry had first made this comparison.[38] If W. Christ, is correct, it may mean that Eusebius was unfamiliar with Porphyry's writings when he wrote *Hierocl.* The purpose of Hierocles' tract was to convict the Christians of "credulity." Hierocles said that Apollonius of Tyana worked greater deeds than Christ but nevertheless was not considered a god by pagans.[39] Eusebius replied by demonstrating the credulity of Hierocles, who placed confidence in the contradictory narrative of Philostratus concerning Apollonius. After Hierocles, pagans continued to put forth the figure of Apollonius of Tyana as a counterpart to Christ. For example, in Chrysostom's homily *Laud. Paul.* 4, an imaginary pagan interlocutor suggests "the one from Tyana" as a magician equal to Christ (PG 50.490). Likewise, in pagan literary salons of Carthage around the year 410, the miracles of Christ were compared unfavorably to those of Apollonius, Apuleius, and other magicians.[40]

(14) In the discourse on Babylas Chrysostom states that

---

[37] Greek text and English translation in *Philostratus: The Life of Apollonius of Tyana,* trans. F.C. Conybeare, Loeb Classical Library (Cambridge, Mass. 1960) 2: 484–605.

[38] Wilhelm von Christ, *Geschichte der griechischen Literatur*[6] 2,2(Munich 1961) 776. Cf. Harnack, *Porphyrius,* frags. 4, 46, 60, 63. Celsus had earlier compared Christ to pagan sorcerers (*Cels.* 1.68).

[39] Eusebius, *Hierocl.* 2. Earlier, the anti-Christian writer Celsus had pointed out many who, despite extraordinary deeds, were not revered as gods by pagans (Origen, *Cels.* 3.22, 26, 31 f.). Celsus, however, does not mention Apollonius.

[40] Augustine, *Ep.* 136.1 (FOTC 20.15–16). Cf. *Ep.* 135.2 (FOTC 20.14–15); 137.13–16 (FOTC 20.29–33); 138.18–20 (FOTC 20.50–53). Elizabeth Hazelton Haight, *Apuleius and His Influence* (New York 1927) 99–100.

Christ is superior to all other teachers, "who had disciples and paraded wonders" (*Bab.* 1). Chrysostom says that no pagan teacher ever said to his disciples what Christ said to his in Jn 14.12: "Amen, amen, I say to you, he who believes in me, the works that I do he also shall do, and greater than these he shall do."[41] By this promise Christ is shown to be superior to pagan teachers in two ways. First, he excels them in philanthropy: the fact that he shared his power with his disciples reveals his infinite goodness.[42] Second, he excels the pagan teachers in power: he predicted that his disciples would do "greater works" (Jn 14.12) and fulfilled his prediction. This is proof of a power which can only be divine.[43] The prophecy of Christ, recorded in Jn 14.12, is fulfilled in the miracles of the apostles. These are recorded in the book of Acts (*Bab.* 9).[44] If, however, one rejects the account of Acts as fiction, the subsequent development of the church suffices to manifest the fulfillment of Christ's prediction.[45]

(15) The pattern of argument is fulfilled prophecy. The empiric fulfillment of Christ's promise in Jn 14.12 proves the wisdom, omniscience, and hence the divinity of Christ. Chrysostom uses the same argument in his other apologetic discourse, translated in the second part of this volume. There

[41] Quoted at *Bab.* 1, 8. Chrysostom omits the end of the verse: "because I am going to the Father"—possibly because the discourse was directed to pagans, and these words were considered inappropriate. See Anne-Marie Malingrey, ed., *Jean Chrysostome: Lettre d'exil,* SC 103 (Paris 1964) 27.

[42] *Bab.* 8: "He would not have shared such honor with them, were he not exceedingly and infinitely good." Earlier, Arnobius argued for the divinity of Christ from the fact that he shared his power with his disciples (*Adversus nationes* 1.50–53; ACW 7.97–101). Since Chrysostom probably had not read Arnobius, this argument may have come from a prior common source.

[43] *Bab.* 3: "For that blessed power alone can make and fulfill such a prediction truthfully." Cf. *Hierocl.* 31: Apollonius of Tyana claimed to have foreknowledge of the future, which Eusebius largely rejects.

[44] In homily 1.1 on Acts Chrysostom says that the book of Acts contains the fulfillment of Jn 14.12 and of other of Christ's prophecies (Mt 10.17 f.; 24.14): "Thus, the predictions which in the Gospels Christ utters, here we may see these actually come to pass; and note in the very facts the bright evidence of Truth which shines in them . . ." (PG 60.13 f.; trans. H. Browne and revised by G.B. Stevens, NPNF 11[1889]: 1. Also *Hom.* 4.7 *in Ac. princ.;* PG 51.107.

[45] *Bab.* 10: "But visible phenomena can shut the blasphemous mouth and shame it, and bridle the licentious tongue."

Chrysostom states the axiom that one cannot use the testimony of the evangelists concerning his miracles to demonstrate the divinity of Christ to pagans, because pagans will not
accept this testimony.[46] The demonstration must be based
upon incontestable facts, which are recognized by both pagans and Christians *(argumentum e concessis)*.[47] Such commonly
accepted facts are that Christ founded the church, and that
Christ's predictions about the invincibility of the church (Mt
16.18) and the destruction of the temple (Mt 24.2) have been
fulfilled.[48] Moreover, it is the special character of Christ's predictions that they become progressively more obvious in the
course of history.[49] Finally, Chrysostom also states that the
fulfillment of Christ's prophecies in the present shows the
trustworthiness of the miracles, which he performed in the
past.[50] It seems that earlier Eusebius of Caesarea had made
extensive use of this argument in a monograph directed to
pagans, whose subject was the fulfilled predictions of Christ.[51]
Book four of Eusebius's *Theophany* is devoted to the same
topic and may be a reedition of this monograph.[52]

(16) In conclusion, there are certain other elements in *Bab.*
which suggest that Chrysostom may have read Eusebius' trea-

---

[46] *Jud. et gent.* 17.8: "I did not speak to you of the dead who were brought
back to life or of the lepers who were made clean. Why? So that you will not
say: 'Those are lies, empty boasts, fairy tales. Who saw these things? Who
heard them?'"

[47] *Jud. et gent.* 1.5: "How shall I persuade him, especially if he is ignorant
and ill-informed? What source of proof can I use other than one on which we
both together agree, one which is undeniable and admits no doubt?"

[48] According to Chrysostom, *Jud.* 5 (PG 48.900–01; FOTC 68.136–40),
emperor Julian wished to see the Jewish temple restored in order to confound Christ's prophecy about the definitive destruction of the sanctuary.
The abortive attempt to rebuild the temple is mentioned in *Bab.* 119.

[49] *Jud. et gent.* 16.1 (McKendrick, *"Quod Christus sit Deus"* 123).

[50] *Jud. et gent.* 11.13 (McKendrick, *"Quod Christus sit Deus"* 106).

[51] Cf. Eusebius, P.e. 1.3.12 (*Eusebius Werke* VIII,1: *Die Praeparatio evangelica*,
ed. K. Mras, GCS 43,1[1954]:13; trans. E. Gifford, *Preparation for the Gospel:
Eusebius*, 2 vols. [Oxford 1903; reprint Grand Rapids Michigan 1981] 1:9.
Gifford's translation has been reprinted in this volume thanks to the kind
permission of Baker Book House.): "There are also countless other sayings
and prophecies of our Saviour, by collecting which in a special work, and
showing that the actual events agree with His divine foreknowledge, we
prove beyond all question the truth of our opinions concerning Him."

[52] Johannes Quasten, *Patrology* (Utrecht 1966) 3:332.

tise against Hierocles. In both *Hierocl.* and *Bab.* the Christian authors cite and analyze the writings of pagan authors (Philostratus, Libanius) for apologetic purposes. This type of literary criticism is characteristic of the epoch—Porphyry practiced a similar analysis of the gospels—and was considered a more convincing form of proof than mere rhetoric.[53] Other similarities between the two works are the discussion of necromancy[54] and of demons.[55] In another place Chrysostom says that Apollonius is not divine because his virtue left no enduring imprint on history.[56] This resembles what Eusebius said in his treatise.[57] It is not certain, however, that Chrysostom had Apollonius of Tyana specifically in mind when he wrote *Bab.*[58]

The Pagan Reaction II: Emperor Julian

(17) Emperor Julian (361–63) attempted to restore paganism as the official creed of the Roman empire. Christian and pagan contemporaries noted the potentially far-reaching effects of his reign on the political and cultural life of the empire. Gregory of Nazianzus, for example, criticized Julian for endangering the stability of the empire by his anti-Christian policy.[59] Libanius, on the other hand, believed that the renewal of traditional pagan religion would benefit rhetorical education, which had undergone a decline under the previous Christian emperor, Constantius (337–61).[60] The Arian continuator of Eusebius, writing in the time of Valens (364–

[53] Joseph-Rhéal Laurin, *Orientations maîtresses des apologistes chrétiens de 270 à 361* (Rome 1954) 140.
[54] *Bab.* 1, *Hierocl.* 24.
[55] *Bab.* 3, *Hierocl.* 31.
[56] *Laud. Paul.* 4 (PG 50.490).
[57] *Hierocl.* 4, 7.
[58] The occasion of the *Inst.* of Lactantius is instructive in this regard. Lactantius states that he wrote the *Inst.* to answer the works of Hierocles and one other anti-Christian writer. He then answers Hierocles briefly and says that his apology will not be addressed to their trivial objections (*Inst.* 5.2 f.).
[59] *Or.* 4.74; PG 35.600.
[60] A.J. Festugière, *Antioche païenne et chrétienne* (Paris 1959) 230–39. In *Bab.* Chrysostom does not mention that Julian forbade Christians to teach rhetoric in the schools. Gregory of Nazianzus, on the other hand, refers to the prohibition at length (*Or.* 4.100 ff.; PG 35.634 ff.).

78), mentions the violence which had erupted against the church in Egypt, Palestine, and Syria when Julian decreed the restoration of idolatry.[61]

Against Christians. (18) Julian wrote three books *Against Christians* in the winter of 362–63 at Antioch.[62] The emperor seems to have expected that responses to his work would follow. For, at the outset he asks that those who reply should answer the objections to Christianity which he has raised, and not introduce extraneous countercharges against paganism.[63] It is possible that Chrysostom in *Bab.* is answering some of the objections, which had been raised by Julian in *Against Christians.* Some of these accusations are: that Christian doctrine is a fiction;[64] that Christ is inferior to pagan teachers;[65] that Christians have used force against pagans and heretics— which is inconsistent with Jesus' teaching;[66] that the practice of giving alms is injurious to society;[67] and that Christians worship a corpse. The first two charges are already to be found in Porphyry and Hierocles. The second two indictments, however, seem to belong to Julian. It is known that emperor Julian was self-conscious about the use of force and hesitated to use it against the Christians.[68] As for giving alms, Julian also attacked it in his *Misopogon,*[69] though he tried to

---

[61] Cited by Joseph Bidez, *Philostorgius Kirchengeschichte mit dem Leben des Lucian von Antiochien und den Fragmenten eines Arianischen Historiographen,* GCS 21 (Leipzig 1913) 227–30. Antioch was the exception, where the masses of people were Christian. Paul Petit, *Libanius et la vie municipale à Antioche au ive siècle après J.-C.* (Paris 1955) 200.

[62] Libanius, *Or.* 17.18; cf. *Or.* 18.178.

[63] Neumann, ed., *Contra Christianos,* 163 f. Gregory of Nazianzus predicted that many would write against Julian (*Or.* 4.79; PG 35.605).

[64] Neumann, ed., *Contra Christianos,* 163, 202, 220, 224, and frag. 16 (p. 238). Cf. *Ep.* 90 in *L'empereur Julien Oeuvres complètes* 1,2: *Lettres et Fragments,* ed. J. Bidez (Paris 1960) 174.

[65] E.g., unfavorable comparison of Christ with Asclepius (Neumann, ed., *Contra Christianos* 197 f.). Cf. Neumann, ed., *Contra Christianos* 184 f.: pagans had lawgivers who were the equal of Moses.

[66] Neumann, ed., *Contra Christianos* 199 f. Cf. *Bab.* 13.

[67] Neumann, ed., *Contra Christianos* frags. 44, 45 (p. 84; cf. pp. 19 f.). Cf. *Bab.* 43 f.

[68] E.g., Libanius, *Or.* 18. 121 (R. Foerster, ed., *Opera,* 12 vols., [Leipzig 1903–27; reprint Hildesheim 1963] 2:287). Gregory of Nazianzus, *Or.* 4.79. Chrysostom, *Pan. Juv.* 1 (PG 50.573). Cf. *Bab.* 13 and note.

[69] *Mis.* 363ab (L'Empereur Julien, *Oeuvres complètes.* Volume 2, Part 2: *Dis-*

incorporate the practice into his reformed paganism.[70] The charge that Christians worship a corpse will be discussed in connection with the polemic against relics (pars. 32–33).

(19) Since Chrysostom treats all these subjects in *Bab.*, it is possible that he was responding to the treatise of Julian. This possibility is enhanced by the fact that the refutation of Julian's *Against Christians* was initiated and carried on by Antiochenes. Evidently, the first Christian to write a formal refutation was Theodore of Mopsuestia. Neumann suggests that Theodore wrote in Antioch, sometime after 378, to gratify his teacher, Diodore.[71] A contemporary of Theodore, Philip Sidetes, answered the books of Julian, perhaps also under the inspiration of Diodore.[72] Cyril of Alexandria wrote thirty books against Julian after 435. The occasion may have been a controversy surrounding the writings of Theodore of Mopsuestia. In 435 Cyril wrote three books against Theodore and possibly became acquainted with Theodore's writing against Julian, which naturally contained Antiochene doctrine. Perhaps Cyril then decided to write his own refutation, which would be more orthodox than Theodore's and also combat the pagans in Alexandria.[73] It seems that no Latin writer ever refuted Julian's *Against Christians*.[74] Maybe the text only circulated locally in the area of Antioch, where it had been composed.[75]

---

cours de Julien Empereur: Les Césars, Sur Helios Roi, Le Misopogon, ed. C. Lacombrade [Paris 1964] 189). *Bab.* 44.

[70]Julian, *Ep.* 84 (Bidez, ed., *Lettres et Fragments* 144–46.). Gregory of Nazianzus, *Or.* 4.111 (PG 35.648).

[71]Neumann, ed., *Contra Christianos* 31. Diodore was also the teacher of Chrysostom (Sozomen, H.e. 8.2). As a leading Christian apologist in Antioch, Diodore was sharply attacked by Julian (*Ep.* 90; Bidez, ed., *Lettres et Fragments* 174).

[72]Neumann, ed., *Contra Christianos* 33 ff. Philip belonged to the school of Antioch, and was the *sunkellos* (associate) of Chrysostom at Constantinople.

[73]Cyril sent his books *Contra Julianum* to Theodoret to be read by the Antiochene teachers (Neumann, ed., *Contra Christianos* 36 ff.). One of the most bitter opponents of Cyril, Alexander of Hierapolis in Syria, is also said to have written against Julian (Neumann, ed., *Contra Christianos* 87).

[74]Jerome mentioned the possibility of writing a refutation of Julian in 397 (*Ep.* 70.3; J.Labourt, ed., *Saint Jérôme: Lettres*, 8 vols. [Paris 1949–63] 3:211f.).

[75]Libanius, for example, apparently had read the work (*Or.* 18.178). Both Chrysostom and Theodore were students of Libanius according to Sozomen

Oracles. (20) Emperor Julian was an ardent believer in the supernatural, in divination, and especially the testimony of oracles, and valued this means of communication with the gods.[76] During the preparation of his Persian campaign, for instance, all manner of mantic arts were employed.[77] Julian also wrote in defense of oracles. In his discourse against Heracleius the Cynic, he attacked the second century Cynic philosopher Oenomaus of Gadara, author of an outspoken treatise against oracles.[78] (Eusebius had utilized the work of Oenomaus in his discussion of oracles in P.e. 5 and 6.[79]) In *Against Christians* Julian refers to the divine spirit which had manifested itself among the Jews and pagans.[80] In the same place he says that both the pagan oracles and the Jewish prophets have yielded to time and no longer have the same prophetic power.[81] This statement may reflect the failure of Julian's personal attempt to reactivate the oracle of Apollo at Daphne, narrated by Chrysostom in *Bab.* 80 ff.

The Oracle of Apollo at Daphne. (21) Seleucus I, founder of Antioch, established the sanctuary of Apollo at neighboring Daphne about 300 B.C. Within the temple stood a colossal acrolithic statue of Apollo, attributed to the Athenian sculptor Bryaxis. Two rivulets from the stream Castalia flowed by

---

(H.e. 8.2), and might have had access to the text for this reason. Cf. Gabriel Rochefort, ed., *Discours de Julien empereur* (Paris 1963) ix.

[76] A. Seitz *Die Apologie des Christentums bei den Griechen des IV. und V. Jahrhunderts in historisch-systematischer Darstellung* (Würzburg 1895), p. 10. Cf. Julian, *Ep.* 87 (J. Bidez, ed., *Lettres et Fragments* 149). Chrysostom, *Bab.* 77.

[77] Ammianus Marcellinus, *Hist.* 22.12.7. The emperor's subsequent defeat and death in Persia made a mockery of such prognostications in the eyes of the Christians. Cf. Ephraem, *Adversus Iulianum* 4, trans. G. Bickell, *Zeitschrift für katholische Theologie* 2 (1878): 356. Theodoret, H.e. 3.21.1–3, 28.1 f. (GCS 44: 200, 206).

[78] Julian, *Or.* 7.5 (L'Empereur Julien, *Oeuvres complètes*, Vol. 2, Part 1: *Discours de Julien Empereur: A Thémistius, Contre Héracleios le cynique, Sur la mère de dieux, Contre les cyniques ignorants,* ed. G. Rochefort [Paris 1963] 50.)

[79] Cf. *Bab.* 80 ff. with notes.

[80] Neuman, ed., *Contra Christianos,* 196 f., The parallel between pagan oracles and Jewish prophets may have been drawn by Porphyry, since Eusebius treated the question in D.e. 5 Proem (GCS 23: 202 f.). The comparison had already been made by Celsus (Origen, *Cels.* 7.3). Cf. *Bab.* 85 and note.

[81] Neumann, ed., *Contra Christianos* 197.

both sides of the temple.[82] Oracles were obtained from the ever-changing agitation of the waters.[83]

(22) In the discourse on Babylas Chrysostom narrates the following sequence of events, which led to the destruction of the oracle of Apollo at Daphne. To cure the licentiousness rampant at Daphne, Gallus Caesar had the relics of Babylas brought from Antioch to Daphne (*Bab.* 67). As a result Apollo became mute and the oracle ceased to function (*Bab.* 73). Emperor Julian attempted to consult the oracle when he took up residence in Antioch. He was told that the silence of the god was due to the presence of corpses, buried in the neighborhood of Daphne (*Bab.* 81). Julian then directed that the coffin of Babylas be removed from Daphne (*Bab.* 87). The coffin was carried back to Antioch and reburied in the Christian cemetery (*Bab.* 93). Immediately afterwards, the temple was ravaged by fire, which destroyed the statue of Apollo and the roof of the building (*Bab.* 93). The emperor was overcome by anger; he tortured the priest of Apollo to discover the human agency responsible for the fire—but in vain (*Bab.* 95 f.). For the flame was sent by a divine opponent, Babylas (*Bab.* 93 f.). The partially burned temple is still standing as a monument of the martyr's victory over the demon Apollo (*Bab.* 127).

(23) Interestingly, the contemporary historian, Ammianus Marcellinus, while omitting all reference to the supernatural, in no way contradicts, and corroborates certain elements of, Chrysostom's narrative.[84]

The Monody of Libanius. (24) Julian's friend, Libanius, the distinguished sophist of Antioch, was distressed by the conflagration, which had destroyed the sanctuary and cult of Apollo

---

[82] Glanville Downey, *A History of Antioch in Syria* (Princeton 1961) 82 ff.

[83] Viktor Schultze, *Altchristliche Städte und Landschaften* 3: *Antiocheia* (Gütersloh, 1930) 215. Julian is said to have reopened the oracular stream of Castalia, which had been blocked up by Hadrian. See Downey, *History,* 222 n. 103. A. Bouché-Leclercq, *Histoire de la divination dans l'antiquité* (Paris 1880) 3: 266–70.

[84] Cf. Ammianus Marcellinus, *Hist.* 22.12.8–13.1–3 (Ammiani Marcellini, *Rerum Gestarum: Libri Qui Supersunt,* vol. 1: Books 14–31, ed. C.U. Clark [Berlin 1910] 280 f.).

at Daphne.[85] Tearfully, he composed a lament for Apollo,[86] in which he defended Julian's attempt to reestablish paganism against the signs of the times. Except for the passages quoted by Chrysostom in *Bab.* the text of Libanius's monody has perished.[87] The monody on Apollo was probably written between 22 October 362, the date of the fire according to Ammianus (*Hist.* 22.13.1), and March/April 363, when Julian mentions the work in a letter to Libanius.[88]

(25) It was thus some years after the events which it commemorates that Chrysostom incorporated the monody of Libanius into his discourse. In view of the length and number of citations from the monody Chrysostom probably had before him an exemplar of the speech, which may have circulated as a pamphlet.[89] There are several factors which may have led Chrysostom to utilize the text of the monody in his discourse on Babylas. First, great evidentiary value was attached to the testimony of one's opponent. According to Eusebius, who cited the writings of Porphyry, such evidence was "unassailable."[90] Chrysostom in *Bab.* 10 enunciated this principle: "I shall not need to obtain from others proof of what is said, since you, the enemy, provide me with it." In

---

[85] Julian states that Apollo had left the temple before the fire, having heard Julian's speech to the senate of Antioch, wherein he upbraided the Antiochenes for neglecting the worship of Apollo (*Mis.* 34–36; *Discours de Julien,* ed. Lacombrade 187–89). Libanius also writes that the fire at Daphne is an indication that Apollo has left the earth (*Or.* 17.30; *Libanii opera,* ed. Foerster 2:218). Cf. *Bab.* 100.

[86] Libanius, *Ep.* 785 (*Libanii opera,* ed. Foerster 10:707 f.). Cf. Libanius, *Ep.* 695 to Acacius, who had written a work in honor of Asclepius, whose temple the Christians had apparently demolished (*Libanii opera,* ed. Foerster 10:629 f.).

[87] The monody is printed among the works of Libanius as *Or.* 60. The manuscripts of Libanius, which contain the monody on Apollo, depend on the citations by Chrysostom in *Bab.* Consult: *Libanii opera,* ed. Foerster 4: 298–321.

[88] *Ep.* 98 (Bidez, ed., *Lettres et Fragments* 181).

[89] Anton Naegele, "Chrysostomos und Libanios," in *Chrysostomika* (Rome 1908) 117. Paul Petit suggests that the monody, because of its literary polish, was a work intended for wide circulation. "Recherches sur la publication et la diffusion des discours de Libanius," *Historia* 5 (1956): 491.

[90] Eusebius, P.e. 4.6.1 (GCS 43,1: 176) and 5.5.5 (GCS 43,1: 232). Also P.e. 1.5,6; 2.8; 3 Preface; 8 Preface; 14.2; 15 Preface. In P.e. 10.11 Eusebius cites Tatian as having used proof from the enemy.

addition to the monody he cited the evidence furnished by the oracle of Apollo (*Bab.* 75, 102) and the priest of Apollo (*Bab.* 95).[91] Therefore Chrysostom quoted the text of Libanius as an unimpeachable proof of his narrative concerning the conflagration at Daphne.[92] Among other things, the discourse attests to the melancholy with which the pagan community at Antioch was affected as a result of the fire.[93]

(26) Furthermore, the monody provided material, not neglected by Chrysostom, for ridiculing pagan religion and rhetoric. There may have been a personal element involved, since Libanius may have been his former professor of rhetoric.[94] The tone of the ironic refutation (*Bab.* 98–113) varies between sympathy for the deluded sophist and bitterness towards an opponent of the truth. Seemingly, the personal religion of Libanius is under attack. Nowhere in the discourse on Babylas is Libanius mentioned by name. Chrysostom refers to him as "the sophist of the city" (*Bab.* 98)— which was probably identification enough, since Libanius was well-known at Antioch. Chrysostom also addresses him as "mourner," "scoundrel," "wretched and miserable man," and "fine fellow" (*Bab.* 99, 104, 105, 111). The gulf has continued to widen since Chrysostom, at the age of eighteen, experienced dissatisfaction with the sophists.[95] Though Chrysostom's refutation of Libanius is clothed in oratorical form, nevertheless his material is more topical than the subjects of speeches in the rhetorical schools.[96] The polemic against Libanius is a strong expression of Chrysostom's anti-Hellenism.[97]

---

[91] Chrysostom also utilized the witness of the opponent in his other apologetic treatise, *Jud. et gent.* 2 (PG 48.814 f.). Cf. *Ep. Olymp.* 7.2d (SC 13bis: 140).

[92] Jerome emphasizes the need for documentary proof in polemics (*Vigil.* 3; PL 23.356).

[93] Cf. *Bab.* 97, 105, 112 f.

[94] Naegele, "Chrysostomos und Libanios" 87 ff., discusses the evidence concerning Chrysostom's relationship to Libanius. See also Paul Maas, "Zu den Beziehungen zwischen Kirchenvätern und Sophisten," *Sitzungsberichte der Preussischen Akademie der Wissenschaften, Phil.-hist. Klasse* (Berlin 1912) 2: 1123–26.

[95] Palladius, *V. Chrys.* 5 (Coleman-Norton, *Palladii Dialogus* 28).

[96] Naegele, "Chrysostomos und Libanios" 113.

[97] G.W. Bowersock calls the discourse "invective." *Julian the Apostate* (Cambridge, Mass. 1978) 2.

Conclusion. (27) That many oracles had stopped functioning was generally acknowledged by pagans like Cicero and Plutarch. Christian authors attributed the silence of the oracles to the coming of Christ.[98] In the discourse on Babylas Chrysostom describes the events leading to the cessation of the oracle of Apollo at Daphne and the subsequent physical destruction of the temple and statue of Apollo. Chrysostom's discourse should also be viewed in light of the previous Christian polemic against divination and the role of oracles in pagan religion, such as Eusebius, P.e. 4–6. Although the obtaining of oracles had been forbidden by Constantinus II (357), emperor Julian's renewal of divination required a revival of the Christian polemic against oracles. Thus Chrysostom's discourse contains an attack upon oracles in the tradition of Eusebius with the addition of a new element (the power of relics) to the argument.[99]

Apotheosis of emperor Julian. (28) In his article, "Die Himmelfahrt des Julianus Apostata,"[100] J. Straub has shown how Chrysostom censured the pagan practice of divinizing its rulers and heroes. The pagan apotheosis, according to Chrysostom, is based only upon deeds done in this life. For example, Alexander the Great does not deserve to be worshiped as a god because he accomplished nothing after death:

> For that whilst alive one should win battles and victories, being a king and having armies at his disposal, is nothing marvelous, no, nor startling or novel; but that after a Cross

---

[98] *Martyrdom of the Holy and Glorious Apostle Bartholomew* (ANF 8: 553, 555). Arnobius, *Adversus nationes* 1.46 (Arnobii *Adversus nationes: Libri VII*, ed. C. Marchesi, 2nd ed. [Turin 1953] 41). Athanasius, *Inc.* 55.1 (*Athanasius De incarnatione: An Edition of the Greek Text*, ed. F.L. Cross, SPCK Texts for Students 39 [London 1939] 86). Chrysostom, *Exp. in Ps.* 44.7 (PG 55.193). Eusebius, P.e. 4.2.8 (GCS 43,1: 167) and 4.4.1 (GCS 43,1: 173). According to Eusebius, V. C. 2.50, emperor Diocletian was persuaded to persecute the Christians because they had rendered the gods mute (the words of the Milesian oracle of Apollo to Diocletian). Cf. John Milton, *Hymn on the Morning of Christ's Nativity*, stanza 19, cited in NPNF 2,4: 62, note 8.

[99] For a later parallel see Hippolyte Delehaye, "Les recueils antiques de miracles des saints," AB 43 (1925) 51: the relics of Thecla silenced the oracle of Apollo Sarpedonius.

[100] *Gymnasium* 69 (1962): 310–26.

and Tomb one should perform such great things throughout every land and sea, this it is which is most especially replete with such amazement, and proclaims His divine and unutterable Power. And Alexander indeed after his decease never restored again his kingdom which had been rent in pieces and quite abolished: indeed how was it likely he, dead, should do so? but Christ then most of all set up His after He was dead.[101]

The fact that Christ accomplished great things after death is in the final analysis a proof of his resurrection.[102]

(29) In this connection Straub points to the apotheosis of the emperor Julian in the funeral oration composed by Libanius in 365.[103] Having narrated Julian's career in great detail, Libanius states that his accomplishments were superhuman.[104] Libanius concludes the funeral oration by divinizing Julian and addressing him as "nursling of demons, pupil of demons, associate of demons."[105] It may or may not be a coincidence that the last sentence of *Bab.* seems to echo this: "So great is the power of the saints, so invincible and fearful, both to emperors, and to demons, and to the chief of the demons himself" (*Bab.* 127). In any case, the ambivalence of the word "demon," which is used in two different senses by the pagan writer, Libanius, and the Christian writer, Chrysostom, is striking.[106] It does not appear, however, that Chrysostom in *Bab.* is concerned with the apotheosis of emperor Julian. He describes the death of Julian (*Bab.* 123) but does not mention the emperor's attempt to drown himself in order to create the illusion of an ascension.[107]

[101] Chrysostom, *Hom.* 26.5 *in* 2 *Cor.* (PG 61.581); trans. J. Ashworth and revised by T.W. Chambers NPNF 12 (1889): 402.
[102] This argument was used previously by Athanasius, *Inc.* 30–32. Cf. Chrysostom, *Jud. et gent.* 9: Christ's accomplishments after death are the fulfillment of the prophecy in Is 11.10, "his sepulchre shall be glorious."
[103] *Or.* 18 (*Libanii opera* ed. Foerster 2:222–371). Cf. Socrates, H.e. 3.23 (PG 67.445).
[104] E.g., *Or.* 18.65, 242 (*Libanii opera*, ed. Foerster 2:264, 341).
[105] *Or.* 18.308 (*Libanii opera*, ed. Foerster 2:370).
[106] Cf. Anne-Marie Malingrey, ed., *Jean Chrysostome: Lettre d'Exil*, SC 103 (Paris 1964) 28 f.
[107] See Gregory of Nazianzus, *Or.* 5.14 (PG 35.681). The story about Alexander the Great was probably the model (Arrian, *Anab.* 7.27.3).

Theodicy: Questions Relating to the Fate of Julian. (30) Both pagans and Christians questioned how God's justice had operated in the life of Julian. Jerome reports that a certain pagan, on learning of emperor Julian's death, charged the god of the Christians with cruelty and lack of forbearance.[108] The writings composed against Julian immediately after his death by Ephraem and Gregory of Nazianzus are characterized by exultation at the defeat of one of God's enemies. By contrast, Chrysostom's discourse on Babylas does not have the same bitter tone.[109]

(31) The discourse on Babylas reveals that the reign of Julian had caused consternation in the Christian community. Chrysostom formulates the misgivings of the Christians as: "why God did not punish the emperor?" (Bab. 124), i.e., why was Julian permitted to reign?[110] In the context of his narrative Chrysostom frames a more specific question: why was the temple of Apollo devastated by fire but the emperor spared? (*Bab.* 114). He attempts to answer this latter question in paragraphs 118–24. His explanation is that Julian was spared, whereas the temple of Apollo was destroyed, through the "goodness and philanthropy of Christ" (*Bab.* 118) and the "long-suffering" of God (*Bab.* 124). The emperor was given time to repent, during which period he was repeatedly warned by various signs, including the conflagration at Daphne. Only when emperor Julian repeatedly abused the forbearance of God did he receive partial retribution for his deeds. With this discussion Chrysostom not only explains to Christians why God permitted the reign of Julian, but he also responds to the pagan accusation concerning the inclemency of God toward Julian. He may have intended to defend divine providence against both parties.

---

[108] Jerome, *Abac.* 2.3.14 (PL 25.1329).

[109] Cf. Johannes Geffcken, "Kaiser Julianus und die Streitschriften seiner Gegner," *Neue Jahrbücher für das klassische Altertum* 21 (1908): 161–95.

[110] Similarly, Gregory of Nazianzus in his two orations against Julian attempts to answer the question: why did God take so long to check Julian's impiety (*Or.* 4.28; 5.27).

Veneration of Martyrs and their Relics

Objections to the Honor Paid to Martyrs and their Remains.
(32) Opposition to the Christian practice of honoring martyrs and their remains was prominent in Neoplatonic circles. Emperor Julian opposed the reverence of martyrs ostensibly because of the impurity associated with the dead. This was the reason he gave for removing the bones of Babylas from Daphne.[111] Julian's concern for ritual purity and avoidance of contamination from the dead is probably due to the influence of Iamblichus.[112] Julian attributed the heroism of martyrs to the influence of evil demons.[113] He calls the martyrs "ill-starred" *(dustucheis)*, a description which expresses the traditional attitude of superficial pagan observers of the martyrs.[114] Gregory of Nazianzus contrasts Julian's contempt for the martyrs with his admiration for the senseless murders of classical mythology.[115] Gregory also mentions the prodigy which took place in Julian's youth and presaged his future hostility towards martyrs.[116] Jerome mentions Julian together with Vigilantius as an opponent of martyrs.[117]

(33) In Julian's treatise against Christians the polemic against the veneration of martyrs follows an attack upon the divinity of Christ. The divine worship of a dead man, says Julian, was devised by the apostle John in his gospel.[118] Christians are described as worshiping a corpse.[119] The later disci-

---

[111] *Bab.* 82. Cf. Ammianus Marcellinus 22.12.8. Philostorgius mentions the profanation of relics which occurred under Julian (H.e. 7.4; GCS 21: 80 f., cf. 228).
[112] J. Bidez, ed., *Lettres et Fragments* 129 ff. Similarly Julian forbade the celebration of funerals during the day to avoid pollution (cf. Plato, *Lg.* 960a).
[113] J. Bidez, ed., *Lettres et Fragments* 155.
[114] Neumann, ed., *Contra Christianos* 198. Hippolyte Delehaye, *Les origines du culte des martyrs*² (Brussels 1933) 19 f.
[115] *Or.* 4.69; PG 35.589–92.
[116] I.e., the collapse of a martyr's shrine built by Julian; cf. Sozomen, H.e. 5.2 (PG 67.1213 f.); Gregory of Nazianzus, *Or.* 4.24–27 (PG 35.552 f.).
[117] *Ep.* 109.1 (J. Labourt, ed., *Saint Jérôme: Lettres*, 8 vols. [Paris 1949–63] 5:203).
[118] Neumann, ed., *Contra Christianos* 223–25.
[119] Neumann, ed., *Contra Christianos* 196, 199.

ples introduced the worship of many other corpses.[120] Julian also says that the reverence paid to martyrs is opposed to the injunction of Christ, who stated that tombs are full of impurity (Mt 23.27).[121] The real reason why Christians "haunt the tombs" is to practice sorcery and receive dreams (cf. Is 65.4).[122] These objections indicate that Julian considered the honor given to martyrs and their relics a kind of dedication to death. As Grabar points out, Julian misunderstood the Christian veneration of martyrs, the essence of which is a proclamation of victory over death.[123]

Defense of the Honor Paid to Martyrs and their Remains. (34) In his discourse on Babylas Chrysostom seems to be answering various charges which had been leveled against the veneration of martyrs.[124] First, he combats the notion that dead bodies are a source of pollution. The argument is specifically directed against Julian and contains an attack upon the emperor's sun worship.[125] Perhaps in response to Julian's polemic, Chrysostom describes the beneficial effects of contact with the tombs and relics of martyrs. The sight of the graves of the saints inspires those who behold them with equal zeal. In these tombs is located a tangible energy, which allows the soul of the visitor to perceive an image of the saint whose relics lie there (*Bab.* 65).

(35) The opinion of Porphyry and Eunomius that the dust of martyrs cannot drive away demons[126] is refuted as a matter of course by the narrative concerning the relics of Babylas,

---

[120] Neumann, ed., *Contra Christianos* 225. Cf. Julian, *Mis.* 344a. Eunapius, V. S. 472b. Libanius describes Christianity as "the tombs" (*Or.* 18.282), and Christians as "those around the tombs" (*Or.* 62.10).

[121] Neumann, ed., *Contra Christianos* 223–25. This objection is answered in *Qu. et resp.* 28 (*Corpus apologetarum Christianorum saeculi secundi*, vol. 5: *Justinus philosophus et martyr,* ed. J.C.Th. Otto, 3rd ed. [Jena 1876–81] 5 [1881]: 42ff.).

[122] Neumann, ed., *Contra Christianos* 226.

[123] André Grabar, *Martyrium: Recherches sur le culte des reliques et l'art chrétien antique* (Paris 1946) 2: 39. Cf. *Bab.* 64 and notes.

[124] Ernst Lucius, *Die Anfänge des Heiligenkults in der christlichen Kirche* (Tübingen 1904) 329 ff., seemingly neglects Chrysostom's defense of relics. Insofar as it is a defense of martyrs and their relics, the discourse on Babylas antedates Jerome's *Vigil.* (406) and Theodoret's *Affect.* 8 (ca. 423).

[125] *Bab.* 82–86.

[126] Jerome, *Vigil.* 10 (PL 23.363 f.).

which silenced the oracle of the demon Apollo (*Bab.* 73–75). The relics of Babylas contain a divine power, which easily overpowered Apollo.[127] To refute the accusation that Christians pay homage to corpses, Chrysostom demonstrates that both Christ and the relics of the martyrs are not dead but possess true life. The death of Christ is life-giving *(zōopoios)*.[128] Similarly, the remains of martyr Babylas are not a corpse but alive and active.[129]

Development of the Apology for Martyrs and Relics. (36) Besides responding directly to the objections raised by Julian and others, Chrysostom uses more sophisticated and complex arguments to defend the practice of honoring martyrs. These arguments may have been intended for the edification of the Christian community as well. In his apologetics Chrysostom often uses a twofold argument, consisting of refutation of the error followed by exposition of the truth for the edification of the church.[130] In the discourse on Babylas there are three topics which constitute such positive argumentation for the veneration of martyrs.

Scriptural Proof of the Miracles of the Martyrs. (37) In the prologue of *Bab.* Chrysostom twice cites the text of Jn 14.12: "Amen, amen, I say to you, he who believes in me, the works that I do he also shall do, and greater than these he shall do . . ." (*Bab.* 1, 8). It has already been shown how Chrysostom argues that this prophecy has been fulfilled in the miracles of the apostles

---

[127]*Bab.* 75, 90, 109. Such power belongs to the remains of all the saints (*Bab.* 127).

[128]*Bab.* 1. The word *zōopoios* is used with reference to the death of Christ by the Syrian liturgies. Cf. PGL s.v. *zōopoios. Liturgies Eastern and Western.* ed. F.E. Brightman and C.E. Hammond (Oxford 1896; reprint, Oxford 1965) 1: 20. Ignatius of Antioch, *Eph.* 7.2. (*Die Apostolischen Väter:* Neubearbeitung der Funkschen Ausgabe von K. Bihlmeyer. Part 1: Didache, Barnabas, Klemens I und II, Polykarp, Klemens I und II, Polykarp, Quadratus, Diognetbrief [Tübingen 1924] 84).

[129]*Bab.* 93, 99. Julian, *Mis.* 361bc (*Discours de Julien,* ed. Lacombrade 187) twice refers to the "corpse" of Babylas. Libanius also refers to Babylas as a "corpse" (*Bab.* 98 f.).

[130]E.g., *Incomprehens.* 4 (SC 28bis: 228.1–15; FOTC 72.115). *Jud.* 5.1 (PG 48.883 f.; FOTC 68.97 f.). Athenagoras, *Res.* is also structured this way; chaps. 1–10 are a discourse against false opinions, and chaps. 12–25 are an exposition of the truth.

recorded in Acts (*Bab.* 9). He also says that the apostolic miracles are authenticated by the miracles worked by the relics of
Babylas (*Bab.* 73). Implicit in this argument is the conclusion
that Christ actually predicted the miracles of Babylas; and
that the miracles of Babylas can be defended on the basis of
Christ's prediction in Jn 14.12.[131]

(38) In this regard it is significant that Origen earlier al-
luded to the prediction (Jn 14.12) in reference to certain contemporary miracles of which he was a witness.[132] Furthermore,
Sulpicius Severus, at the beginning of the fifth century, may
have used this text to justify the miracles worked by Martin of
Tours. Sulpicius says that the miracles of Martin were predicted by the Lord:

> The Lord Himself testified that such deeds would be done
> by all the faithful. These Martin performed. Anyone who
> does not believe that Martin has done these things denies
> the very words of Christ.[133]

Newman and others believed that Sulpicius was appealing to
Mk 16.17–18.[134] It is more likely that he had in mind Jn 14.12,
the verse used by Chrysostom in *Bab.* implicitly to justify the
miracles worked by the relics of Babylas. Chrysostom's attempt to justify scripturally the miracles worked by relics
might well respond to Julian's accusation that a veneration of
tombs was foreign to the teachings of Christ.[135] An argument

---

[131] Cf. Chrysostom's exegesis of Jn 14.12 in his commentary on John: "In
future the working of miracles is your prerogative because I am going away."
(*Hom.* 74.2 *in Jo.* [PG 59.402], trans. T. Goggin, *St. John Chrysostom: Commentary
on St. John the Apostle and Evangelist, Homilies 48–88,* FOTC 41 [New York
1959] 296): Chrysostom does not attribute the destruction of Apollo's temple
directly to the relics, but says that Babylas beseeched God to rain fire on the
temple (*Bab.* 93); in *Bab.* 118 he says that Christ threw fire on the temple. This
corresponds to Christ's promise in Jn 14.13–14. Cf. Augustine, *Civ.* 22.9
(FOTC 24.450–51).

[132] *Cels.* 2.8 (GCS 2: 134). But cf. *Cels.* 2.48 (GCS 2: 169–70).

[133] Sulpicius Severus, *Dial.* 1.26.5 (C. Halm, CSEL 1 [1866] 178; trans.
B. Peebles in *Niceta of Remesiana: Writings; Sulpicius Severus: Writings;* Vin-
cent of Lerins: *Commonitories;* Prosper of Aquitaine: *Grace and Free Will,*
FOTC 7 [Washington 1949] 197).

[134] Benjamin B. Warfield, *Counterfeit Miracles* (New York 1918; reprint,
London 1972) 45, 250 n. 20.

[135] Neumann, ed., *Contra Christianos* 225 f.

based upon scripture would also be useful to quell the antagonism of certain Christians and heretics towards the veneration of relics.

The Superiority of the Christian Religion. (39) In his discourse on
Babylas Chrysostom contends that through his actions the
martyr Babylas revealed the nobility *(eugeneia)* of the Christians and the shame *(aischunē)* of the Greeks[136] *(Bab.* 40). In
other sermons of the martyrs Chrysostom understands the
reverence paid to the martyrs as the shame of the pagans. He
speaks of the festival of the martyr Phocas this way: "It is the
shame of the Greeks, the reproach of their error, the destruction of the demons; it is our nobility and the crown of the
church" (PG 50.699). The commemoration of the martyrs
entails the shame of the Greeks because of the multitude
which assembles to honor the martyr. The yearly gatherings
and encomiums testify that the memory of the martyr cannot
be extinguished.[137] Also, the pagans are put to shame by the
recollection of the inhumanity and defeat of those who tortured the martyrs.[138] Thus for Chrysostom the martyrs exem-
plify the nobility of Christianity vis-à-vis the baseness of
paganism. Hence Babylas is the hero of a discourse directed
against the pagans, where the history of the martyr and his
relics constitute a *de facto* apology for the Christian religion.

(40) In *Bab.* Chrysostom employs a number of comparisons
to demonstrate the superiority of Christianity in all spheres.[139]
He compares Christian independence with pagan depen-
dence on the state *(Bab.* 40–44). He shows the difference

---

[136] I.e., pagans. The word *Hellēnes* is translated "Greeks" rather than "pagans" because a specific subgroup of pagans is meant. Implied in the use of
the word *Hellēnes* is the linguistic and cultural legacy of pagan Greece. The
Greeks are contrasted not with the Romans but with barbarians and uneducated people in general, as in Rom 1.14: "To Greeks and to foreigners, to
learned and unlearned, I am debtor."

[137] Chrysostom, *Pan. Pelag. Ant.* 3 (PG 50.582 f.). *Pan. Phoc.* 1 (PG 50.699 f.).

[138] Cf. Chrysostom, *Pan. Aeg.* 1 f. (PG 50.695 f.). *Pan. mart.* 3.1 (PG 50.708).

[139] Gregory of Nazianzus also uses the rhetorical device of comparison
(sunkrisis) in his first oration against Julian. Gregory compares the martyrs'
love of truth with the philosophers' love of glory *(Or.* 4.59 f.; PG 35.581). He
also compares the accomplishments of the monks with those of the Greek
philosophers *(Or.* 4.72 f.; PG 35.593 f.).

between Christian truth and pagan vanity (*Bab.* 45–50). Bishop Babylas is shown to be the true Stoic sage. His act of expelling the emperor from the church embraced many moral achievements *(katorthōmata),*[140] including frankness, courage, and moderation (*Bab.* 34–36). Chrysostom compares the outspokenness of Babylas towards a Roman emperor with the bravado of Diogenes, who requested Alexander the Great to step out of his light (*Bab.* 45 ff.).[141] The common good is used as the standard to measure the superiority of Babylas (*Bab.* 47). The nobility of Babylas puts to shame the most distinguished of the pagan philosophers (*Bab.* 49). In making common utility the criterion of virtue, Chrysostom is faithful to traditional Greek ethical theory. Tyrtaeus, for example, in the seventh century. B.C., defined virtue *(aretē)* according to the value it had for the common welfare of the polis.[142] Thus Chrysostom uses the principles of Greek ethical theory to demonstrate that the Hellenic ideal of virtue is realized only among Christians.[143]

Miracles Worked by the Relics of a Martyr: Evidence of the Resurrection. (41) Like Athanasius (*Inc.* 30 ff.), Chrysostom demonstrates the resurrection of Christ on the basis of the continuing activity of the Lord after the crucifixion. Unlike pagan teachers, Christ communicated his power to his disciples (*Bab.* 1). The signs worked by the apostles in the book of Acts—the "greater works" predicted in Jn 14:12—are one example of the prolongation of Christ's power in the world (*Bab.* 9).[144] The en-

---

[140] According to the Stoics only the sage can perform true acts of virtue (SVF 3: 5.28–29). Chrysostom often describes the deeds of the martyrs as *katorthōmata: Pan. Ign.* 1 (PG 50.587). *Pan. Macc.* 2.1 (PG 50.623). *Pan. Barl.* 1 (PG 50.675 f.).

[141] Cf. Geffcken, "Julianus und Streitschriften" 187. *Bab.* 45 note.

[142] Frag. 9.15 f. (*Anthologia lyrica graeca,* ed. E. Diehl, 3rd ed., 3 fascicles to date [Leipzig 1949–] 1:16).

[143] This theme was later developed by Theodoret, *Affect.* 12; SC 57: 419 ff.

[144] Elsewhere Chrysostom states that the miracles worked by the apostles after the intervention of the cross are indisputable proof of the resurrection; if Christ were dead, the signs would have ceased and others would not have worked miracles in his name. *Hom.* 4.6–7 *in Ac. princ.* (PG 51.105 ff.). *Hom.* 63.3, 72.2 *in Jo.* (PG 59.351 f., 392 [FOTC 41.185f., 275]). The book of Acts is a demonstration of the resurrection (*Hom.* 1.2 *in Ac.;* PG 60.16).

ergy of the risen Christ is also manifested in the martyrs. Chrysostom says in his panegyric on Ignatius:

> For in reality it is the greatest proof of the resurrection that the slain Christ should show forth so great power after death, as to persuade living men to despise both country and home and friends, and acquaintance and life itself, for the sake of confessing him, and to choose in place of present pleasures, both stripes and dangers and death. For these are not the achievements of any dead man, nor of one remaining in the tomb but of one risen and living.[145]

Christ lives and acts in the souls of the martyrs.[146]

(42) A third manifestation of Christ's undiminished power are the miracles worked by the relics of the martyrs. The miracles produced by the remains of Babylas in the time of Julian witness to the resurrection and prove the existence of another life (*Bab.* 64). At *Bab.* 90 Chrysostom says: "Therefore, if someone denies the resurrection, let him henceforth be ashamed, observing the more brilliant works of the martyr after his decease." Likewise in his homily on Babylas he says:

> Do not then look at the fact that the mere body of the martyr lies destitute of energy of soul; but observe this, that a greater power takes its place by the side of it, different from the soul itself—I mean the grace of the Holy Spirit, which pleads to all on behalf of the resurrection, by means of the wonders which it works.[147]

Chrysostom thus cites the miracles performed by the relics of Babylas as evidence of the resurrection of Christ. Later on Augustine will argue that miracles worked by the remains of martyrs testify to faith in the resurrection of Christ and faith in the eternal resurrection of the flesh.[148] It has not been

---

[145] PG 50.593; trans. T.P. Brandram, NPNF 9 (1889): 139. See also Chrysostom, *Hom.* 4.8 *in Ac. princ.* (PG 51.109). The argument that contempt for death on the part of Christians proves the reality of Christ's resurrection is used by Athanasius, *Inc.* 27–29. Cf. *Diogn.* 7.9.

[146] Chrysostom, *Pan. Dros.* 2 (PG 50.686).

[147] Chrysostom, *Pan. Bab.* 1; PG 50.529; trans. T.P. Brandram, NPNF 9(1889): 141.

[148] *Civ.* 22.8–9 (FOTC 24.431–51). Cf. Eugene TeSelle, *Augustine's Strategy as an Apologist* (Villanova, Pa. 1974) 39.

hitherto noticed that Chrysostom, like Eusebius, antedates
Augustine in making contemporary miracles serve an apologetic purpose.[149]

(43) The discourse on Babylas is an apology, in which
Chrysostom defends Christianity against certain accusations.
The various charges and responses have already been detailed; two principal themes emerge. One is that the apostolic
miracles are not fictions (against Porphyry, Hierocles, etc.).
The other is that martyrs and their relics are worthy of the
highest praise and veneration (against Julian, Libanius, etc.).
The narrative concerning Babylas offers proof of both these
assertions.

(44) While it is clear that the discourse is an apology, it is
more difficult to determine its precise literary genre.[150] Although the work contains references to hearing[151] and speaking,[152] and direct addresses to the audience,[153] it does not seem
to be a sermon. The discourse on Babylas far exceeds any of
Chrysostom's sermons in length. Furthermore, it was composed before Chrysostom was ordained to the priesthood and
permitted to preach (386).[154] Also, Chrysostom actually says
that he is writing (*Bab.* 78). The fact is that the patristic apology and apologetic treatise were oratorical in style and always

---

[149]Cf. Delehaye, "Les recueils antiques," 79: "Encore moins chercherait-on
chez les Grecs une déclaration de principes comparable à la théologie du
miracle que S. Augustin tire des faits qu'il vient de rapporter." Cf. Theodoret,
Affect. 8.65 (SC 57: 334) for a similar demonstration.
     [150]See M. Schatkin, "The Authenticity of St. John Chrysostom's *De sancto
Babyla, contra Iulianum et gentiles,*" *Kyriakon: Festschrift Johannes Quasten,* ed.
Patrick Granfield and Josef A. Jungmann (Münster Westf. 1970) 1: 475–77.
     [151]*Bab.* 22, 25, 31.
     [152]*Bab.* 2, 22, 27, 96, 110, 125 *(erō). Bab.* 3, 22, 30, 50, 73, 78, 96 *(eipon).*
Bab. 16, 55, 97 *(phēmi). Bab.* 23, 47, 67, 98 *(legō).*
     [153]*Bab.* 22, 75.
     [154]*Const. App.* 2.57.9 (F.X. Funk, ed., *Didascalia et Constitutiones Apostolorum*
[Paderborn 1905] 1: 163).

retained something of the character of living speech.[155] Moreover, works of ancient literature were often intended to be read aloud, in which case such rhetorical devices were appropriate.[156] (45) The discourse *Bab.* is carefully constructed according to the rules of classical rhetoric. An outline of its structure is found below in paragraph 85. The main body of the discourse, comprising the narrative about Babylas and extensive proofs of it,[157] constitutes in its entirety a demonstration of the thesis stated in the prologue. The prologue (*Bab.* 1–21) contains a refutation of the charge that apostolic miracles are a fiction. Chrysostom counters that Christ predicted that his disciples would do "greater works" (Jn 14.12), and that his prediction has been fulfilled in the apostolic miracles. The main body (22–126) consists of a narrative concerning the martyr Babylas and is divided into two sections. The "ancient history" concerns the heroic actions and resultant martyrdom of bishop Babylas; the "modern history" concerns the miracles performed by his relics. The connection between the two parts of the narrative is the power manifested by Babylas equally in life and in death. The twofold narrative about the accomplishments of Babylas in life and after death would seem to correspond to the dichotomous eulogy of the hero in ancient Greek literature.[158] Many examples are found in Plato: e.g., veneration of the hero in life and in death (*Resp.* 468b–69b); the reward of virtue, which belongs to the just man during life and after death (*Resp.* 612b ff.); honor paid to

---

[155] H. Jordan, *Geschichte der altchristlichen Literatur* (Leipzig 1911) 211. Cf. *Bab.* 81: direct address to Apollo and Julian; *Bab.* 99: direct address to Libanius. Throughout Christians are referred to as "we" and pagans as "you" (e.g., *Bab.* 85, 121; 20, 75, 86). Chrysostom also introduces an imaginary pagan opponent, whose challenges he regularly overcomes (*Bab.* 43, 46, 47, 48, 78). The device of an imaginary opponent derives from the Cynic diatribe. It is not unusual to find elements of the diatribe in a treatise (see W. Capelle and H.I. Marrou, "Diatribe," RACh 3: 992, 998, 1002).

[156] Lenain de Tillemont, *Mémoires pour servir à l'histoire ecclésiastique des six premiers siècles* (Venice 1732) 11: 564.

[157] E.g., *Bab.* 75, 78, 95, 98, 100, 102.

[158] Werner Jaeger, *Paideia: The Ideals of Greek Culture,* trans. Gilbert Highet, 2nd ed. 3 vols., (Oxford 1965) 2: 367.

the public examiner in life and after death (*Lg.* 946e–47b);
and the superhumanity of the good man in life and in death
(*Cra.* 398c). The same bipartite scheme is applied to the eulogy of Elisha by Sirach (48:14).[159]
(46) In the discourse on Babylas the ancient and modern
histories are each preceded by a proem, which in each case
establishes that the narrative is a proof of the thesis advanced
in the general prologue.[160] In addition, the proem to the modern history also contains a defense of the veneration of relics,
which is a principal theme of the apology. The last paragraph
(127) is a summary which repeats the main points of the
proof, i.e., the accomplishments of Babylas during life and
after death. The use of asyndeton marks off this paragraph as
a true peroration.[161] In terms of its structure and length, the
discourse on Babylas most closely resembles the epideictic
orations of Libanius.[162]

THE MARTYRDOM OF BABYLAS

"One must say that there is almost no history so difficult to
investigate and so involved as that of saint Babylas, when
we limit ourselves to what Eusebius and Chrysostom have
written. For, if we wish to add the testimony of later writers,
I believe that it will be impossible to entangle."

"On peut dire qu'il n'y a guere d'histoire si difficile à examiner, & si embrouillée que celle de S. Babylas, quand
nous ne nous arresterions qu'à ce qu'Eusèbe & S. Chrysostome en ont écrit. Car si nous y voulons ajouter le témoig-

---

[159] The encomium of martyr Theodore, written by Chrysippus of
Jerusalem (died ca. 478), is also structured this way. The first part of the
encomium treats the martyrdom of Theodore; the second part narrates
twelve miracles worked by Theodore after death. See Delehaye, "Les recueils
antiques," 41.
[160] In classical rhetoric the main proofs may each begin with their own
proem. Richard Volkmann, *Rhetorik der Griechen und Römer*, Handbuch der
klassischen Altertumswissenschaft 2,3 (Munich 1901) 27.
[161] Aristotle, *Rh.* 3.19. Volkmann, *Rhetorik der Griechen und Römer* 32.
[162] E.g., Libanius, *Or.* 1.55 and 4.8.

nage des auteurs posterieurs, je croy qu'il n'y aura aucun moyen d'en sortir."

Lenain de Tillemont[163]

(47) In this section an analysis will be made of the major texts which deal with the martyrdom of Babylas, starting with Chrysostom's discourse. By this method, new light may be shed upon the martyrdom of Babylas. Also: the writer expects to clarify to the extent possible the relationship of the literary sources.

Chrysostom

(48) Chrysostom's discourse on Babylas contains a rather detailed account of the circumstances of the martyrdom. It describes a certain Roman emperor *(basileus)*,[164] to whom a foreign monarch had entrusted his son as a pledge of peace *(Bab.* 23f.). The emperor treacherously murdered the child *(Bab.* 25 f.). Then he hastened to the church *(Bab.* 27). Babylas, the bishop of Antioch, expelled him from the church on account of his crime *(Bab.* 30). In return, the emperor imprisoned Babylas in chains *(Bab.* 54), and subsequently had him executed *(Bab.* 60). At the behest of Babylas, the chains were buried with his body *(Bab.* 63). In this account Chrysostom gives no proper names except that of the protagonist, Baby-

---

[163] Tillemont, *Mémoires* 3: 727.
[164] The word *basileus* was used regularly in later Greek of Roman emperors. W.F. Arndt and F.W. Gingrich, *A Greek-English Lexicon of the New Testament and Other Early Christian Literature: A Translation and Adaptation of the Fourth Revised and Augmented Edition of WALTER BAUER's Griechisch-Deutsches Wörterbuch zu den Schriften des Neuen Testaments und der übrigen urchristlichen Literatur*, 2nd ed., revised and augmented by F. Wilbur Gingrich and Frederick W. Danker from Walter Bauer's fifth edition, 1958 (Chicago 1979) s.v. *basileus*. At *Bab.* 30 the emperor is described as: "Not the tetrarch of a few cities, not the king of a single nation, but the ruler of the greater part of the whole world . . . possessing many nations, many cities, and an immense army, formidable in every respect by reason of the magnitude of his power and his reckless disposition. . . ." The *Alia Acta,* printed in the AASS, emphasize that it was a Roman emperor, not merely a judge, whom Babylas withstood (AASS, *Jan.* 3: 187 f.).

las. The Roman emperor and foreign king are both nameless. Such anonymity was characteristic of sophistic discourses and the Christian panegyrics modeled on them.[165] Of course, it is also possible that Chrysostom could not or did not choose to name the *basileus* responsible for the death of Babylas.[166]

(49) Although he does not name names, Chrysostom does provide significant details concerning the expulsion of the emperor from the church. The data, mostly linguistic, suggests that Babylas was imposing an ecclesiastical penance on the emperor for his crime.[167] To describe the expulsion Chrysostom employs the words *ekballō* (*Bab.* 30), *exōtheō*, and *aphorizō* (*Bab.* 34). These terms are regularly associated with penitential discipline in Greek patristic literature.[168] In the *Const. App.*, for example, written in Syria in the second half of the fourth century,[169] the bishop is admonished to eject the sinner from the congregation in the following manner:

> When thou seest the offender, with severity command him to be cast out; and as he is going out, let the deacons also treat him with severity, and then let them go out and seek for him, and detain him out of the Church. . . .[170]

[165] Hippolyte Delehaye, *Les passions des martyrs et les genres littéraires*[2] (Brussels 1966) 150 ff.

[166] Cf. *Bab.* 23: "There was a certain *basileus* in the time of our forefathers. What this *basileus* was like in other respects I cannot say; but once you have heard the crime which he dared to commit, you will understand the complete savagery of his nature." Manlio Simonetti, "Sulla struttura dei panegyrici di S. Giovanni Crisostomo," *Rendiconti del R. Istituto Lombardo di scienze e lettere* 86 (1953): 179.

[167] Henri Crouzel denies this, but the linguistic evidence, which has never been cited before, seems to favor this interpretation. "Le christianisme de l'empereur Philippe l'Arabe," *Gregorianum* 56 (1975): 546.

[168] PGL, s.vv., *ekballō*, *exōtheō*, and *aphorizō*.

[169] F. X. Funk, ed., *Didascalia et Constitutiones Apostolorum* (Paderborn 1905) 1: xix. Thus the *Const. App.* were written close to the time and place of composition of *Bab.*

[170] *Const. App.* 2.16.1 (*Didascalia et Constitutiones Apostolorum*, ed. Funk 1:61; trans. W. Whiston and J. Donaldson in *The Ante-Nicene Fathers: Translations of the Writings of the Fathers Down to A.D. 325*, ed. A. Roberts and J. Donaldson in 24 vols. [Edinburgh 1866–72], new impression ed., A. Coxe in 8 vols. [(Buffalo 1884–86; reprint Grand Rapids, Michigan: William B. Eerdmans Publishing Company 1978) 7:402]. This translation as well as any other translation from the *Ante-Nicene Fathers* series (hereinafter ANF) in this volume is reprinted with the permission of the William B. Eerdmans Publishing Company. Subsequent translations from ANF will be cited by translator's name,

The same direction is given to the bishop in the *Didasc. Apost.*
2.16:

> But when thou hast seen one who has sinned, be stern with
> him, and command that they put him forth; and when he is
> gone forth let them be stern with him, and take him to task,
> and keep him without the Church; and then let them come
> in and plead for him.[171]

The Syriac version of the *Didascalia*, quoted above, probably
represents the custom of the Syrian church in the early third
century, approximately at the time of Babylas. Evidently, the
sinner was physically expelled from the church building by
the bishop, who acted as a kind of prosecuting officer. It
should be mentioned here that catechumens were subject to
penance just like the baptized members of the community. It
is wrong to assume that the ancient church only inflicted penance on baptized people.[172] The catechumens who sinned

---

volume, date published by Coxe, and page.) The continuation of this passage
on excommunication, which concerns the reconciliation of the repentant
sinner is also relevant: "'Let her be shut out of the camp seven days, and
afterwards let her come in again' (Nm 12.14). We therefore ought to do so
with offenders, when they profess their repentance—namely, to separate
them some determinate time, according to the proportion of their offence,
and afterwards, like father to children, receive them again upon their repentance." (*Const. App.* 2.16.3–4; *Didascalia et Constitutiones Apostolorum*, ed. Funk
1:63; trans. W. Whiston and J. Donaldson, ANF 7 [1886]: 402). Possibly the
use of *aphorizein* in penitential language derives from the *Septuagint* (e.g., the
passage just quoted, Nm 12.14). The same may be true of *exōtheō*, which is
also used by *Const. App.* 2.20.4 (*Didascalia et Constitutiones Apostolorum*, ed.
Funk, 1:73) in connection with excommunication: "'Bring again that which is
driven away' (Ez 34.16), that is, do not permit that which is in its sins, and is
cast out by way of punishment, to continue excluded; but receiving it, and
bringing it back, restore it to the flock, that is, to the people of the undefiled
Church" (trans. W. Whiston and J. Donaldson, ANF 7[1886]: 404). The Old
Testament may have provided a model for the immediate expulsion of the
sinner from the community; cf. *Const. App.* 2.9.3 (*Didascalia et Constitutiones
Apostolorum*, ed. Funk 1:45), 2.10.3 (*Didascalia et Constitutiones Apostolorum*, ed.
Funk 1:47).

[171] R. Hugh Connolly, *Didascalia Apostolorum: The Syriac Version Translated
and Accompanied by the Verona Latin Fragments* (Oxford, 1929; reprint Oxford
1969) 52. Permission to reprint this translation in this volume has been given
by the Oxford University Press.

[172] É. Amann, "Pénitence-sacrement," *Dictionnaire de Théologie Catholique* 12,
1: 775. Hereinafter this article will referred to as Amann, DTC 12,1.

were treated analogously to the faithful, and placed in the ranks of the penitents.[173] Thus, for example, in his second homily against the Jews Chrysostom says that a catechumen guilty of Judaizing was to be kept outside the doors of the church.[174]

(50) There are other similarities between the description of penitential discipline given in *Const. App.* and Chrysostom's account of the expulsion of an emperor. The same emphasis is placed on the bishop's duty to expel a sinner from the church. The duty of expelling the sinner is associated with the episcopal power of binding and loosing.[175] According to *Const. App.* 2.9–10,[176] the bishop who allows the sinner to remain in the church, as Saul spared Agag (1 Sm 15) and Eli, his sons (1 Sm 2.15, 3.13–14), has polluted his own office and the church of God in his diocese. Such a bishop will be punished and his people will perish with him. Similarly, Chrysostom argues that the bishop who thus diminishes the power of his office by not expelling the sinner injures his flock and will be punished (*Bab.* 51).

(51) Both the *Const. App.* and Chrysostom say that the bishop must not be guilty of partiality in his treatment of sinners.[177] The bishop should rebuke the sinner with *parrhēsia* (boldness), according to *Const. App.* 2.6.12, 2.8.4.[178] Chrysostom demonstrates the *parrhēsia* of Babylas from the fact that he expelled an emperor (*Bab.* 35, cf. 31, 46 f.). He emphasizes, however, that Babylas exercised great restraint in his

---

[173] P. de Puniet, "Catéchuménat," *Dictionnaire d'Archéologie Chrétienne et de Liturgie* 2,2: 2584.
[174] *Jud.* 2.3 (PG 48.861); trans. FOTC 68. 45. Cf. *Bab.* 31: "The emperor was driven from the vestibule of the church." In Syria the catechumens worshiped within the basilica proper, seated directly behind the faithful. Jean Lassus, *Sanctuaires chrétiens de Syrie* (Paris 1947) 193, 212.
[175] Cf. *Const. App.* 2.18.3 (*Didascalia et Constitutiones Apostolorum*, ed. Funk 1:65; trans. W. Whiston and J. Donaldson, ANF 7 [1886]: 403): "Be sensible, therefore, O bishop, of the dignity of thy place, that as thou hast received the power of binding, so hast thou also that of loosing." *Bab.* 51: ". . . the magnitude of priestly power is not to be diminished. . . ."
[176] *Didascalia et Constitutiones Apostolorum*, ed. Funk 1:45–47.
[177] *Const. App.* 2.9.1 f., 2.17.1 (*Didascalia et Constitutiones*, ed. Funk 1:45, 63). *Bab.* 51.
[178] *Didascalia et Constitutiones Apostolorum*, ed. Funk 1:41, 45.

parrhēsia towards the emperor (*Bab.* 36–39). In *Const. App.* it is stated that all men, including kings, are subject to the bishop.[179] According to Chrysostom, Babylas demonstrated that the office of priest is higher than that of emperor:

> He showed that one appointed to the priesthood is a more responsible guardian of the earth and what transpires upon it than one who wears the purple (*Bab.* 51).

Thus the relationship between *sacerdotium* and *imperium* is similar in both documents.

(52) Another significant parallel is the medical imagery associated with penance in the *Const. App.* and patristic literature in general.[180] Chrysostom employs such medical imagery to describe the expulsion of the emperor from the church. He compares Babylas to a physician and the act of expelling the emperor to surgery (*Bab.* 29, 37, 39, 52, 56).[181] Chrysostom also uses medical imagery to describe penitential discipline in his treatise on the priesthood, which contains certain of the same observations as are found in *Bab.* For example, in both works Chrysostom states that the "surgery" must be carefully adapted to the requirements of the patient (*Sac.* 2.4; *Bab.* 37). The success of the "cure" depends on the will of the patient, not of the doctor (*Sac.* 2.3; *Bab.* 52). Finally, in both places Chrysostom says that the sinner should be grateful for the penance imposed on him by the bishop (*Sac.* 2.3; *Bab.* 54).[182] Another medical image associated with penance is that of the "mangy sheep," found in both *Const. App.* and *Bab.* The "mangy sheep" symbolizes the sinner who must be expelled

---

[179] *Const. App.* 2.11.1 (*Didascalia et Constitutiones Apostolorum*, ed. Funk 1:47; trans. W. Whiston and J. Donaldson, ANF 7 [1886]: 399.): "Upon this account, therefore, O bishop, endeavour to be pure in thy actions, and to adorn thy place and dignity, which is that of one sustaining the character of God among men, as being set over all men, over priests, kings, rulers, fathers, children, teachers, and in general over all those who are subject to thee. . . ."

[180] *Const. App.* 2.41.5–9 (*Didascalia et Constitutiones Apostolorum*, ed. Funk 1: 131–33). Examples from Methodius, Cyprian, Augustine, and Aphraates in Amann, DTC 12, 1: 770, 786, 805, 808, 813.

[181] Earlier, Origen had characterized excommunication as surgery, citing Mt 5.30 (*Hom.* 7.6 *in Jos.;* SC 71: 210).

[182] Cf. Cyprian, *Laps.* 14 (CSEL 3,1: 247).

from the church in order to prevent the spread of his contagion (sin):

> So one mangy sheep, if not separated from those that are whole, infects the rest with the same distemper (*Const. App.* 2.17.4; *Didascalia et Constitutiones Apostolorum*, ed. Funk, 1: 63 ff.)[183] (The emperor) like a vile and worthless slave was ejected from the church (by Babylas) with the calmness and fearlessness of a shepherd who separates a mangy and diseased sheep from the flock to prevent the disease of the infected one from spreading to the rest (*Bab.* 30).

The image of the mangy sheep, which was used earlier by Origen, signifies that the participation of a sinner in the mysteries soils the community.[184]

(53) Thus there are definite similarities between the description of penitential discipline found in the *Const. App.* and Chrysostom's account of the expulsion of an emperor in *Bab.* Do these similarities constitute evidence that Babylas expelled the emperor from the church according to the prescribed rite of ecclesiastical penance? Chrysostom seems to imply this at *Bab.* 47: "He punished the scoundrel as is lawful for a priest to punish . . . ." That the emperor was subject to the authority of a bishop suggests that he was a member of the Christian community. In the discourse on Babylas, in fact, there are several indications that the unidentified emperor was a Christian, possibly a catechumen. This is implied first of all by the desire of the sovereign to enter the church.[185] Second, Chrysostom says that the emperor was a disciple *(mathētēs)* of Babylas (*Bab.* 57). The designation of the emperor as *mathētēs* may imply that he was a member of Babylas's congregation or was receiving instruction from the bishop.[186] The same inference per-

---

[183] Cf. *Const. App.* 6.18.10 (*Didascalia et Constitutiones Apostolorum*, ed. Funk 1:345; trans. W. Whiston and J. Donaldson, ANF 7 [1886]: 458.): "But those that were incurable we cast out from the flock, that they might not infect the lambs with their scabby disease . . ." This pertains to heretics.

[184] Origen, *Hom.* 7.6 *in Jos.* (SC 71: 210). Cf. Amann, DTC 12,1: 776.

[185] *Bab.* 27, 47, 52, 60. The catechumens attended the first part of the service (Lassus, *Sanctuaires chrétiens* 212 f.).

[186] Cf. Const. App. 2.6.5 (*Didascalia et Constitutiones Apostolorum*, ed. Funk 1:39 ff.; trans. W. Whiston and J. Donaldson, ANF 7 [1886]: 398): "For if the

haps may be drawn from the characterization of Babylas as "the philoprogenitive father" with respect to the emperor (*Bab.* 60). Here the context intimates that the emperor was the spiritual son of Babylas (*Bab.* 57 ff.).[187]

(54) Other details which appear in Chrysostom's narrative also may have historical significance. It is clear that the ruler whom Babylas expelled from the church is the same person who martyred him.[188] This is in accord with the *Passio* tradition, but conflicts with Eusebius (see below). In contrast to the accounts of the *Passiones*, Babylas was not executed for confessing the Christian faith before a pagan emperor. Chrysostom's account does not contain any mention of the emperor's attempt to impose pagan worship on Babylas, or the latter's defense of Christianity, as the *Passiones* do.[189] Also, Chrysostom discloses the sequence of events following the expulsion; seemingly, a progression is involved:

> When he had slain the youth he hastened from the murder to the insult against the sanctuary; and again after this, advancing on the road, he stripped for his mad combat against the priesthood. Having put the saint in irons and thrown him into prison, he punished him for a while this way in retaliation for his benefaction (*Bab.* 54).

The emperor's actions, according to Chrysostom, were dic-

---

pastor be unblameable as to any wickedness, he will compel his own disciples, and by his very mode of life press them to become worthy imitators of his own actions." The later *Passiones* of Babylas emphasize that Babylas was a celebrated teacher (*Marturion,* ed. A. Papadopoulos–Kerameus 78 to be found in his *Sullogē palaistinēs kai suriakēs hagiologias* I, Pravoslavnyj Palestinskij Sbornik XIX.3 [= 57], [Petropolis (Leningrad) 1907] pp. 75–84. Hereinafter this study will be referred to as *Marturion,* ed. Papadopoulos–Kerameus; cf. AASS *Jan.* 3:186). His status as a teacher is the occasion for introducing three children, who subsequently share his martyrdom (*Marturion,* ed. Papadopoulos–Kerameus 79; AASS *Jan.* 3: 186).

[187] Lenain de Tillemont, *Histoire des empereurs* (Venice 1732) 3: 497: "il est impossible de douter que ce Prince ne fust un Chrétien: tous les termes de S. Chrysostome le marquent."

[188] *Bab.* 60. This is also suggested by Chrysostom's comparison of Babylas with John the Baptist (*Bab.* 56, cf. *Hom.* 9 *in Eph.;* PG 62.71).

[189] The *Marturion* of Papadopoulos–Kerameus says that Babylas "insulted" the emperor (no. 5, p. 78), which recalls Chrysostom's account. Also the *Alia Acta* 3 (AASS *Jan.* 3: 188).

tated by the growing power of sin, which is compared to the progress of a forest fire (*Bab.* 53) and rabid horses (*Bab.* 55). It appears that a certain space of time may have elapsed between the emperor's frustrated attempt to enter the church and the arrest of Babylas. Possibly, Babylas was not seized immediately after the expulsion but after a period of brooding by the emperor.[190] The same text reveals that Babylas was kept in prison in chains for an unspecified length of time before he was executed (*Bab.* 54). While in prison, Babylas is said to have mourned the progressive deterioration of the emperor (*Bab.* 60). Finally, the emperor ordered his execution (ibid.).[191] Possibly, these events (the expulsion from the church, arrest, and execution of Babylas) did not immediately succeed each other, but took place over a more extended period of time. This seeming lapse of time enables one to reconcile Chrysostom's account with that of Eusebius, which will be discussed next.

Eusebius

Texts. (55) Eusebius, H.e. 6.29. 1, 4[192]: "Gordianus succeeded Maximinus as Roman emperor . . . About that time Zebinus, bishop of Antioch died, and Babylas succeeded him."

(56) Eusebius, H.e. 6.34[193]: "Gordianus had been emperor

---

[190] This is what seems to be implied by the *Passio* of Babylas cited by Philostorgius (H.e. 7.8; GCS 21: 90. 10–15): the emperor yielded, resenting the opposition of the bishop. When the emperor returned to his palace, however, he ordered Babylas to appear in court to be accused. The *Alia Acta* 2 (ASS Jan. 3: 188) relate the psychology of the emperor's withdrawal from the church and the clandestine arrest of Babylas which followed.

[191] Babylas's execution by the sword is attested by the *Passiones.*

[192] G. Bardy, ed., SC 41 (1955): 131 f.; trans. A. McGiffert in 1890 in *A Select Library of Nicene and Post-Nicene Fathers of the Christian Church,* 2nd Series, ed. Ph. Schaff and H. Wace (New York 1890–1900; reprinted Grand Rapids, Michigan: William B. Eerdmans Publishing Company 1978) 1:274f. Permission to reprint from the second series of *A Select Library of Nicene and Post Nicene Fathers* (hereinafter NPNF 2) here and elsewhere in this volume has been granted by the William B. Eerdmans Publishing Company. Subsequent references to NPNF 2 will include the translator's name, NPNF 2, volume number, date published by Schaff and Wace, and page(s).

[193] G. Bardy, ed., SC 41 (1955): 137; trans. A. McGiffert, NPNF 2,1(1890): 278.

for six years when Philip, with his son Philip, succeeded him. It is reported that he, being a Christian,[194] desired, on the day of the last paschal vigil, to share with the multitude in the prayers of the Church,[195] but that he was not permitted to enter by him who then presided, until he had made confession and had numbered himself among those who were reckoned as transgressors and who occupied the place of penance. For if he had not done this, he would never have been received by him, on account of the many crimes which he had committed. It is said that he obeyed readily, manifesting in his conduct a genuine and pious fear of God."

(57) Eusebius, H.e. 6,39.1, 4[196]: "After a reign of seven years Philip was succeeded by Decius. On account of his hatred of Philip, he commenced a persecution of the churches . . . Babylas in Antioch, having like Alexander passed away in prison after hi[s] confession, was succeeded by Fabius in the episcopate of that church."[197]

Evaluation. (58) Probably Eusebius determined the dates of the accession and martyrdom of Babylas, twelfth bishop of

---

[194]Catechumens were included in the name Christian. Tillemont, *Histoire des empereurs* 3: 498. Cf. Friedrich Lauchert, ed., *Die Kanones der wichtigsten altkirchlichen Concilien* (Freiburg i.B., 1896) 136: Concilium quinisextum can. 95.

[195]Rufinus in his translation of this passage says that Philip came to the church on easter eve to communicate in the mysteries ("communicare mysteriis," GCS 9,2: 591). This, however, is not an accurate translation of the Greek text of Eusebius. Chrysostom says that a catechumen takes part in the lenten fast but not in the sacrifice: "Although the catechumen keeps the fast each year, he does not celebrate the Pasch since he does not share in the sacrifice" (*Jud.* 3.5; PG 48.868; trans. P. Harkins, FOTC 68.63).

[196]G. Bardy, ed., SC 41 (1955): 141; trans. A. McGiffert, NPNF 2,1(1890): 280 f.

[197]Cf. *Hieronymi Chron.* Decius 1 (*Eusebii Pamphili Chronici canones latine vertit, adauxit, ad sua tempora produxit S. Eusebius Hieronymus*, ed. J. K. Fotheringham [London 1923] 300. Reprinted with the permission of the Oxford University Press): "Alexandro Hierosolymarum episcopo apud Caesaream Palestinae ob martyrium interfecto et Antiochiae Babyla, Mazabanus et Fabius episcopi constituuntur." In addition to the translation of Jerome, the *Chronicle* of Eusebius exists in an Armenian translation and two extensive Syriac excerpts. In the case of the notice on Babylas, these versions are garbled and add nothing of value. Cf. Adolf von Harnack, *Geschichte der altchristlichen Literatur bis Eusebius*, 2nd ed., 2,1 (Leipzig, 1893–1901; reprint Leipzig 1958) 70 ff. (Hereinafter *Geschichte der altchristlichen Literatur²* 2,1).

Antioch, on the basis of his own private research and conjecture. The *Chronicle* of Sextus Julius Africanus, upon which Eusebius relied in his *Chron.*, contained a list of Antiochene bishops, which extended only to Philetus, tenth bishop of Antioch.[198] For the accession dates of the following nine bishops of Antioch (Zebennus, Babylas, Fabius, Demetrianus, Paulus, Domnus, Timaeus, Cyrillus, Tyrannus), Eusebius could no longer rely upon Africanus. Nor did he possess another list giving this information. He therefore had to rely upon his own research to calculate approximately the dates of their office.

(59) The accession date of Babylas "under Gordian" is not given in the *Chron.*, but appears in H.e. 6.29.4. Apparently, Eusebius arrived at this date, synchronized with the beginning of the reign of emperor Gordian (238), by further study after the publication of the *Chron.* As Tillemont has shown, there is nothing firm about this date, because in the same passage (H.e. 6.29.1) Eusebius states that Anteros and then Fabian became bishop of Rome at the accession of Gordian (238)—whereas the correct dates are 235 and 236.[199]

(60) With regard to the accession date of Babylas it may be significant that the post-Eusebian chronographers differ as to the length of Babylas's episcopate.[200] The *Chronographeion syntomon* of 853, Syncellus, and Nicephorus, who apparently rely on a common source, say that Babylas served for thirteen years. This figure may be based on the span of Babylas's episcopate according to Eusebius, i.e., from the accession of Gordian, 238, through the reign of Decius, 251. On the other hand, the oriental chronographers, Eutychius and Barhe-

---

[198] Harnack has demonstrated that the dates of Julius Africanus, which Eusebius used in his *Chronicle* but discarded in his *Church History*, are largely worthless, because the reigns of the first seven bishops of Antioch are artificially synchronized with Rome. *Geschichte der altchristlichen Literatur*² 2,1: 208 ff.

[199] Tillemont, *Mémoires* 3: 727 f. Lawlor and Oulton believe it possible that the contents of Eusebius, H.e. 6.29 belong to the reign of Maximinus (235–38). See Hugh Jackson Lawlor and John Ernest Leonard Oulton, trans., *Eusebius, Bishop of Caesarea, The Ecclesiastical History and The Martyrs of Palestine* (London 1954) 2: 221.

[200] Cf. Harnack, *Geschichte der altchristlichen Literatur*² 2,1: 95.

braeus, give the length of Babylas's episcopate as eight years. The existence of two different traditions regarding the length of Babylas's rule is evidence that the date was not firmly established in antiquity. (61) Eusebius, H.e. 6.34 is the first text which mentions the Christianity of Philip the Arab, and the public penance to which he was subject during a paschal vigil by an unidentified bishop. Eusebius does not give the name of the bishop or the specific charges made against the sovereign. Evidently he was ignorant of these details or saw fit not to mention them. He does state, however, that Philip is said to have readily submitted to the penance. To designate the source of his account Eusebius employs the phrase, "it is reported." According to Zahn, this phrase indicates an authentic tradition, which lacks sufficient documentary (written) proof.[201] The use of the phrase, "it is said," may also imply oral tradition. The fact that Eusebius's account lacks so many pertinent details (name of the bishop, site of the event), may be explained by the supposition that his immediate source was rumor.[202]

(62) What have been said to be inconsistencies between the accounts of Eusebius and Chrysostom may be explained as selective differences of detail and emphasis. Reduced to bare essentials, the action of the story told by both writers is that of an emperor who came to the church and was excluded by a bishop. Eusebius says that Philip "obeyed readily."[203] Philip's act of obedience, however, must be viewed in light of the penitential practice of the Syrian church, which involved expulsion from the church building, detention outside the

---

[201] Cited by Adolf Harnack, *Die Zeit des Ignatius und die Chronologie der antiochenischen Bischöfe bis Tyrannus* (Leipzig 1878) 7 n. 3.
[202] H. Crouzel, "Le christianisme de l'empereur Philippe l'Arabe," *Gregorianum* 56 (1975): 547f., suggests that Eusebius's information came from the correspondence of Origen, which Eusebius had collected and used as a source for H.e. 6.1–39. A few lines after the story about Philip's penance, Eusebius cites two letters of Origen to emperor Philip and his wife, Severa (H.e. 6.36.3).
[203] Philip's obedience is all the more remarkable in the light of *Doct. Apost.* 25 (trans. B.P. Pratten, ANF 8 (1886): 669): "The apostles further appointed: That those kings who shall hereafter believe in Christ should be permitted to go up and stand before the altar along with the Guides of the Church. . . ."

church by the deacons, followed by an examination within the
church by the bishop and imposition of a sentence decreeing
separation from the church for a certain space of time.[204]
Chrysostom states that Babylas expelled the emperor; this is
really the same action described from another point of view—
that of bishop Babylas. A further difference between the two
accounts is that Eusebius does not mention what follows according to Chrysostom, namely, the arrest and execution of
Babylas by the emperor. It would be useless to speculate on
why this omission by Eusebius unless further information
comes to light.

(63) Eusebius in both *Chron.* and H.e. puts the martyrdom
of Babylas "under Decius."[205] It has already been mentioned
that Eusebius was not well informed on the succession of
Antiochene bishops, and for the last nine (Zebennus–
Tyrannus) was only able to estimate the years of their respec-
tive offices. Hence he was probably ignorant of the exact time
and circumstances of the death of Babylas. Possibly he conjectured that Babylas was a victim of the Decian persecution on
the basis of his own researches.

(64) In this connection it is significant that three post-
Eusebian chronographers date the martyrdom of Babylas
earlier than the reign of Decius. The *Chronographeion syntomon*
and, apparently, Syncellus, place the martyrdom in the time
of Gordian (238–44); Eutychius, in the time of Maximinus
(235–38).[206] Their evidence serves to weaken the authority of
Eusebius, who states that Babylas was martyred under Decius
(249–51).

(65) A few remarks are in order about Eusebius's account
of the manner of Babylas's death. The relevant text is H.e.
6.39.4, which is usually interpreted to mean that Babylas died
in prison. For example, A. McGiffert translates: "Babylas in

[204] Cf. *Const. App.* 2.16 (*Didascalia et Constitutiones Apostolorum*, ed. Funk, 1: 61 ff.). *Didasc. Apost.*, trans. Connolly, *Didascalia Apostolorum*, 52 f.
[205] In placing the martyrdom of Babylas "sub Decio," Eusebius was fol-lowed among others by Jerome, *Vir. ill.* 54, 62. Gregory of Tours, *Hist.* 1.30 (*Monumenta Germaniae Historica: Scriptores Rerum Merovingicarum:* Vol. 1, Part 1: *Gregorii Episcopi Turonensis Libri Historiarum X*, ed. B. Krusch and W. Levi-son, 2nd ed. [Hannover 1951] 22). *Chron. Pasch.*, ed. Dindorf, 1: 503.
[206] Harnack, *Die Zeit des Ignatius*, 59.

Antioch, having like Alexander passed away in prison after hi[s] confession. . . ." (NPNF 2,1[1890]: 281). Jerome also seems to have understood the text in this way.[207] This rendering, however, contradicts the evidence of Chrysostom and the *Passiones* that Babylas was executed by the sword. There is, however, another possible translation of this passage in Eusebius which would read: "In like manner to Alexander Babylas at Antioch after confession in prison departed this life." The implication of this version is that subsequent to the imprisonment Babylas died in an unspecified manner. Actually the context suggests that the words "after confession in prison" should be taken closely together. The description of Origen's sufferings which immediately follows (H.e. 6.39.5) makes it plain how imprisonment and concomitant torture constituted a confession. Therefore the text of Eusebius under discussion (H.e. 6.39.4) may be interpreted to mean that Babylas spent time in prison as a confessor,[208] and died afterwards, the exact manner of his death being omitted by Eusebius, perhaps from ignorance.

The Passiones

(66) The *Passio*, or literary account of the martyrdom, of Babylas is known in several recensions prior to the compilation of Simeon Metaphrastes in the tenth century. The more important of these are the *Passiones* of Philostorgius (H.e. 7.8), Papadopoulos-Kerameus (BHG 205), and the AASS (BHL 889). In addition to the Greek and Latin redactions, there are

---

[207] Jerome, *Vir. ill.* 54 (Hieronymus und Gennadius, *De viris inlustribus*, ed. C. Bernoulli [Freiburg and Leipzig 1895] p. 34): "Alexander and Babylas, pontiffs of the churches of Jerusalem and Antioch, fell asleep in prison for their confession." Jerome's understanding may have been affected by the account of bishop Alexander's death in prison, which precedes the mention of Babylas's death in Eusebius, H.e. 6.39.3. Rufinus, however, seems to have relied upon a different tradition, which referred to Babylas's death in chains rather than in prison. See T. Mommsen, GCS 9.2 (1908): 595 on this point. The chains in which Babylas was imprisoned and executed are prominent in Chrysostom's account (e.g., *Bab.* 60).

[208] Babylas's incarceration is also recorded by Chrysostom (*Bab.* 54 ff.). Also the *Passio* of Basil of Epiphania contains the exhortation to martyrdom, which Babylas is said to have composed in prison.

Armenian, Syriac, and Georgian versions.[209] These texts all allude to the circumstance—not mentioned by Chrysostom in the discourse on Babylas—that Babylas was martyred along with three children.[210] The three children are also attested as fellow martyrs with Babylas by the ancient Syrian martyrology of the year 412,[211] and the *Mart. Hier.*[212]

(67) As already stated, Chrysostom does not mention the three children in his discourse on Babylas. He does, however, mention them in a sermon on the martyrs Juventinus and Maximinus. Here Chrysostom recalls the recent celebration of the feast day of Babylas: "The blessed Babylas together with three children just now gathered us here. . . ." (*Pan. Juv.* 1; PG 50.571). This statement indicates that Chrysostom was acquainted with the tradition concerning three children, who suffered martyrdom with Babylas. It is unlikely that the reference to the three children is an interpolation, because Chrysostom subsequently refers to Babylas and the three children as a "team" of martyrs in contrast to the "pair" of martyrs, Juventinus and Maximinus (*Pan. Juv.* 1; PG 50.571). Probably the encomium on Babylas and the three children, referred to here by Chrysostom, had been delivered by another Antiochene cleric; no such work is to be found among the panegyrical sermons of Chrysostom.

(68) If Chrysostom was acquainted with the tradition concerning the three children, why did he fail to mention them in his discourse on Babylas? Most likely it was on artistic grounds that he omitted all reference to the children. The discourse

[209] Paul Peeters, "La passion de S. Basile d'Épiphanie," AB 48 (1930): 309, 310 n.4.
[210] E.g., Philostorgius (Phot.) 7.8 (GCS 21: 88 f.) says that the three children were quite young and brothers. The three brothers are said to have been pupils of Babylas (e.g., *Marturion,* ed. Papadopoulos-Kerameus, no.6). Their ages are given as twelve, nine, and seven by their mother, who appears briefly (*Marturion,* ed. Papadopoulos-Kerameus, no. 7). Meletius, bishop of Mopsuestia around 432, mentions the infant of seven years who suffered with Babylas, according to Tillemont, *Mémoires* 3: 404.
[211] W. Wright, "An Ancient Syrian Martyrology," *Journal of Sacred Literature,* (January 1866): 424: "January 24. At Nicomedeia, Babylas, bishop of Antioch, and the three boys, confessors."
[212] AASS *Nov.* 2,2: 59–60: "Ian. 24. Antiochia passio sancti Babilae episcopi cum tribus parvulis."

on Babylas was carefully composed; any details which might tend to obscure the symmetrical structure of the *logos* or diminish its hero, would naturally have been omitted.[213]

(69) The panegyric on Juventinus and Maximinus, in which Chrysostom mentions the three children, was apparently delivered at Antioch. The information about the three children may therefore be considered part of the Antiochene tradition concerning Babylas. Theodoret, a native of Antioch, also bears witness to this tradition. In his H.e. 3.10[214] Theodoret says that the remains of Babylas and the three children who were martyred with him were housed in a single coffin.[215] Since Theodoret had personal knowledge of the church at Antioch, it is probable that his testimony about the three children depends upon local tradition. Thus it appears that the *Passiones* of Babylas preserve an important detail: that Babylas was martyred along with three young disciples. This piece of information accords with the tradition of Antioch, as witnessed by Chrysostom in his homily on Juventinus and Maximinus and by Theodoret, and appears to be authentic.[216]

(70) In this connection may be mentioned the *Passio* published by Halkin from an eleventh century Moscow manuscript.[217] This pre-Metaphrastic *Passio* is summarized by the *Synaxarium Constantinopolitanum* in its notice of a second Babylas on the same day as Babylas of Antioch (Sept. 4). The second Babylas was said to be a teacher at Nicomedia mar-

[213] Chrysostom's extant homily on Babylas likewise makes no mention of the three children (PG 50.527–34). In this case the absence of any reference to the three children may be explained by the fact that this homily deals with the miracles associated with Babylas's relics. It is evidently to this homily which Chrysostom refers in *Laz.* 4.1 (PG 48.1007), where Babylas is mentioned alone.

[214] GCS 44: 186 f.

[215] The *Passio* BHL 889 (no. 12) also states that Babylas was buried together with the children (AASS *Jan.* 3: 187). Chrysostom says that one coffin was removed from Daphne (*Bab.* 90).

[216] Gregory of Tours gives the names of the three children as Urban, Prilidan, and Epolon. Gregory was evidently relying upon a Syriac source, since the names of the three children which he gives concur with the names found in the thirteenth-century Syriac martyrology of Rabban Sliba. See Paul Peeters, "Le martyrologe de Rabban Sliba," AB 27 (1908): 173.

[217] François Halkin, *Inédits byzantins d'Ochrida, Candie et Moscou*, Subsidia hagiographica 38 (Brussels 1963) 328–39.

tyred under Diocletian along with eighty-four infants.[218] The appearance of this second Babylas is evidently owing to a false reading of the abbreviation "pd" in the title of a *Passio* of Babylas and his three young companions (pd´ = 84).[219] The error, which created another Babylas, testifies indirectly to the tradition that Babylas was martyred along with three companions.

(71) While the evidence of the *Passiones* appears to be trustworthy with regard to the three children, in other respects their testimony is suspect. According to the *Passiones*, Babylas suffered martyrdom under emperor Numerian.[220] But Numerian was emperor in 283–84, when there was another bishop of Antioch (Cyril).[221] To solve the dilemma, Baronius suggested that in the *Passiones* of Babylas the emperor Numerian was confused with the general Numerius, who persecuted Christians under Decius according to the *Acta Isidori*.[222] The identification of the emperor who martyred Babylas as Numerian is as old as the fourth/fifth centuries, because the name of Numerian occurs in the *Passio* utilized by Philostorgius. That the emperor was called Numerian (rather than Philip or Decius) may imply that at this time there was no fixed tradition concerning the identity of the sovereign responsible for the death of Babylas. The view of Eusebius, that Decius martyred Babylas, was not universally accepted. As Tillemont has said: it is inconceivable that Numerian (or Decius) would have come to the church of Christ as friends; and, if they came as persecutors, it is unlikely that Babylas could have prevented them from entering.[223] In reading the *Passiones* one senses the confusion which has arisen from iden-

[218] *Synaxarium Ecclesiae Constantinopolitanae, Propylaeum ad AASS Novembris* 12.

[219] Hippolyte Delehaye, "Les deux saints Babylas," AB 19 (1900): 5–8.

[220] Ioannes Malalas also identifies the emperor as Numerian (*Chron.* 12; *Chron. Pasch.*, ed. Dindorf 303).

[221] Downey, *History*, 316.

[222] *Caesaris Baronii Annales Ecclesiastici* 3: no. 126. The same Numerius is also called Numerianus in the *Synaxarium Constantinopolitanum, Propylaeum ad AASS Novembris*, p. 818, lines 19–20 (cf. p. 683, line 13). It is possible that many martyrs were wrongly said to have suffered under emperor Numerian owing to this confusion, according to Tillemont, *Mémoires* 3: 729.

[223] *Mémoires* 3: 727.

tifying the emperor as a pagan (Numerian). The desire of the sovereign to enter the church is not satisfactorily explained.[224] In the *Passiones* the real nature of the conflict between Babylas and the emperor is not perceived; instead you find a stereotyped dialogue concerning religion between Numerian and Babylas.

Chronicon Paschale

(72) Text of *Chron. Pasch.* 1: 503.9–504.6 (ed. Dindorf): "In the beginning of the reign of Decius there was a persecution against Christians . . . . Babylas, bishop of Antioch, was perfected in the course of martyrdom . . . . And this piece of information concerning holy Babylas came to us by transmission of tradition, as blessed Leontius, bishop of Antioch, related to those before us: Decius killed the holy Babylas, not only because he was a Christian, but because he also dared to prevent the wife of emperor Philip and Philip himself, who were Christians, from entering the church, because Philip had transgressed. And this was the nature of the transgression: Philip Junior,[225] who was a governor in the time of his predecessor, emperor Gordian, had taken Gordian's son from him in trust; and when emperor Gordian died, Philip murdered his child and reigned."

(73) The *Chron. Pasch.* was composed during the reign of emperor Heraclius (610–41), probably by a cleric in the retinue of Sergius, patriarch of Constantinople.[226] The *Chron. Pasch.* contains two accounts of the martyrdom of Babylas, the first of which is under consideration here.[227] For this account

---

[224] Philostorgius says that the emperor was led to enter the church by demonic inspiration (H.e. 7.8; GCS 21: 89).

[225] Leontius seems to confuse emperor Philip and his son, M. Iulius (Severus) Philippus. For another confusion see Jerome, *Vir. ill.* 54 (*De viris inlustribus,* ed. Bernoulli 33; trans. E.C. Richardson, NPNF 2,3[1892]: 373): "[Origen] sent letters to the Emperor Philip . . . and to his mother, letters which are still extant." According to Eusebius, Origen wrote to Philip and his wife, Otacilia Severa, who was mother of Philip Junior (H.e. 6.36.3; SC 41: 139).

[226] Heinrich Gelzer, *Sextus Julius Africanus und die Byzantinische Chronographie* (Leipzig 1885) 2: 138.

[227] The second account, which evidently derives from the *Passio* tradition,

the compiler of the *Chron. Pasch.* used at least two sources.
Eusebius probably supplied the date of Babylas's martyrdom
under Decius (H.e. 6.39.4). The other source is known as the
"Arian historiographer," from whom came the rest of the ex-
cerpt which is translated here. The honorable mention of
Leontius, bishop of Antioch, and the reference to "transmission of tradition" *(diadochē)* suggest that the informant was an
Arian of the generation after Leontius rather than the compiler of the *Chron. Pasch.*[228] Evidently Leontius, who was
bishop of Antioch from 348–57 and Arian, had passed along
this piece of information regarding Babylas.[229]

(74) It is noteworthy that Peeters gave great weight to this
testimony of Leontius, and called it the "fond primitif" of the
entire tradition concerning Babylas.[230] Certain information
conveyed by Leontius may possibly be accurate. According to
the Arian historiographer, Leontius names Philip as the emperor whom Babylas excluded and says that Philip's wife was
also excluded. Both Philip and his wife are said to be Christians. This is in accord with the statement of Eusebius that
Origen wrote letters to emperor Philip and to Severa, his wife
(H.e. 6.36.3). Hence it is possible that Philip's wife, Marcia
Otacilia Severa, was also excluded by Babylas. At the same
time it is understandable that this fact might have been unknown to later writers. Possibly, this may be a genuine piece of
tradition.

(75) The rest of Leontius's statement, on the contrary,
seems not to be supported by the evidence of history and to
lack all intrinsic probability. First: Leontius says that Decius
killed Babylas, not only because he was a Christian, but because Babylas had injured Philip. Other sources, however,
attest that Decius was hostile to Philip and connect the Decian

---

resembles that of Malalas, and states that Babylas was martyred in the time of
Carinus (283–85) and Numerian. See *Chron. Pasch.*, ed. Dindorf, 1: 510.1 ff.

[228] Gelzer, *Sextus Julius Africanus* 2: 138.

[229] There is no evidence, however, that Leontius wrote up the acts of Babylas, as is suggested in AASS *Jan.* 3: 183. Indeed, Leontius's account differs
substantially from the tradition of the *Passiones.*

[230] Peeters, "La passion de S. Basile" 314.

persecution with the Christianity of Philip.[231] It is unlikely that Decius would have wished to avenge Philip. Second: Leontius says that Philip killed the son of emperor Gordian, whom Gordian had entrusted to Philip's care. This statement must be challenged. There is no evidence that emperor Gordian III had any children.[232] And, no other source attests that Philip murdered Gordian's son.[233] Even the *Historia Augusta* does not mention the murder of Gordian's son, though it details Philip's other crimes, including his murder of Gordian's father-in-law and of emperor Gordian himself.[234] Is it possible that Leontius or his informant confused Philip's murder of emperor Gordian III, who was quite young,[235] with the murder of a young hostage, described by Chrysostom? According to Chrysostom, the young prince had been entrusted to the emperor as a hostage and guarantor of a treaty (*Bab.* 24). This detail corresponds to Leontius's statement that Philip took Gordian's son from him "in trust" or "as a hostage" *(parathēkē).*

(76) The eighteenth-century Jesuit scholar Merlin doubted that Leontius was the source of the text attributed to him by the *Chron. Pasch.*, because a bishop of Antioch could not have been mistaken in regard to such an important piece of local tradition.[236] It is significant, however, that Leontius was not actually a native of Antioch; he was Phrygian, according to

---

[231] John M. York, Jr., "The Image of Philip the Arab," *Historia* 21 (1972): 329 ff., 332, with the correction of Crouzel, "Le christianisme," *Gregorianum* 56 (1975): 549 f.

[232] Tillemont, *Histoire des Empereurs* 3: 252.

[233] Cf. Peeters, "La passion de S. Basile," 305, 313.

[234] *Scriptores Historiae Augustae*, ed. E. Hohl, editio stereotypa editionis prioris 1927 cum addendis ad vol. 1 et 2 (Leipzig 1927; reprint Leipzig 1955) 20.28.1, 5 f.; 20.30.8 f. Hereinafter cited as S.H.A.

[235] Gordian is said to have assumed the purple, according to various authors, at the age of eleven, thirteen, or sixteen (S.H.A. 20.22.2). Throughout his biography he is called "parvulus" (S.H.A. 20.22.2), "adulescens" (S.H.A. 20.22.5), and "puer" (S.H.A. 20.23.1). The senate and army called him "son" (S.H.A. 20.31.6), and Gordian regarded Philip as his father (S.H.A. 20.29.1).

[236] Père Merlin, "Dissertation sur ce que rapporte Saint Chrysostome du Martyre de Saint Babylas, contre la censure injurieuse que fait M. Bayle de la Narration du Saint Docteur," *Mémoires de Trévoux,* Juin 1737: 1073–74.

Theodoret, H.e. 2.10.2.[237] Moreover, as a crypto-Arian bishop, Leontius was not close to the orthodox Christian community of Antioch. In fact, Flavian, a native and later bishop of Antioch (381–404), whom Chrysostom implies was a source of the tradition concerning Babylas,[238] was an outspoken opponent of Leontius.[239] For these reasons Leontius probably did not derive his information about Babylas directly from the orthodox tradition of Antioch.

(77) In this regard it may be significant that the image of Philip the Arab was apparently deformed by succeeding generations of historians.[240] Moreover, with regard to Philip's murder of emperor Gordian, there is an additional reason why the crime may have become distorted in the popular tradition. According to the *Historia Augusta* Philip dissembled his crime, and led the Roman senate to believe that Gordian had died a natural death.[241] Furthermore, the epitaph set up by Gordian's loyal soldiers somewhere in the Persian empire, which insinuated the truth about Gordian's death, was torn down by Licinius, the alleged descendant of Philip.[242] Accordingly, any recollection of Gordian's murder which survived in the popular memory would probably have been garbled and confused. Such indeed appears to be the testimony of Leontius in the *Chron. Pasch.*

[237] GCS 44: 121.

[238] *Pan. Bab.* 1. Is it possible that Chrysostom in writing *Bab.* proposed to record the authentic tradition concerning the illustrious bishop of Antioch, in opposition to the false information which circulated among the Arians? The Arian historiographer cited in *Chron. Pasch.* omits all reference to the miracles worked by the relics of Babylas during the reign of Julian. The Arians, i.e., Eunomians, were opposed to the veneration of relics (Jerome, *Vigil.* 8, 10; PL 23.362 ff.).

[239] Theodoret, H.e. 2.24.6–8 (GCS 44: 153 f.). Cf. Philostorgius, H.e. 3.18 (GCS 21: 46).

[240] Philip was the alleged ancestor of Licinius, who was defeated by Constantine in 324; it seems that historians favorable to the Constantinian dynasty could not do justice to him. Likewise, pagans apparently wrote from a point of view hostile to Philip. York, "The Image of Philip the Arab" 320–24.

[241] S.H.A. 20.31.2 f.; ed. Hohl 2: 53. As Leontius implies (*Chron. Pasch.*, ed. Dindorf 1:504.4–5).

[242] S.H.A. 20.34.2–5; ed. Hohl 2:56.

Passio *of Basil of Epiphania*

(78) The eleventh-century Georgian legendary of Iviron contains the *Passio* of a bishop named Basil, whose episcopal seat is the village of Hamah (Epiphania) on the Orontes river. This document, which makes extensive reference to the martyrdom of Babylas, was brought to light by Kekelidze in 1918.[243] Peeters has published an extensive study of the work, which includes a Latin translation in twelve paragraphs.[244]

(79) The contents of the *Passio* of Basil of Epiphania are as follows. The action takes place under emperor Numerian, who was ruling at Antioch when Babylas was bishop. The Persians and "Greeks" have just concluded a peace treaty, according to which the king of Persia, Sapor, gives his son as a hostage to Numerian. When Sapor dies, Numerian has the young hostage assassinated and seizes his inheritance. Babylas learns of the crime. When Numerian, who was nominally Christian, appears at the gates of the church, Babylas forbids him entrance. Numerian has Babylas arrested, and issues a general edict of persecution. Pastors of the churches everywhere are arrested, including Basil, bishop of Hamah. An officer named Tullius, accompanied by Julianus and Liberianus, Syrians, go to the village of Hamah. Basil is summoned before their tribunal and subjected to interrogation and torture. Finally, Basil is remanded to prison for three days to give time for reflection. In prison, he receives a letter which the patriarch of Antioch, Babylas, had written to the imprisoned bishops. The text of the letter is reproduced. Basil's desire for martyrdom is strengthened by the letter. At the end of three days he is led back to the tribunal. Again he is tortured but unmoved. At last Basil is condemned to the beasts.

(80) The *Passio* of Basil of Epiphania sheds light upon several aspects of the Babylas tradition. First: according to the *Passio* of Basil, Numerian is the Roman emperor whom Baby-

---

[243] K. Kekelidze, *Monumenta Hagiographica Georgica. Pars Prima: Keimena* (Tiflis [Tbilisi, U.S.S.R.] 1918) 1:5–10.

[244] Peeters, "La passion de S. Basile" 302–23.

las confronted. This identification accords with the *Passio* tradition of Babylas. In the *Passio* of Basil, however, Numerian is depicted as a nominal Christian,[245] whereas in the *Passio* tradition of Babylas he is pagan. Second: The *Passio* of Basil contains the story of a young hostage murdered by a Roman emperor, which Chrysostom narrates in *Bab.* The same incident is found, in distorted form, in Coptic monophysite legends.[246] Compared to Chrysostom's version, the account found in the *Passio* of Basil is more detailed. The foreign people who concluded a treaty with the Roman emperor are identified as Persians, and their king is named Sapor.[247] The *Passio* of Basil also states that Sapor's death was the occasion of the murder of his hostage son. Since Sapor died ca. 272,[248] this detail is irreconcilable with the chronology of Babylas. It is interesting, however, that according to the tenth-century chronographer Eutychius, Sapor died in the second year of the reign of emperor Maximinus, i.e., 236 (cf. Eutychius, *Annales;* PG 111.994). The identification of the foreign monarch as a Persian may be related to the fact that Gordian with Philip campaigned against the Persians and Philip concluded a treaty with Sapor.[249] The third point to be mentioned is that, according to the *Passio* of Basil, Babylas composed an exhortation to martyrdom, which was sent to his fellow bishops in prison. This detail is compatible with the history of the third century, when such exhortations were composed. Origen, for example, wrote his *Exhortation to Martyrdom* ca. 235, at the beginning of the persecution of Maximinus (Eusebius, H.e. 6.28; cf. H.e. 4.15.47; 6.39.5; 8.10).

---

[245] Cf. para. 2 (Numerianus) "qui nomine quidem christianus sed reapse a deo et religione alienus erat." Peeters, "La passion de S. Basile" 318.

[246] Peeters, "La passion de S. Basile" 311.

[247] The notice on Babylas in the *Synaxarium Constantinopolitanum* (Sept. 4) also identifies the hostage as son of the Persian king (*Propylaeum ad AASS Novembris* 11). This may indicate a common source for the *Synaxarium Constantinopolitanum* and the *Passio* of Basil. Peeters, "La passion de S. Basile" 310.

[248] Peeters, "La passion de Saint Basile" 318.

[249] A.T. Olmstead, "The Mid-Third Century of the Christian Era," *Classical Philology* 37 (1942): 255 f.

The Tradition of Antioch

(81) One may suggest that Chrysostom's account of the martyrdom of Babylas derives from the tradition of the church of Antioch. Chrysostom was a native of Antioch, and lived there while writing the discourse on Babylas. In *Pan. Bab.* 1 Chrysostom reveals that the events of Babylas's episcopacy and martyrdom were known to the elder teachers and to the bishop of Antioch:[250]

> How, indeed, he presided over the Church which is among us, and saved that sacred ship, in storm, and in wave, and billow;[251] and what a bold front he showed to the emperor, and how he lay down his life for the sheep and underwent that blessed slaughter; these things and such as these, we will leave to the elder among our teachers, and to our common father[252] to speak of.[253] For the more remote matters, the aged can relate to you . . .

Evidently, facts of the episcopacy and martyrdom of Babylas were known to the elders and bishop of Antioch. It can hardly be doubted that Chrysostom relied upon the same tradition for his narrative concerning Babylas's martyrdom. This conclusion was already made in the eighteenth century by the Jesuit, Père Merlin.[254] Merlin also pointed out that the dis-

---

[250] PG 50.529; trans. T.P. Brandram, NPNF 9 (1889): 141.

[251] Peeters interprets the storm to mean a time of persecution, i.e., the reign of Decius ("La passion de S. Basile" 307). Other examples of nautical imagery, however, show that the storm may symbolize the world in general. E.g., *Clem. ep.* 14 (PG 2.49): "For the whole business of the Church is like unto a great ship, bearing through a violent storm men who are of many places, and who desire to inhabit the city of the good kingdom (trans. ANF 8 [1886]: 220)." In *Pan. Bab.* 1 Chrysostom may have used the storm image to symbolize the special problems which affected the church in Babylas's time.

[252] Bishop Flavian, who ordained Chrysostom to the priesthood.

[253] The practice was for several presbyters and then the bishop to preach at each service. *Const. App.* 2.57.9 (*Didascalia et Constitutiones Apostolorum,* ed. Funk 1: 163). A. Neander, *Der heilige Johannes Chrysostomus,* 2 vols. (Berlin 1848) 1:20.

[254] Père Merlin states: "il est plus clair que le jour qu'un témoignage de la nature de celui de S. Chrysostome sur la cause et les autres circonstances du Martyre de S. Babylas est le témoignage de l'Evêque, de tout le Clergé, de tout le peuple d'Antioche, fondé sur une tradition qui ne pouvoit être fausse,

course on Babylas was a published work, directed against the
pagan community of Antioch, in which Chrysostom employed the history of Babylas as a fact of established certitude,
to confound the adherents of paganism and establish the va-
lidity of Christianity. There is no evidence that any attempt
was ever made to refute what Chrysostom wrote.[255]

TEXT AND TRANSLATION

(82) Editions of the Greek text of Chrysostom's discourse
on Babylas were previously made by Erasmus (Basel 1527);
Fronto Ducaeus, S.J. (Paris 1609); Sir Henry Savile (Eton
1612); Bernard Montfaucon, O.S.B. (Paris 1718; editio
Parisina altera 1838); and Johann Friederich Dübner (Paris
1861). The text of Montfaucon was reprinted by Migne in
1862 (PG 50.533–72). A new critical edition of the Greek text,
based upon nineteen manuscripts, has been prepared by the
present writer for the series, *Sources chrétiennes*. The *Sources
chrétiennes* edition provides the Greek text, subdivided into
one hundred twenty-seven paragraphs, which has been
translated in this volume.

(83) Previous translations of the discourse on Babylas include the Latin versions of Iohannes Oecolampadius (1523),
Germanus Brixius (1528), and Montfaucon (1718). In pre-
paring this translation, which appears to be the first English
version, the writer consulted the Latin translation of Montfaucon, and the French translations of Jeannin-Vierrjski
(1863) and Cécile Blanc et al. (forthcoming in *Sources chrétiennes*). The present translation aims at fidelity to the original
Greek and avoidance of paraphrase as much as possible. Biblical texts are translated according to the Douay version.

---

parce que regardant un fait aussi éclatant que public, elle n'étoit que de
quarante ou de cinquante ans au plus depuis la mort des derniers témoins
oculaires. . . . Car une opinion populaire qui défigurât absolument l'histoire
du martyre de S. Babylas, ne pouvoit s'établir à Antioche, qu'après la mort
non seulement de tous ceux qui l'avoient vû souffrir, mais encore de tous
ceux à qui les témoins oculaires ont pû parler." *Dissertation* 1061 ff.
[255] Merlin, *Dissertation* 1056 ff.

(84) In conclusion, it is fitting to quote from Erasmus's *Epistola de modestia profitendi linguas*, which constitutes the preface to his edition of *Bab.* (Basel: Froben, Aug. 1527). In this letter, written to Nicholas Varius, principal of the Collegium Trilingue, a college which Erasmus had helped to organize in Louvain for the study of Hebrew, Greek, and Latin, Erasmus states that the discourse on Babylas ought to become part of the curriculum of the Collegium Trilingue:

This writing of Chrysostom, despite its brevity, seems to be worthy to be studied in your college for many reasons. It is so unique and skillful a blend of the loftiest piety with wonderful eloquence that in my opinion no other text can be more suitably presented to young men occupied with the writing of themes. What do Aphthonius, Lysias, or Libanius have that can be compared with this argument—I do not mean with the piety which characterizes it, but with its eloquence of style, acuity of reasoning, and in a word abundance? What could be more useful to this age than that language and eloquence be early imbibed simultaneously from these authors whose speech breathes Christ no less than Demosthenes? The argument is simple: Babylas, bishop of Antioch, tried to keep Caesar out of the church on account of his defilement by an impious murder; was killed by him; buried outside the city; and much later transported into the city. It is amazing how the truly golden artisan takes this theme, which is neither versatile nor contains anything impressive or remarkable, and paints it with the colors of rhetoric and enriches it with a wealth of talent.[256]

(85) Outline of *Bab.* (see above, paragraphs 10, 43–46).

Bab. 1–21	*Prologue*
1	Novel prediction of Christ: his disciples would do "greater works" than he (Jn 14.12).
2	No pagan teacher ever made such a prediction.

---

[256] Translated from *Opus Epistolarum Des. Erasmi Roterodami 7: 1527–1528*, ed. P. S. Allen (Oxford 1928) 126–27 (*Ep.* 1856). Another appreciation of the literary style of *Bab.* is found in P. Albert, *S. Jean Chrysostome considéré comme orateur populaire* (Paris 1858) 371 f.

DISCOURSE ON BLESSED BABYLAS
AND AGAINST THE GREEKS

INTRODUCTION

UR LORD, JESUS CHRIST, as he was about to go to his passion and die a life-giving death,[1] on the very last night called his disciples aside and, conversing with them at length, gave them counsel. In addition to other words he said, he spoke thus: "Amen, amen, I say to you, he who believes in me, the works that I do he also shall do, and greater than these he shall do."[2] Yet there have been many other teachers, who had disciples and paraded wonders, even as the Greeks[3] boast.[4] Nonetheless none of them ever con-

---

[1] The adjective "life-giving" is applied by Greek Fathers to the passion, cross, death, and burial of Christ. See the examples listed in PGL, s.v. *zōopoios* 4g.

[2] Jn 14.12. See Introduction 37–38. Cf. Chrysostom, *Hom.* 4 *in Ac. princ.* (PG 51. 107–08. A. Neander, *The Life of St. Chrysostom,* trans. J.C. Stapleton [London 1845] 310–11.): "Christ performed miracles; he raised the dead; he cleansed lepers; he cast out devils: he was afterwards crucified; and, as the wicked Jews say, he arose not from the dead. What then shall we say to them? If he arose not, whence came it, that greater miracles were afterwards wrought in his name? For no one, who ever lived, wrought after his decease miracles greater than before. But here they became more wonderful both in the manner of their performance and their own nature. In their own nature, because the shadow of Christ never awakened the dead; but the shadow of an Apostle performed many such miracles. In the manner of their performance, because, before the crucifixion, Christ wrought the miracles by his own personal presence; but, after the crucifixion, they were his servants, who, by virtue of his holy and adorable name, performed greater and sublimer miracles; and thus his power shone forth more gloriously; for it was the same power, which wrought both before and after the crucifixion—first directly from himself; afterwards by means of his disciples."

[3] "The Greeks" here stands for "children of the Greeks," a circumlocution found in classical Greek and analogous to the biblical phrase "children of Israel." On the translation of *"Hellēnes"* as "Greeks" rather than "pagans" see Introduction note 136.

[4] Thus the anti-Christian writer Hierocles mentioned wonder-workers of

75

ceived of or dared to express such a notion. Nor can certain among the Greeks, for all their impudence, point to the existence of such a prediction or saying among themselves. Rather, many say that many of their wonder-workers evoke apparitions of the departed and phantoms of certain dead men. They also say that certain individuals elicit voices from tombs.[5] But never can any of them assert concerning any human being, whom they admired during his lifetime, or concerning those whom after death they considered gods, that he said such a thing to his disciples.

(2) Permit me to explain the reason why they never dared to invent a fiction of this kind, though lying impudently and brazenly[6] in regard to all else.[7] They did not desist from this stratagem casually without some purpose. These malefactors shrewdly perceived that one who intends to deceive must contrive something plausible, ingenious, and hard to detect. And in fact skillful hunters of fish and of birds do not expose bare traps, but carefully cover them all round with bait, and thus both prevail in their hunting. But if they uncovered their traps and allowed them to be seen by those about to be captured, neither fish nor bird would ever enter those nets—or rather they would not approach them in the first place, and the hunter on the sea and on the land would each go home

---

the past including Aristeas and Pythagoras, as well as Apollonius (*Hierocl.* 2). Earlier, Celsus enumerated a whole list of such men, whom the pagans did not consider gods in spite of their extraordinary works (note 39 to Introduction). Cf. Eugene V. Gallagher, *Divine Man or Magician? Celsus and Origen on Jesus,* SBL Dissertation Series 64 (Chico, California 1982).

[5] Necromancy, defined as "the pretended art of revealing future events, etc., by means of communication with the dead" (OED), was associated with Persian magi and the followers of Zoroaster. Eusebius accuses Apollonius of necromancy (*Hierocl.* 24). Chrysostom makes the accusation against emperor Julian (*Bab.* 79).

[6] Literally, "with bare head." Chrysostom reports that in the theater a prostitute appeared on stage with a bare head (*Theatr.* 2; PG 56.266). Hegesippus earlier applied the image of bareheadedness to gnostic heretics (Eusebius, H.e. 3.32.8; SC 31: 145). The image reoccurs in *Bab.* 76 with reference to emperor Julian.

[7] Chrysostom accuses the pagan wonder-workers of deceit. Cf. *Bab.* 10: everything said about Zoroaster and Zamolxis was fiction. Earlier, Clement of Alexandria made the same accusation against Orpheus, Amphion of Thebes, and Arion of Methymna (*Prot.* 1.3.1; SC 2:55).

empty-handed. Thus since these proposed to ensnare human beings in their nets, they did not toss bare deceit into the sea of life, but composed fictions able to catch the less intelligent. They forebore to advance further in falsehood, afraid of exaggeration and fearing that they might nullify their first prevarication by the extravagance of the second.

(3) If they said that one of theirs made a promise such as our Savior made to his disciples, even those who had been duped would have laughed at them for not being able to invent plausible lies. For that blessed power alone can make and fulfill such a prediction truthfully. If demons ever were able to delude and deceive people a little,[8] it was when the source of light was still unknown to the multitude.[9] And even then it was obvious that demons had wrought the works from the duplicity, especially the sacrifices.[10] The command to redden their altars with human blood, and the order for such victims to be slain by their parents, surpasses extreme madness.

[8] In this discourse Chrysostom accepts the traditional view of demons and their activities found in apologetic literature starting with Justin. The deceit and delusiveness of demons is emphasized by Athanasius, *Inc.* 12.6, 14.3 f., 47.2, 48.3 and 9, 49.6. Athanasius states in *Inc.* 55.1–3: "since the Saviour has come among us . . . demons, so far from cheating any more by illusions and prophecies and magic arts, if they so much as dare to make the attempt, are put to shame by the sign of the Cross. . . . 3. For as, when the sun is come, darkness no longer prevails, but if any be still left anywhere it is driven away; so, now that the divine Appearing of the Word of God is come, the darkness of the idols prevails no more, and all parts of the world in every direction are illumined by His teaching." (trans. A. Robertson, NPNF 2,4 [1892]: 66).

[9] Cf. Jn 8.12, 12.46.

[10] Human sacrifice, especially the sacrifice of children by their parents, is proof of the depravity of demons, who ordained such offerings. The goodness of Christ is evident from the fact that he abolished the practice of human sacrifice for all humanity (*Bab.* 3–7). Chrysostom may rely on Eusebius, *P.e.* 4.15–21. Eusebius endeavored to prove from the writings of Porphyry and others that pagan gods are evil demons because they delighted in human sacrifice. Citing Porphyry, Eusebius gives a long list of cities and lands where human sacrifice was practiced (*P.e.* 4.16.1–11; GCS 43,1: 190–93). Eusebius also cites from Porphyry the fact that human sacrifices were officially abolished in the time of Hadrian (117–38) (*P.e.* 4.16.7; GCS 43,1: 192). Elsewhere, Chrysostom states that before the coming of Christ human sacrifice was common among both Greeks and Jews (*Hom.* 5.4 *in Tit.*; PG 62.692 f.). Chrysostom knows of human sacrifice carried on in his own day (*Laz.* 2.2; PG 48. 983). Archaeological evidence of child sacrifice has recently

(4) These (demons) never have their fill of our miseries, nor do they know any boundary or limit in the battle against us, but, ever provoked by eternal rage, when the slaughter on their altars of women and children instead of sheep and cattle did not suffice to appease their anger, they contrived an alien crime of manslaughter and introduced a novel fashion of misfortune. They persuaded people who should have mourned the slaughter of these victims to act as sponsors of the deplorable carnage.

(5) Lest human statutes only be transgressed, they also utterly uprooted the very laws of nature; which they frenzied against herself by introducing into human life the most atrocious murder of all. Henceforth everyone feared their parents more than any enemy. Instead of placing special confidence in them, they suspected and rejected them most of all. God had introduced them to the spectacle of this universe through their parents. These destructive spirits sought to deprive them of this gift by making parents who had fostered their life the cause of their death, as if wishing to show that they have profited not at all from the goodness of God: they will not require other executioners than their parents.

Even if a great miracle had resulted (not something small, insignificant, and full of chicanery, but even if something great occurred), what I have said is able to show those not completely bereft of reason the identity of the perpetrators, their total depravity, and their constant effort to upset the tranquillity of our life.

(6) No such command was imposed on us by our Lord Jesus. Though he is admired as a wonder-worker, everyone should rightly worship him and believe that he is God on account of his precepts no less than his miracles. His coming put an end to this transgression. Even more amazing, he rescued not only us who worship him but even those who blaspheme him from the fierce and savage tyranny; for no Greek is required to offer such sacrifices to demons anymore.

---

been discovered at Carthage. See Philip J. King, *American Archaeology in the Mideast* (Philadelphia 1983) 225–27.

(7) Such is the philanthropy[11] with which he always treats our race. The good which God did for his enemies was greater than the evil which demons perpetrated upon their friends. For the demons forced their servants and worshipers to become executioners of their own children; whereas Christ freed those who reject him from these injunctions. He did not limit to his own the exemption from savage worship and this marvelous peace, but extended it to outsiders. He showed that they are tyrants, enemies, and destroyers of our race; whence they treated their own as aliens, as indeed they were. But he was the King, Creator, and Savior of the whole human race; whence he spared his enemies and treated them as his own.

(8) And indeed all of human nature was his special concern, just as his disciple says: "He came unto his own, and his own received him not."[12] But now is not the time to recount all of his philanthropy. But even if one discusses it for all the ages, even if one is as eloquent as the incorporeal powers, not even then will he grasp its worth. He alone knows the extent of his goodness, since he alone is good to this degree.[13] See what he says to his disciples: "Amen, amen, I say to you, he who believes in me, the works that I do he also shall do, and greater than these he shall do."[14] He would not have shared such honor with them, were he not exceedingly and infinitely good.

(9) However, if someone should argue with me as to where this oracle was accomplished, let him take in hand the book which is called Acts of the Apostles. In it are described not all

---

[11] *Philanthrōpia*, in classical and hellenistic Greek literature describes the love of the gods for man and the love of men for one another. G. Downey, "Philanthropia in Religion and Statecraft in the Fourth Century after Christ," *Historia* 4 (1955): 199 f. Philanthropy is an important attribute of God already in Justin (1 *Apol.* 10.1). For Chrysostom philanthropy is characteristic of God, "who wishes all men to be saved and to come to the knowledge of the truth" (1 Tm 2.4; cf. *Bab.* 125). See Maksimilijan Žitnik, "*Theos philanthrōpos* bei Johannes Chrysostomus," *Orientalia Christiana Periodica* 41 (1975): 76–118.
[12] Jn 1.11.
[13] Cf. Mt 19.17.
[14] Jn 14.12.

the acts, nor all the apostles, but a few acts of one or two apostles. He will see sick men lying on couches, who regain their health when touched by the shadows of those blessed men,[15] and many madmen who were released from the demon assaulting them by nothing more than the robes of Paul.[16]

(10) Someone may say that this is nonsense and an unconvincing tale of wonder-mongering. But visible phenomena can shut the blasphemous mouth and shame it, and bridle the licentious tongue. In our world there is no land, no nation, no city, where these miracles[17] are not celebrated, which, if fiction, would never have attracted notice. You can supply me with evidence of this statement. I shall not need to obtain from others proof of what is said, since you, the enemy, provide me with it. Tell me why it is that the great Zoroaster[18] and Zamolxis[19] are unknown to most people except for a few? Because all that was said about them was fiction.[20] And yet

---

[15] Cf. Acts 5.15.

[16] Cf. Acts 19.12

[17] I.e., the miracles of Christ and the apostles and the whole Christian preaching.

[18] Zoroaster (most common Greek spelling of the Persian name Zarathustra), Persian religious reformer of the sixth century B.C., was known to the Greeks as early as Xanthus of Lydia (fifth century B.C.). Towards the end of the hellenistic period, works attributed to Zoroaster were translated into Greek; the writings listed under his name in the library of Alexandria amounted to two million lines. J. Bidez and F. Cumont have collected all classical references to Zoroaster in their two volume study, *Les mages hellénisés* (Paris 1938). Chrysostom's testimony is listed there as frag. B10c (vol. 2) and also in A. Jackson, *Zoroaster* (New York 1898) Appendix 5 (25). Nowhere else does Chrysostom refer to Zoroaster (Baur 1: 179). Other church fathers who mention Zoroaster include Origen (*Cels.* 1.16), Pseudo-Melito (ANF 8: 753), and Arnobius 1.52. Contrary to Chrysostom's statement, the books ascribed to Zoroaster "enjoyed a prodigious authority until the end of paganism," according to F. Cumont, *Oriental Religions in Roman Paganism* (Chicago 1911; reprint ed., New York 1956) 189.

[19] The enigmatic figure of Zamolxis is discussed in the OCD, s.v. Zalmoxis. Other references to him are found in the *index nominum* of Bidez-Cumont, s.v. Clement of Alexandria says that Zamolxis was a disciple of Pythagoras (*Str.* 4.8; ANF 2: 419). Zamolxis is also mentioned by Origen (*Cels.* 2.55, 3.34 and 54). Apparently this is the only reference to Zamolxis in the writings of Chrysostom (cf. PG 64.416).

[20] Chrysostom repels the pagan accusation that the new testament narratives are fiction.

both they and the ones who wrote about them are said to have been proficient in the theory and practice of magic, and the use of persuasive language to conceal falsehood.

(11) But all is in vain and futile, when the basis of what is said is unsound falsehood; just as when the basis is powerful truth, everything which is contrived by the enemy for its subversion is in vain and futile. For the power of truth needs no assistance.[21] Even if there is an infinite number who extinguish it, the truth not only is not suppressed but overcomes the attempt to destroy it with added lustre and stature, while mocking those who senselessly strike themselves in rage.[22]

Our doctrine, which you say is fiction, has been assailed by tyrants, kings, orators of invincible eloquence, as well as by philosophers, sorcerers, magicians, and demons, and "their tongues against them are made weak," according to the prophetic saying, and "the arrow of children are their wounds."[23] Emperors benefited from their attack upon us only insofar as they gained a reputation for savagery worldwide. They were carried away by their anger against the martyrs into inhuman

[21] Cf. 1 Esdras 4:35,38,41. See also *Bab.* 21. Elsewhere Chrysostom says: "Error is such that it is dissipated even without opposition, but truth prevails in the midst of hostile forces" (*Laud. Paul.* 4; PG 50.496; St. John Chrysostom, *In Praise of St. Paul,* trans. T. Halton [Boston 1963] 71. Permission to quote from this translation here and elsewhere in this volume has been granted by the Daughters of Saint Paul and Doctor T. Halton.). The autonomy of Christian truth is described by Arnobius 3.1: "For neither is the Christian religion unable to stand though it found no advocates, nor will it be therefore proved true if it found many to agree with it, and gained weight through its adherents. Its own strength is sufficient for it, and it rests on the foundations of its own truth, without losing its power, though there were none to defend it, nay, though all voices assailed and opposed it, and united with common rancour to destroy all faith in it." (trans. H. Bryce and H. Campbell, ANF 6 [1886]: 464)

[22] Chrysostom says: to attempt to suppress the truth of Christianity is insanity. Arnobius likewise accuses the opponents of Christ of insanity (1.24, 31, 42). Indeed Arnobius states concerning the divinity of Christ: "only a raving and reckless madman can be in doubt" (2.60).

[23] Ps 63 (64): 8–9. The invincibility of the gospel is a recurring theme in the Greek apologists. E.g., Clement of Alexandria, *Str.* 6.18: "But our doctrine on its very first proclamation was prohibited by kings and tyrants together, as well as particular rulers and governors, with all their mercenaries, and in addition by innumerable men, warring against us, and endeavouring as far as they could to exterminate it. But it flourishes the more" (trans. W. Wilson, ANF 2 [1885]: 520). Origen, *Cels.* 1.3: "But in the case of the Christians the

cruelty, and did not realize that they were incurring untold disgrace.[24] The philosophers[25] and talented orators[26] had a great reputation with the public on account of their dignity and ability to speak. After the battle against us they became ridiculous and seemed no different from foolish children. From so many nations and peoples, they were not able to change anyone, wise, ignorant, male, female, or even a small child. The estimation of what they wrote is so low that their books disappeared a long time ago, and mostly perished when they first appeared.[27] If anything at all is found preserved, one finds it being preserved by Christians.[28]

(12) Far from suspecting any injury from their treachery, we scorn the fruitless effort of all their machinations. If our bodies were adamantine and incorruptible, we would not be afraid to hold in our hands scorpions and serpents and fire, but would do it ostentatiously. Christ prepared our souls with such faith that we do not fear to have the poisons of the

---

Roman Senate, the contemporary emperors, the army, the people, and the relatives of believers fought against the gospel and would have hindered it; and it would have been defeated by the combined force of so many unless it had overcome and risen above the opposition by divine power, so that it has conquered the whole world that was conspiring against it" (Origen, *Contra Celsum*, trans. H. Chadwick [Cambridge, 1953; reprinted 1979] 8. Permission to reprint from this translation here and elsewhere in this volume has been granted by the Cambridge University Press.). Likewise Eusebius states that the Christian nation is invincible because it always receives assistance from God: H.e.1.4.2. P.e. 1.4 (9d).

[24] Tertullian describes the emperors who persecuted Christianity as "impious, unjust, base, savage, mindless, insane" (*Apol.* 5.7).

[25] Ancient philosophers who combatted Christianity include Celsus and Porphyry, on whom see John S. Whale, "Great Attacks on Christianity: Celsus," *The Expository Times* 42 (1930): 119–24. James Moffatt, "Great Attacks on Christianity 2: Porphyry *Against Christians*," *The Expository Times* 43 (1931): 72–78. Chrysostom may also be thinking of the philosopher emperor Julian.

[26] One of the most famous orators to write against Christianity was M. Cornelius Fronto. See *Handbook of Church History*, ed. Hubert Jedin and John Dolan, vol. 1 (1965): K. Baus, *From the Apostolic Community to Constantine* with a General Introduction to Church History by H. Jedin (New York 1965–81) 166. Perhaps Chrysostom has Libanius in mind.

[27] Cf. Introduction 7 and note 16.

[28] In fact, the text of Celsus's and emperor Julian's anti-Christian treatises is found mostly in the subsequent refutations of Origen and Cyril of Alexandria, *resp.* Also Libanius's monody (*Or.* 60) survives only in excerpts in *Bab.* 98–113 (see Introduction 24 and note 87).

enemies. If we have been ordered to tread upon serpents and scorpions, and all the tyranny of the devil,[29] much more upon worms and beetles. So great is the difference between their mischief and his treachery. (13) Such is the character of our doctrine; what about yours? No one ever persecuted it, nor is it right for Christians to eradicate error by constraint and force, but to save humanity by persuasion and reason and gentleness.[30] Hence no emperor of Christian persuasion enacted against you legislation such as was contrived against us by those who served demons.[31] Just as a body given over to a long and wasting disease perishes of its own accord, without anyone injuring it, and gradually breaks down and is destroyed, so the error of Greek superstition, though it enjoyed so much tranquillity and was never bothered by anyone, nevertheless was extinguished by itself and collapsed internally. Therefore, although this satanic farce has not been completely obliterated from the earth,[32] what has already happened is able to convince you concerning the future.

(14) The greater part has been destroyed in a very short time; henceforth no one will argue about the remainder. Nor

---

[29] Cf. Lk 10.19.

[30] Chrysostom "discovered himself an adversary to the employment of force in religious affairs, and by this truly Christian Spirit he afterwards distinguished himself above many of his cotemporaries" (Neander, *The Life of St. Chrysostom* 52). Neander compares the similar view of Isidore of Pelusium (*Ep.* 3.363): "Since it seemeth not good forcibly to draw over to the faith those who are gifted with a free will, employ at the proper time conviction and by thy life enlighten those who are in darkness." (Neander, *The Life of St. Chrysostom* 52). Isidore also says: "Human salvation is procured not by force but by persuasion and gentleness" (*Ep.* 2.129; PG 78.573).

[31] Cf. Chrysostom, *Pan. Dros.* 2 (PG 50.686): "No pious emperor ever chose to torture and punish an unbeliever so as to force him to withdraw from error." However, pagans would change their religion if threatened with fines (Chrysostom, *Laud. Paul.* 4; PG 50.495). Cf. *History of the Church*, ed. Hubert Jedin and John Dolan, vol. 2 (1980): K. Baus, H.-G. Beck, E. Ewig, and H.J. Vogt, *The Imperial Church from Constantine to the Early Middle Ages*, trans. A. Biggs (New York 1965–1981) 219. Future references to this volume will be abbreviated to Jedin, ed., *History of the Church* 2. Robert E. Carter, "Saint John Chrysostom's Rhetorical Use of the Socratic Distinction between Kingship and Tyranny," *Traditio* 14 (1958): 370–71.

[32] Cf. *Bab.* 43 on the practice of pagan religion at the time when Chrysostom was writing.

yet, when a city has been captured, its walls razed, its public buildings, theatres, and promenades burned down, and all those in the prime of life slain, because someone observes half–burned porticoes, a few houses partially preserved, and old women and small children, will he argue that the victor who has prevailed over the greater part cannot conquer what remains.

This is not the case with the fishermen: their doctrine is flourishing daily, despite the fact that it did not enter freely and easily into our life, but through affliction, wars, and combat.

(15) The religion of the Greeks had been spread all over the earth and controlled the souls of all humanity; only later, after gaining so much strength, was it destroyed by Christ's power.[33] Contrariwise, our preaching was opposed before it spread everywhere and was firmly established. Before it was firmly planted in the souls of those who heard it, from its very inception, it was forced to battle against the whole world: "against the principalities and the powers, against the world-rulers of the darkness of this age, against the spiritual forces of wickedness."[34] The spark of faith had not yet been kindled, when rivers and oceans streamed in upon it. As you well know, it is not the same thing to pull up the plant which has been firmly rooted for a long time and one that has just been set in the earth. Just so, the sea of adversaries was already deluging what I have called the spark of piety, which not only was not extinguished by it, but became greater and brighter. It approached with alacrity every obstacle, easily destroying and consuming the enemy, while restoring its own and raising

---

[33] The destruction of polytheism and idolatry by the power of Christ is a recurrent theme in the works of Eusebius. E.g., P.e. 1.5 (14b): "BUT to understand the sum of the first and greatest benefit of the word of salvation, you must take into consideration the superstitious delusion of the ancient idolatry, whereby the whole human race in times past was ground down by the constraint of daemons: but from that most gloomy darkness, as it were, the word *by its divine power* [italics mine] delivered both Greeks and Barbarians alike, and translated them all into the bright intellectual daylight of the true worship of God the universal King" (*Preparation for the Gospel: Eusebius.* trans. Gifford 16). See also P.e. 4.1 (129d); 5.1 (180d). *Bab.* 16.

[34] Eph 6.12.

them to unheard of heights, though its servants were of little wealth or fame.

(16) The cause was not these fishermen's words and miracles, but the words and miracles of Christ's power, which was working in them.[35] One of those who did this, Paul, was a tent maker;[36] another, Peter, was a fisherman.[37] It would never have occurred to people so ordinary and humble to invent such a thing, except if someone is prepared to say that they were raving lunatics.[38] That they were not lunatics is clear from what they accomplished when they spoke, and from those who are still persuaded by them even now. Accordingly, such claims could never be lies or rash boasting. For, as I said at the beginning, the person who intends to deceive tells lies, but not the sort of lies that are manifest to everyone.

(17) The events have been accomplished and great numbers bear witness to the consummation, including those who believed at that time and those who afterwards everywhere celebrate these events, not only among us, but also among even the most savage barbarians.[39] If nevertheless, after so much proof and, so to speak, the testimony of the whole world, there are certain individuals who refuse to believe that these events occurred (and many without examination or inquiry), who would have accepted this religion at the begin-

---

[35] Cf. Origen, *Cels.* 1.62: ". . . to people who can study the question about Jesus' apostles intelligently and reasonably it will appear that these men taught Christianity and succeeded in bringing many to obey the word of God *by divine power* [italics mine]" (trans. Chadwick *Contra Celsum* 57). Eusebius, H.e. 2.32: "*the power of Christ* [italics mine] operating through the teaching and the wonderful works of his disciples" (trans. A. McGiffert, NPNF 2,1 [1890]: 107). H.e. 3.5.2: "But the rest of the apostles . . . went unto all nations to preach the Gospel, relying upon *the power of Christ* [italics mine]" (trans. A. McGiffert, NPNF 2,1 [1890]: 138). Chrysostom, *Laud. Paul.* 4: "He [Christ] was a reformer and possessed divine and *invincible power* [italics mine]. That was the cause of His superiority and the reason why He could inspire this tent-maker [Paul] with the power that his deeds attest" (trans. Halton, *In Praise of St. Paul* 60).

[36] Cf. Acts 18.3.

[37] Cf. Mt 4.18.

[38] Prof. Morton Smith has stated that the disciples of Jesus were "schizophrenics." *New York Times*, May 29, 1973, p. 39.

[39] Cf. *Bab.* 119. A. Fliche and V. Martin, *Histoire de l'église* 3 (Paris 1950) 489–90.

ning, if he did not see the events or have trustworthy evidence of them?

(18) What in the world could have incited them to devise such a fiction? They did not rely on eloquence; how could they, when the one did not even know how to read and write?[40] Nor did they rely on great wealth. In fact, they both barely had enough to maintain life, supporting themselves by the skill of their hands. They could not even be proud of a distinguished ancestry: the one's father was so obscure and undistinguished, that we do not even know his name; while Peter's father is known, but is superior to the other only in that the Scriptures informed us of his name alone, and that on account of his son.[41] If you care to examine their country and nation, you will find that the one was a Cilician,[42] the other a citizen of an obscure city. Rather, it was not a city, but the smallest of villages, for he was from Bethsaida. (This is the name of a place in Galilee, from which that blessed one came.)[43] Also, when you hear their occupations, you will see that they are not imposing and dignified: though the tent-maker has more prestige than the fisherman, yet he is lower than all the other artisans.

(19) Therefore tell me whence, whence their boldness in feigning so great a matter. What hopes excited them? What did they rely on? The fishing rod and the fish hook, or the knife and the borer? Go off and hang yourselves or throw yourselves off a cliff as a penalty for being so foolish.[44]

[40] Cf. Acts 4.13.
[41] Cf. Jn 1.42.
[42] Cf. Acts 22.3.
[43] Cf. Jn 1.44. Chrysostom, *Hom. in Ac.* 4.3 (PG 60.47): "Where now is Greece, with her big pretensions? Where the name of Athens? Where the ravings of the philosophers? He of Galilee, he of Bethsaida, he, the uncouth rustic, has overcome them all. Are you not ashamed—confess it—at the very name of the country of him who has defeated you? But if you hear his own name too, and learn that he was called Cephas, much more will you hide your faces" (trans. H. Browne and G. Stevens, NPNF 11 [1889]: 29).

[44] A retortion of the pagan accusation against the apostles that they were ignorant and uneducated. Chrysostom says that this accusation should be acknowledged by Christians and used as an argument for the divinity of Christianity. See *Hom.* 3.4 *in* 1 *Cor.* (PG 61.27 f.) quoted above in note 31 of the notes to the Introduction.

(20) Permit me to assume, according to your point of view, that the following impossibility was possible, and that someone returned from the lake and said: "the shadow of my body raised the dead," while another leaped from the skins of the tent-maker's workshop and boasted this very same thing as the other about his clothes.[45] What person who heard this was so insane as to believe mere words about such matters? How come an artisan of that time never said such a thing about himself, or someone else about him? And yet, if our doctrine were fiction, the successors (of the apostles) would probably have uttered such lies more easily. Whereas the apostles could not hope to succeed in the business by appealing to others for vindication, their successors would more readily have ventured upon the fabrication after observing them and having their example as an inducement to be bold—as if no one on earth possessed intelligence, but all were stark raving mad, and everyone who is so inclined might say exactly what they wish about themselves and be believed.

(21) This is drivel and nonsense and utterances of Greek folly. Someone who is prompted to shoot at heaven hoping to rend it with his missiles, or to drain the ocean by emptying it with his own hands, will be mocked by the more witty, and the more serious will weep for him with many tears.[46] Just so when the Greeks contradict us is it right to laugh and weep for them, for they are undertaking much more difficult tasks than one hoping to wound the sky and empty the deep.[47] Light will never be darkness so long as it is light; neither will

[45] Cf. *Bab.* 9 and notes.

[46] Cf. J.D. Duff, ed., *D. Iunii Iuvenalis Saturae XIV: Fourteen Satires of Juvenal* (Cambridge 1898; reprint ed., Cambridge 1962) 330 on *Sat.* 10.28–30: "A tradition, constantly recurring in Latin authors, represents Democritus as unable to restrain his laughter, and Heracleitus his tears, at the spectacle of human life."

[47] The poetic device of the *adunaton* or impossibility, studied by Ernest Dutoit, *Le thème de l'adynaton dans la poésie antique* (Paris 1936). In *Pan. Bab.* 1 Chrysostom quotes Mt 24.35 and says concerning emperor Julian's attempt to destroy Christianity: "But this was impossible, O wretched and miserable man! as it was impossible to destroy the heaven and to quench the sun, and to shake and cast down the foundations of the earth. . . ." (trans. T.P. Brandram NPNF 9 [1889]: 141).

the truth of the facts asserted by us ever be refuted: for they are the truth, and there is nothing stronger than this.[48]

PROEM TO THE HISTORY OF BABYLAS

(22) Accordingly, everyone who is not insane and mindless will acknowledge that events of the past, which we know of by hearsay, are no less credible than present events which we observe.[49] However, in order to win total victory, I wish to mention a miraculous event that occurred in our generation. Do not be confused if after promising to mention a contemporary miracle, I begin to compose the beginning of the narrative from ancient history. I will not stop there, nor will I relate events of the past which are foreign to the modern subject: for both are connected with each other, and it is not possible to separate their natural sequence. You will understand perfectly once you have heard the events themselves.

THE EMPEROR'S FIRST CRIME: MURDER OF A YOUNG HOSTAGE

(23) There was a certain emperor[50] in the time of our forefathers. What this emperor was like in other respects I cannot say; but once you have heard the crime which he

[48] This sentence is attributed to Justin Martyr by John of Damascus, *Sacra Parallela*. See J.C.Th. Otto, *Corpus Apologetarum Christianorum saeculi secundi*[3] 3.2 (Jena 1879) 258, frag. 7. Otto compares Justin, *Res.* 1: "Nothing is more powerful than truth." The concept of the invincibility of truth seems to derive from 1 Esdras 4 (cf. *Bab.* 11).

[49] The consensus of antiquity was that the evidence of the eyes is more reliable than that of the ears. Edward Kennard Rand, *The Building of Eternal Rome* (Cambridge, Mass. 1943; reprint ed., New York 1972) 116 note 2. Cf. Jb 42.5. Chrysostom, however, in defending the credibility of events recorded in the Bible, challenges the traditional view that seeing is believing. E.g., *Hom.* 8.3 *in* 1 *Thess.* (PG 62.443): "For to me indeed the former things were not incredible, but things not seen were equally credible with things that were seen" (trans. J. Tweed, NPNF 13 [1890]: 358). But cf. *Bab.* 56, 78.

[50] "Emperor" is a translation of *basileus*, the word regularly used by Greek patristic writers for Roman emperors. E.g., Justin, 1 *Apol.* 14.4 etc.

dared to commit, you will understand the complete savagery of his nature. What was the crime? One of the nations at war with this emperor decided to end the war and neither to attack others nor be attacked by others henceforth, but to be delivered from trouble, danger, and fear, being contented with their possessions and seeking nothing more than these: for it was better to enjoy modest means with serenity than through greediness to be in constant fear and trembling, and to live inflicting evil on others and receiving it back from them.

(24) It was resolved to end the war and to live in tranquillity, and they decided to confirm this good decision by a tough law and secure boundaries. When they had made a treaty and exchanged oaths, they attempted, in addition, to persuade their king to deposit his son (quite a young child) as security for the peace[51] in order to make his former enemies confident and to proffer evidence of his own mind and the good faith in which he had made peace with them. With these words they persuaded the king, who surrendered his son, as he thought, to friends and allies, but as it later appeared, to a beast of unsurpassed savagery. For after he received that royal child according to the treaty of friendship, he despised and subverted it all: the oaths, the treaty, human honor, divine reverence, and compassion for youth.

(25) Neither did infancy sway the beast, nor did penalty, which follows such pollutions, terrify the savage, nor did the entreaties of the donor father come to mind as he entrusted his son, beseeching him to take good care of him, calling him the child's father, requesting that he bring him up as if he had begotten him, and that he make him worthy of the nobility of his own ancestors, and with these words placing the right

---

[51] The practice of taking children as hostages was current in the Greco–Roman world. See M. Rostovtzeff, *The Social and Economic History of the Hellenistic World* (Oxford 1941) 3: 1512 note 35. Jean Gagé, *Res gestae divi Augusti*[2] (Paris 1950) 142. Cf. Tacitus, *Ann.* 2.1; 12.10.4; 13.9. Chrysostom states that the foreign king expected his child to be reared and educated by the (Roman) emperor (*Bab.* 25). This is credible in view of the widespread practice of rearing and educating children taken as hostages. Cf. Suetonius, *Aug.* 48: "Augustus reared and educated the children of very many kings together with his own."

hand of the child in the right hand of the murderer and dissolving into tears. The blackguard took none of this into consideration, but abruptly dismissed it from his mind, and committed the most foul of all murders. For this crime is worse than killing one's own child. And you are witnesses, who would not have been so pained if you had heard that he murdered his own son. In that case the ordinances of nature, together with the laws of society, would have been over-thrown, but here many things coincided which in the aggre-gate are stronger than the bond of nature.

(26) When I reflect on the innocent lad, who was surren-dered by his father, who was snatched from his ancestral palace, and exchanged the magnificence, glory, and honor due him for life in a foreign country, in order to give that blackguard confidence in the treaty; and who, when he was in his power and deprived of his domestic splendor, was then killed by him—I experience the contradictory emotions of anger and despair simultaneously. When I reflect on how the blackguard armed himself, and brandished his sword, and grasped the child's neck, and pushed the sword into it with the right hand with which he had received him as a ward—I burst and am choked with anger. Again, when I see the youth trembling with fear, lamenting bitterly, calling on his father, saying that he is to blame, crediting the murder not to the one who plunges the sword into his throat, but to the one who begot him, being unable to escape or defend himself, but now vainly blaming his father, receiving the wound, gasping, kick-ing the ground with his feet, defiling the earth with streams of blood—my insides are rent, my mind is darkened, and a mist of despair is poured over my eyes.

THE EMPEROR'S SECOND CRIME: IMPENITENCE

(27) But that beast did not have any such feelings, but his attitude toward this foul murder was that of one about to kill a lamb or calf. The boy lay dead after receiving the blow; the murderer, however, increased the pollution in an attempt to cover the first crime with a second. Perhaps someone thinks

that I shall speak of the burial, and that after the murder he did not allot even a patch of earth to the slain man.[52] No; I shall mention something else, more insolent than this. When he had defiled his impious hands with such blood, and enacted the new tragedy, as if he had done nothing, this shameless and stone-hard[53] character hastened to the church of God.[54]

REFLECTIONS ON THE SLOWNESS OF DIVINE JUSTICE

(28) And certain ones are probably wondering why he was not stricken by a blow from heaven for such arrogant behavior, or why God did not discharge a thunderbolt at him from above and destroy the shameful spectacle with lightning before he entered. If certain ones conceived this thought, although I praise them and admire their ardor, nevertheless my admiration and praise for them are highly qualified. For, they were rightfully indignant over the unjust slaying of the child and over the reckless violation of the laws of God; but due to their seething anger they did not comprehend as much as was necessary. For in heaven there is another law, much higher than this justice.

(29) What is this law? That sinners not be punished immediately, but that the transgressor be given respite and a set period of time to divest himself of the transgression and by means of repentance to become the equal of those who have not done evil.[55] This is exactly how God treated the malefactor

---

[52] Great importance was attached to an honorable burial in antiquity, as the *Antigone* of Sophocles attests. On pagan and Christian funeral rites see Rudolph Arbesmann, ed., *Aurelius Augustinus, Die Sorge für die Toten* (Würzburg 1975) ix–liii.

[53] I.e., impenitent, like emperor Julian (*Bab.* 121) and the pharaoh (*Bab.* 122). Cf. Rom 2:5.

[54] Evidently to attend the service. Cf. Eusebius, H.e. 6.34 (Introduction 56).

[55] The slowness of divine justice was a recurring theme in ancient Greek literature, discussed in Plutarch's dialogue on that topic. See Anne–Marie Malingrey, "Les délais de la justice divine chez Plutarque et dans la littérature judéo-chrétienne," *Actes du VIIIe Congrès de l'Association Guillaume Budé* (Paris 5–10 Avril 1968) 542–50. Whence the Greek proverb (translated from the German of F. von Logau by H.W. Longfellow in "Retribution": "Though the

at that time. But it profited nothing, and he remained incorrigible. Although he foreknew it, nevertheless the philanthropic Lord did not disdain him or cease from his efforts, but himself visited the sick man and did what was necessary for his recovery; he, however, was not willing to accept the medicine and killed the physician sent for this purpose. The medicine and the method of treatment were as follows.[56]

BABYLAS EXPELS THE MURDERER FROM CHURCH

(30) It happened when this cruel and pitiful drama was boldly enacted[57] that our flock was guided by a great and wonderful man—if he is to be called a man at all—whose name was Babylas.[58] He had then been entrusted by the grace of the Spirit with the local church of Christ.[59] That he excelled Elijah and his imitator, John, I will not say, because it would sound excessive, but he attained to the point where he was not in the least inferior in courage to those brave men.[60] Not the

---

mills of God grind slowly, yet they grind exceeding small; though with patience he stands waiting, with exactness grinds he all." Chrysostom combined the traditional Greek idea of the slowness of divine punishment with the biblical teaching of repentance, as in *Poenit* 7.4 (PG 49.328 f.). Reflections on the slowness of divine punishment also occur in connection with the narrative concerning emperor Julian (*Bab.* 124 f.).

[56] On the medical imagery, associated with penance, see Introduction 52.

[57] Chrysostom frequently employs imagery taken from the Greek theater, particularly tragedy. See *Bab.* 27, 56, 76, 81. *Ep. Olymp.* 7.1a9, 3c37, 4a16, 4b35 (SC 13bis: 132, 144, 148).

[58] Possible meaning of the name Babylas: "a person from Byblos (or Babylon)"?

[59] Babylas was the twelfth bishop of Antioch (Introduction 58).

[60] Chrysostom conjoins John the Baptist and Elijah in *Hom.* 58.4 *in Mt.* (PG 58.571): "if thou wouldest show me that thou art noble, show the freedom of thy soul, such as that blessed man had (and he a poor man), who said to Herod, 'It is not lawful for thee to have thy brother Philip's wife;' such as he was possessed of, who before him was like him, and after him shall be so again; who said to Ahab, 'I do not trouble Israel, but thou, and thy father's house'" (trans. S.G. Prevost and M.B. Riddle, NPNF 10 [1889]: 362). Chrysostom again commends Elijah for reproaching Ahab in *Hom. in Petrum et Heliam* 3 (PG 50.732). Elsewhere Chrysostom draws a parallel between Babylas and John the Baptist: "The blessed martyr Babylas was bound, and he too for the very same cause as John also was, because he reproved a king in his transgression" (*Hom.* 9.2 *in Eph.*; trans. W.J. Copeland and G. Alexander

tetrarch of a few cities,[61] nor the king of a single nation,[62] but the ruler of the greater part of the whole world, the murderer himself, possessing many nations, many cities, and an immense army, formidable in every respect by reason of the magnitude of his power and his reckless disposition, like a vile and worthless slave he ejected from the church with the calmness and fearlessness of a shepherd who separates a mangy and diseased sheep from the flock to prevent the disease of the infected one from spreading to the rest.[63]

(31) Doing this he confirmed in deed the word of our Savior that he alone is a slave who commits sin,[64] even though he may have numerous crowns on his head and seem to rule all the earth's people; whereas a person who is conscious of no evil in himself, even though numbered in the rank of a subject, is more kingly than all kings.[65] Thus, the subordinate gave orders to the chief, and the subject judged the ruler of all and cast the vote which condemned him. But you, o man, who hears these things, do not fail to heed what has been said. This report, that the emperor was driven from the vestibule of the church by someone under his rule, suffices even by itself to excite and astound the soul of those who hear.

NPNF 13 [1890]: 96). John the Baptist was beheaded "for the sacred laws that were despised" (*Stat.* 1.12; trans. C. Marriott and W.R. Stephens NPNF 9 [1889]: 343); likewise Babylas refused to overlook "the violation of the law of God" (*Bab.* 51).

[61] Viz., Herod Antipas. Cf. Mt 14.3 f.

[62] Ahab? Cf. 1 Kgs (3 Kgs) 18.17–18.

[63] The image of the mangy sheep, which must be separated from the rest of the flock, is associated with penance in patristic literature (Introduction 52). See also Cyprian, *Ep.* 59.15.2 (*Saint Cyprien: Correspondance*, ed. and trans. L. Bayard, 2 vols. [Paris 1925] 2: 184): "Nor is that pastor serviceable or wise who so mingles the diseased and affected sheep with his flock as to contaminate the whole flock with the infection of the clinging evil" (trans. E. Wallis, ANF 5 [1886]: 345).

[64] Cf. Jn 8.34.

[65] An echo of the Stoic paradox, found in Philo, that "every bad man is a slave," and "every good man is free." Samuel Sandmel, *Philo of Alexandria: An Introduction* (New York 1979) 32. Cf. Augustine, *Civ.* 4.3, trans. D. Zema and G. Walsh, Saint Augustine: *The City of God Books 1–7*, FOTC 8 (New York 1950) 194: "Thus a good man, though a slave, is free; but a wicked man, though a king, is a slave. For he serves, not one man alone, but, what is worse, as many masters as he has vices. For, it is in reference to vice that Holy Scripture says: 'For by whom a man is overcome, of the same also he is the slave.' [2 Pt 2.19]." *Bab.* 61.

(32) But if you want to discover the exact extent of the miracle, do not pay attention to a prosaic account, but picture the spearmen, armor bearers, military leaders, governors, including those who live in the royal palace and those who are assigned to cities, the pride of the officers, the multitude of pompous attendants, and all the rest of the retinue. Then picture him in the midst, advancing with great haughtiness, appearing more dignified from his clothes, purple robe, and the gems scattered all over his right hand, the buckle of his coat, and his head, whence they gleamed from the diadem.

(33) And do not end the picture here, but extend it also to God's servant, the blessed Babylas, his modest bearing, simple dress, contrite soul, and spirit free from arrogance. Picture them both, compare them, and then you will understand the miracle well, or rather not even then will you grasp the exact nature of it. For such liberty[66] cannot be grasped by language or sight—only by experience and practice. And the courage of that generous soul can only be comprehended by one who has been able to reach the same high degree of liberty. How did the old man approach, push aside the guards, open his mouth, speak, convict, rest his right hand on the breast still flaming with anger and seething with murder, repulse the murderer? None of these actions frightened him or swayed him from his purpose. O, unshakeable soul and sublime resolve! O, heavenly disposition and angelic constancy! Viewing the whole spectacle like a wall painting, the intrepid man acted with total imperturbability.

---

[66] I.e., *parrhēsia*, boldness of speech, an important concept, which would merit a separate study in Chrysostom. Freedom of speech is one of the basic elements of ancient Greek culture; its most famous representative in Greek literature was Aristophanes, who may have influenced Chrysostom. See R.W. Livingstone, *The Greek Genius and its Meaning to Us* (London 1915), chap. 2: "The Note of Freedom" 64–69. Werner Jaeger, *Paideia: The Ideals of Greek Culture*[2], trans. Gilbert Highet (Oxford 1965) 1:364. J.A. Nairn, ed., *De sacerdotio of St. John Chrysostom* (Cambridge 1906) xxxiii–xxxiv. For Chrysostom *parrhēsia* is usually an attribute of biblical personages (above note 60) and monks. In fact, Chrysostom says that the boldness of contemporary monks proves the existence of the boldness of the apostles in the past (*Stat.* 17.2; PG 47,175; trans. NPNF 9:455). Chrysostom emphasizes the *parrhēsia* of Babylas, says it proves the *parrhēsia* of the apostles, and favorably contrasts it with the *parrhēsia* of the Greek philosopher, Diogenes (*Bab.* 35, 38, 46 f.).

APOSTOLIC BOLDNESS DISPLAYED

(34) For he was instructed by the divine teaching that all worldly activities are a shadow,[67] and a dream,[68] and less significant than these.[69] Therefore, none of this made him cower, but inspired him with greater fearlessness. The spectacle which he beheld directed his mind to the king above, who sits upon the cherubim and gazes at abysses, to the glorious and sublime throne, to the heavenly host, to the myriads of angels, to the thousands of archangels, to the terrible tribunal, to the impartial judgment, to the river of fire, to the judge himself.[70] Accordingly, he repaired altogether from earth to heaven, and, as if standing beside that assessor and hearing his command to expel the defiled excommunicate from the holy flock, he ejected him and separated him from the rest of the sheep, and paid no attention to the visible and seemingly frightful scene, but courageously and valiantly banished him and vindicated the outraged laws of God.

(35) Besides, how much liberty did he probably exercise towards others? After contending so mightily with a sovereign, what other person would he fear? My guess or rather my conviction is that this man never did or said anything out of partiality or antagonism, but nobly and courageously withstood fear, flattery, which is more powerful than fear, and other such factors which abound in human affairs, and did not vitiate right judgment even a little. For, if "the attire of the body, and the laughter of the teeth, and the gait of the man, shew what he is,"[71] much more do such accomplishments sufficiently exhibit to us all the virtue of the rest of his life. One must not only admire his boldness, but also that he imposed a limit on his boldness and did not exceed it.

[67] Cf. 1 Chr (1 Paralipomenon) 29.15. Jb 8.9. Ps 143 (144).4. Wis 2.5.

[68] Cf Jb 20.8.

[69] An echo of the pessimistic commonplace of Greek poetry: "man is the dream of a shadow" (Pindar, *Pyth.* 8.99 f.). Cf. Aeschylus, *Ag.* 1327 f. Sophocles, *Aj.* 125 f. Euripides, *Med.* 1224.

[70] Cf. *Bab.* 51. The eschatological perspective is characteristic of Chrysostom (e.g., *Thdr.* 2.8–14; SC 117: 118–64; trans. NPNF 9:97–103). In general see Fr. Leduc, "L'eschatologie, une préoccupation centrale de saint John Chrysostome," *Proche-orient chrétien* 29 (1969): 119–24.

[71] Sir 19.30.

(36) Such is the wisdom of Christ: it does not permit either deficiency or excess in combat, but everywhere maintains the proper measure.[72] And yet, if he wanted, he could have gone even further. As one who had renounced life—he would not have approached at all, if he had not armed himself with such thoughts—he could do anything with impunity: shower the emperor with insults, remove the diadem from his head, strike his face when he rested his right hand on his breast. But he did none of this, for his soul was seasoned with spiritual salt,[73] whence he did nothing with rashness and futility but everything according to correct reasoning and sound judgment.

(37) Not so the Greek sages, who are never measured, but always, so to speak, employ more or less liberty than is necessary. Therefore they acquire a reputation never of courage but always of irrational passions, and everyone convicts them of cowardice, where they were deficient, and of arrogance and vanity, where they were excessive. But not that blessed man. He did not simply act on impulse, but carefully analyzed everything, and conformed his thoughts to the divine laws before putting them into action. Therefore the incision he made was not superficial, so as not to leave remaining the greater part of the diseased tissue, nor deeper than necessary, so as not to injure his health in another way by radical cutting, but he adapted the operation to the sickness and thus effected the best cure. Whence I confidently asserted that he was free of anger, cowardice, arrogance, vanity, hostility, fear, and sycophancy.

(38) If I may say something paradoxical, I admire the blessed one not so much because he confronted the sovereign's fury, as because he recognized the limit to which

---

[72] Cf. Plato, *Phlb.* 64e: "measure and symmetry are beauty and virtue." The concept of the mean and moderation in Greek culture is discussed by C.M. Bowra, *The Greek Experience* (New York 1959) 46 ff., 91, 99 f. William Chase Greene, *Moira: Fate, Good and Evil in Greek Thought* (Cambridge, Mass. 1944; reprint ed., New York 1963) 22, 267, 411. The concept of the mean is employed by Chrysostom in various contexts. He says, for example, that Plato's teaching on the soul lacks symmetry (*Hom.* 2.3 *in Jo.;* PG 59,33; trans. FOTC 33.19).
[73] Cf. Col 4.6.

he should go, and did not exceed this limit in deed or in word. And because this is more wonderful than that, one finds many individuals who achieved the first, but have been defeated by the second. Simple boldness is the attribute of many ordinary folk, but to employ it for a needful purpose, at an opportune time, and with the proper moderation and discretion requires a very great and wonderful soul. For example, Schimei very forcefully censured David and called him a "man of blood;"[74] I cannot, however, call this courage, but an unbridled tongue, an insolent spirit, vulgarity, folly—anything but courage. It is necessary, in my opinion, that one who intends to reproach should distance himself as far as possible from audacity and pride, and display energy only in the quality of his words and actions.

(39) And indeed physicians, when it is necessary to amputate limbs which are gangrenous or reduce inflammation in others, do not first fill themselves with wrath and then proceed to administer medical treatment. On the contrary, then especially do they strive to maintain the proper equilibrium so their art will not be injured by mental confusion. If one who intends to treat the body has need of so much tranquillity, in what category shall we place the doctor of souls, tell me, and how much self–mastery shall we require of him? Much more, obviously, and as much as that good martyr displaced. For, when he ousted that miserable man from the sacred precincts, he established for us certain rules and principles, which might serve as guidelines for our conduct in similar situations in the future.

CHRISTIANITY SHOWN SUPERIOR TO PAGANISM

(40) Seemingly, this event represents a single act of heroism.[75] But, if you examine and unfold it and carefully observe it all round, you will find conjoined a second and third exploit and a great treasure of edification.[76] Only one

---

[74] 2 Sm (2 Kgs) 16.7.
[75] Cf. Introduction 40 with note 140.
[76] At the beginning of *Bab.* 50 Chrysostom characterizes paragraphs 40–50

person was then chased from the church, but the people who profited through him were many. Within the tyrant's realm, which constituted most of the inhabited world, all unbelievers were struck with astonishment and admiration upon learning how much courage Christ imparted to his servants; they derided their own servility, bondage, and humiliation, and saw the great distance between the nobility of the Christians and the degradation of the Greeks.

(41) The administrators of pagan religion honor their gods[77] and idols less than the emperors, and from fear of the latter minister to the statues, so that the evil demons are indebted to the emperors for the honor paid them.[78]Certainly, as soon as a nonpagan becomes emperor, one cannot enter the idol temples without seeing spider webs stretched all over the walls, and dust lying on the statue in such a quantity that neither nose nor eye nor any other part of the face is visible.[79] Of the altars only the ruins of some remain, of which the greater part has collapsed; others are covered on every side with a grass so thick that the unknowing person assumes what appears is a heap of manure. The reason is that formerly the idol cult was an occasion for them to steal as much as they wanted and gorge themselves;[80] but now, why should they bother? They expect no recompense for their assiduousness and expenditure from the statues, for these are of wood and of stone, and the incentive to feign this worship, the honor

---

as a digression. The digression or excursus was a literary device commonly used by ancient historians starting with Thucydides (1.97.2). See M.L.W. Laistner, *The Greater Roman Historians* (Berkeley 1947; reprint ed., Berkeley 1966) 50, 98, 109, 155. It appears that in his discussion of Babylas's influence on the pagan world, Chrysostom has adopted with slight changes of emphasis a general polemic against pagan religion and morality to fit the history of Babylas. Cf. R. Asmus, "Die Invektiven des Gregorius von Nazianz im Lichte der Werke des Kaisers Julian," *Zeitschrift für Kirchengeschichte* 31 (1910): 331–34.

[77] Literally, "lords, masters." The idols are called "masters" of the pagans in *Clem. Recogn.* 5.14 (ANF 8: 146). *Hom. Clem.* 10.7 (ibid. 281). Cf. *Hom. Clem.* 10.25 (ibid. 284).

[78] Tertullian says that the emperors are "masters" of the pagan gods in *Apol.* 13.8 (FOTC 10.44).

[79] Cf. *Epistula Ieremiae* 1:11, 16.

[80] Cf. *Bab.* 43, where Chrysostom associates gluttony and other vices with pagan worship.

paid by the rulers, is also gone, since the emperors have become wise and worship the Son of God.

(42) Our situation is entirely different. When a Christian ascends the imperial throne, far from being shored up by human honors, Christianity deteriorates. On the other hand, when rule is held by an impious man,[81] who persecutes us in every way and subjects us to countless evils, then our cause acquires renown and becomes more brilliant, then is the time of valor and of trophies, then is the opportunity to attain crowns, praises, and every distinction.[82]

(43) If someone tells me that even now there are cities which display the same superstition and madness of idolatry, first, you will respond, they are few in number and small.[83] But in any case, this does not affect our argument. The theory is the same: in place of the ruler, the inhabitants of the city pay honor to the idols. The inducement to worship is the revelry, the daily and nocturnal feasts, the flutes and kettledrums, the license to use obscene language and to act even more obscenely, gluttony to the point of bursting, delirium from intoxication, degeneration into most shameful madness.[84] These disgraceful expenditures are keeping the

---

[81] The contrast between a Christian emperor and an impious one points to the conclusion that true piety is identical with Christianity. On the piety of Christian emperors see Dieter Kaufmann-Bühler, "Eusebeia," RACh 6: 1043–47.

[82] Chrysostom expresses the sane point of view in *Oppugn.* 2.9 (PG 47.344): "Our cause is not the same as the cause of the Greeks; it is not dependent upon the disposition of a ruler, but it rests on its own internal strength, and shines forth with greater luster, the more vehemently it is assailed." The church is more illustrious in times of persecution than when enjoying peace (*Hom.* 26.4 *in* 2 *Cor.*; PG 61.580): "For now indeed that we are in the enjoyment of peace, we are become supine and lax, and have filled the Church with countless evils; but when we were persecuted, we were more soberminded, and kinder, and more earnest, and more ready as to these assemblies and as to hearing. For what fire is to gold, that is affliction unto souls; wiping away filth, rendering men clean, making them bright and shining" (trans. J. Ashworth and revised by T. Chambers, NPNF 12 [1889]: 401). Chrysostom thus questions the advantage of the Constantinian alliance between the church and the Roman empire; his attitude is "un-Byzantine."

[83] Evidently Chrysostom is writing at a time when paganism is on the wane.

[84] Idolatry was practiced for the sake of gluttony, drunkenness, obscenity, and sexual immorality, according to the early Christian apologists. E.g., Tertullian, *Idol.* 1.4: "In it are *lasciviousnesses* and *drunkennesses;* since it is, for the most part, for the sake of food and stomach and appetite, that these solem-

decrepit system of error from total collapse. For instance, the more affluent single out those persons whom indolence has made victims of hunger,[85] and keep them as parasites and dogs fed at the table: they stuff their shameless bellies with the remains of the iniquitous banquets and use them as they wish.[86]

(44) We, who once for all loathe your folly and iniquity, do not support individuals living in idleness and therefore necessarily suffering hunger, but convince them to work and to provide for themselves and others.[87] As for the physically disabled, we allow them to receive only the necessary support from the well-to-do.[88] Revelry, carousal, and every other mad and shameful practice has been expelled, and in their place introduced "whatever honorable, whatever holy, whatever just, whatever of good repute, if there be any virtue, if anything worthy of praise."[89]

(45) In addition, Babylas demonstrated that the philosophers, of whom they boast, are characterized by vainglory, impudence, and puerility.[90] He did not shut himself up in a large wine cask, nor did he go round the market place

---

nities are frequented" (trans. S. Thelwall ANF 3 [1885]: 61). Emperor Constantine, *Or. s.c.* 11: "Away then, ye impious . . . begone to your sacrifices, your feasts, your scenes of revelry and drunkenness, wherein, under the semblance of religion, your hearts are devoted to profligate enjoyment, and pretending to perform sacrifices, yourselves are the willing slaves of your own pleasures" (trans. E.C. Richardson NPNF 2,1 [1890]: 568).

[85] Hunger attends the idle: Hesiod, *Op.* 302.

[86] See OCD, s.v. Parasite. Chrysostom, however, emphasizes the moral and social implications of parasitism here and in *Hom.* 48.7 *in Mt.* (PG 58.496; trans. NPNF 10:303).

[87] Cf. 2 Thes 3.10.

[88] Cf. Introduction 18. Adolf Harnack, *The Mission and Expansion of Christianity in the First Three Centuries*, trans. James Moffatt (London and New York 1908; reprint ed., New York 1962) 173–76. Igino Giordani, *The Social Message of the Early Fathers* (Patterson, N.J. 1944; reprint ed., Boston 1977) 282–83.

[89] Phil 4.8.

[90] Chrysostom frequently states that the passion for glory was the motive for all the amazing deeds of the philosophers. No apologist expressed this so forcefully since Tertullian's "philosophus gloriae animal" (*An.* 1.2), according to Elser, "Der hl. Chrysostomus und die Philosophie," *Theologische Quartalschrift* 76 (1894): 561–63. Other patristic references to the vainglory of the philosophers are given by J.H. Waszink, ed., *Quinti Septimi Florentis Tertulliani De anima* (Amsterdam 1947) 87.

clothed in rags.[91] These actions, although they seem to be astounding and to involve much labor and extreme pain, nevertheless are deprived of all praise. This too is the malice of the devil: to subject his servants to such labors, which both torment the deceived and make them appear most contemptible. Indeed, useless labor is deprived of every encomium. Thus even now there are still depraved men, filled with innumerable vices, who display much greater feats than the philosopher: some eat pointed and sharpened nails, some chew up and devour sandals, some take other risks much greater than these.[92] Such phenomena are much more impressive than the wine cask and the rags, but we do not accept either, and equally censure and bewail the philosopher and all those who perform similar tricks to no purpose.

(46) "But he also addressed a king with great liberty."[93] Let us consider this great liberty; it is possibly more inane than the marvelous tale of the wine cask. What liberty was it? The Macedonian, on the way to his expedition against Persia, encountered him and urged him to state what he needed; he said, "nothing, except that the king should not cast a shadow on him,"—for the philosopher was then in the process of warming himself in the sun. Retire from sight! Don't show your face! Depart and bury yourselves in some cave, you who take pride in what ought to entail shame. How much better would it have been to put on a sturdy garment and be energetic and on that occasion to ask the king for something

---

[91] Diogenes of Sinope, founder of the Cynic sect of philosophy. Coleman-Norton cites other places where Chrysostom refers to Diogenes, often favorably. "St. Chrysostom and the Greek Philosophers," *Classical Philology* 25 (1930): 308–09. Chrysostom's criticism of Diogenes here resembles that of contemporary Cynic philosophers, against whom emperor Julian directed his oration on the uneducated Cynics written in 362. See *L'empereur Julien Oeuvres complètes* 2,1, ed. Gabriel Rochefort (Paris 1963) 135–73.

[92] See Herbert Musurillo, "Ascetical Fasting in the Greek Patristic Writers," *Traditio* 12 (1956): 25 and note 12 for the following reference to mountebanks in Chrysostom: "Some chew the soles of worn-out sandals; others drive sharp spikes through their heads; others jump naked into waters frozen with cold; still others endure things even more outlandish than these." The source of the quotation has yet to be identified.

[93] *Parrhēsia:* see above note 66. The story of Alexander the Great and Diogenes in Corinth occurs frequently in ancient literature. On this see P. Natorp, "Diogenes," *RE* 5:767.

useful, rather than to sit with his rags warming himself like the suckling infants whom nurses, after bathing and anointing, lay down the way the philosopher was then reclining, as he asked for a favor due an unfortunate old woman. (47) "But liberty is surely commendable." But his was eccentricity. For, it is necessary that the good man refer all his actions to the common welfare and improve the lot of humanity.[94] What city, what household, what man, what woman did he benefit, asking not to be put in the shade? Tell the fruit of his liberty. We have exhibited that of the martyr and, as we go on, shall reveal it even more clearly. But up to this point: he punished the scoundrel as is lawful for a priest to punish; he curbed the insolence of those in power; he protected the laws of God from instability; and, in behalf of the murder victim, he exacted the most rigorous of all punishments, at least in the eyes of thinking people. Doubtless you remember how, when I recounted the murder, each of the listeners was inflamed and desired to get his hands on the assassin, and prayed that someone would appear from somewhere to avenge the murder. That blessed man was the avenger and inflicted on him the proper punishment, sufficient to restore him to his senses, if he had not been very insensible.[95] He did not request the emperor to step out of his light as he warmed himself, but, when he impudently invaded the sacred precinct and upset everything, chased him, like a dog and an unruly servant, from the master's courtyard. You see that I was not boasting when I said that he demonstrated the childishness of your philosophers' marvelous deeds.

(48) "But the man from Sinope was also temperate and lived abstinently, even refusing to contract a legitimate marriage." But add how and in what way! You will not add it, but

---

[94] Cf. Plato, *Clitopho* 410b: "The just person does everything to benefit everyone." 1 Cor 10.33.

[95] Repentance is a recovering of sanity as in Lactantius, *Inst.* 6.24.6: "For he returns to a right understanding, and recovers his mind as it were from madness, who is grieved for his error; and he reproves himself of madness, and confirms his mind to a better course of life . . ." (trans. W. Fletcher, ANF 7 [1886]: 191).

prefer to deprive him of praise for temperance than tell the mode of his temperance, so foul and full of so much shame.[96] (49) I could also recount the absurdity, futility, and turpitude of the rest. Tell me, what is the use of eating human seed, as the Stagirite did?[97] What profit to have intercourse with mothers and sisters, as the philosopher in charge of the Stoa legislated.[98] As for the director of the Academy[99] and his teacher[100] and those whom they admire still more, I would expose their still greater depravity[101] and, stripping off all the allegory, I would unveil pederasty, which they consider respectable and a part of philosophy,[102] if my discourse were not so lengthy and did not hasten to another subject and had not amply convicted all by deriding one. For, when he who prevails in courage and temperance, according to the seemingly more austere branch of philosophy,[103] appears so disgraceful, eccentric, and unbalanced—he even said it is "indifferent" to eat human beings[104]—what argument against the others is left us, if one who eclipsed the rest at the acme of the profession is convicted of absurdity, puerility, and stupidity in the eyes of all.

[96] Diogenes habitually did the works of Aphrodite in public (Diog. Laert. 6.69).
[97] It has been suggested that Chrysostom might have found this statement in a lost work of Aristotle, in a gossipy source, or might have inferred it from a passage like *Pr.* 4.29 (880a23 ff.). It may also refer to homosexual activity; cf. Tertullian, *Apol.* 9.12; J.P. Waltzing, *Tertullien Apologétique: Commentaire analytique, grammatical, et historique* (Paris 1931) 23.
[98] It is reported that the Stoic philosopher Chrysippus (ca. 280–207 B.C.) approved incest (frags. 743–46; SVF 3:185). A retortion of the slander of "Oedipodean intercourse," i.e., incest, made against the early church (e.g., Athenagoras, *Leg.* 3; trans. ANF 2:130).
[99] Plato (ca. 429–347 B.C.).
[100] Socrates (469–399 B.C.).
[101] Cf. Rom 1.27.
[102] The pederasty practiced by Socrates and Plato is discussed by H.I. Marrou, *A History of Education in Antiquity*, trans. George Lamb (New York 1956; reprint ed., New York 1964) 59. A good analysis of Greek homosexuality is found in K.J. Dover, *Greek Homosexuality* (Cambridge, Mass. 1978).
[103] Viz., Cynicism.
[104] Diog. Laert. 6.73. In effect, a retortion of the slander of "Thyestean feasts" (cannibalism) made against the early Christians (Athenagoras, *Leg.* 3; ANF 2:130).

(50) Let us return to the subject from which we digressed in the preceding discussion.[105] Accordingly, the blessed one put down the unbelievers and made the believers more dedicated, not only private citizens but also soldiers, generals, and governors. He showed that among Christians the emperor and the "last of all"[106] are only titles, and that he who wears the diadem is no more venerable than the least important when punishment is mandated.[107] Furthermore, he bridled the impudence of those who say that our religion is boasting and fiction, for he manifested by his actions the probability that men of such character existed in the past, when the prominence of miracles gave them even greater authority.

THE OFFICE OF BISHOP MAGNIFIED

(51) There is also a third remarkable achievement: he emboldened future priests and intimidated future emperors. He showed that one appointed to the priesthood is a more responsible guardian of the earth and what transpires upon it than one who wears the purple, and that the magnitude of priestly power is not to be diminished but one's life is to be surrendered sooner than the authority which God has assigned to this office from above.[108] For he who dies in this way

---

[105] End of the digression which began at *Bab.* 40.

[106] Cf. Mk 9.35.

[107] I.e., even the emperor, if a Christian, is subject to penitential discipline. Cf. Introduction 51. This may help to explain why Constantine apparently deferred even becoming a catechumen till the end of his life (Eusebius, *V.C.* 4.61.3; trans. NPNF 2,1: 556 and note 2). Even the status of catechumen entailed accountability to episcopal authority and subjection to penitential discipline (Introduction 49). Emperor Theodosius, on the contrary, was baptized when he fell ill; he then recovered and subsequently was subjected to penance by Ambrose for the massacre of Thessalonica (Sozomen, H.e. 7.4,25; trans. NPNF 2,2: 378, 393 f.).

[108] Chrysostom addresses the deacons in Hom. 82.6 on Matthew and tells them it is necessary to hinder from communion anyone who approaches unworthily, even the emperor, since their authority is greater than his. He continues: "But if thou darest not to do it thyself, bring him to me; I will not allow any to dare do these things. I would give up my life rather than impart of the Lord's blood to the unworthy; and will shed my own blood rather than impart of such awful blood contrary to what is meet" (PG 58.744–46; trans. S.G. Prevost and revised by M.B. Riddle, NPNF 10 [1888]: 496).

could benefit everyone even after death, whereas he who abandons his post not only benefits no one after death, but even while alive weakens most of those under his command, and becomes an object of scorn and ridicule to the pagans. And when he departs this world, he will "stand at the judgment seat of Christ"[109] with much shame and dejection, and from there the powers assigned this task will drag him again and carry him off to the furnace.[110] This is why a wise precept admonishes: "Accept no person against thy own person."[111] If it is unsafe to dissemble the injury done to a man, of what punishment is he worthy who silently overlooks the violation of the laws of God?

(52) Besides this he gave us another lesson, no less salutary: namely, that each person ought to do his duty, even if no one profits from what ensues.[112] Despite his courage, he did not succeed in edifying the emperor, but nevertheless fulfilled his entire duty and omitted nothing. The patient, however, through his own folly, ruined the science of the doctor and angrily removed the dressing applied to the wound. As if murder and shameless assault on the temple of God did not suffice for impiety, to murder he added another murder; and as if he strove to surpass the first by the second and at the same time not to efface the excesses of the preceding by the enormity of the latter (for such is the madness of the devil, that he unites even opposites), he gave to both murders a corresponding peculiarity. The first, that of the child, was more pitiful than the second; whilst the second, that of blessed Babylas, was more sacrilegious than the first.

THE EMPEROR CONTINUES TO DETERIORATE OWING TO SIN

(53) For a soul which once has tasted sin and become unfeeling, intensifies the malady more and more. Just as a spark

[109] Cf. Rom 14.10, 2 Cor 5.10.
[110] Cf Mt 13.42, 50.
[111] Sir 4.22.
[112] The obligation to perform one's duty was an important teaching of Stoic

falls into a huge forest and immediately ignites what it meets, and does not stop at that alone but extends to all the rest; and the more it captures with its flame, the more strength it acquires for the destruction of the remainder, and the multitude of stricken trees becomes a danger to the trees about to be vanquished, since the flame always arms itself against the trees that remain by what it has already captured—such is also the nature of sin: when it captures the mind and there is no one to extinguish the evil, it becomes more serious and intractable, as it gains ground. This is why the subsequent wrongdoings very often are more serious than the initial ones, because by additional sins the soul is continually aroused to greater madness and presumption, which weaken its own power and foster that of sin. In this way, to be sure, many fall into every kind of sin inadvertently, because they do not extinguish the incipient flame. Whence also that miserable man added to his earlier sins other worse ones.

THE EMPEROR'S THIRD CRIME: MURDER OF BABYLAS

(54) When he had slain the youth he hastened from the murder to the insult against the sanctuary; and again after this, advancing on the road, he stripped for his mad combat against the priesthood. Having put the saint in irons and thrown him into prison, he punished him for a while this way in retaliation for his benefaction. Instead of admiring, crowning, and honoring him more than his parents, as he should have, he forced him to endure the misery of criminals, for he inflicted on him the punishment of chains.[113]

(55) Thus, as I said, sin which from its inception has no one to hinder its further progress, becomes violent and uncontrollable, analogously to rabid horses, which, casting the bit from their mouth and throwing the rider off their back head over

---

philosophy readily accepted by early Christians. See Johannes Stelzenberger, *Die Beziehungen der frühchristlichen Sittenlehre zur Ethik der Stoa* (Munich 1933) 217–44.
    [113] The *Passiones* corroborate the fact that Babylas was put in chains. Introduction 66.

heels, are ungovernable by those they encounter, and if no one stops them, frantically throw themselves down a precipice.[114] Accordingly, the enemy of our salvation drives such persons mad in order to destroy them and afflict them with myriad evils by isolating them from those who could heal them. Indeed, people who are physically infirm as long as they visit their physicians have great hope of recovery; but when their brain becomes inflamed, and they kick and bite those who wish to deliver them from their infirmity, then their disease becomes incurable, not because of the nature of the disease, but because of the absence of those able to deliver them from delirium, into which the emperor also had fallen.

(56) For he seized the doctor, still operating on his wound, and immediately drove him away and removed him far from his domicile. It was the drama of Herod,[115] no longer made known by hearsay, but beheld with the eyes and more catastrophic, which the devil again introduced onto the stage of life with even more solemnity and display. The tetrarch he replaced with an emperor, and substituted for a single action a double plot, much more sordid than the original. Hence the tragedy became more spectacular not only by the number, but also by the nature of the events. For it was not a question here, as there, of a violated marriage or an illicit union; but the evil one wove this history from a defilement more abominable than infanticide, a most savage tyranny, and a crime committed not against a wife but against holiness itself.

(57) When imprisoned, the blessed one rejoiced in his chains[116] but grieved at the destruction of the one who had bound him. Likewise, neither a father nor even a gymnastic teacher, who gains notoriety from the misdeeds and failures of a child or a pupil, experiences the pleasure of this renown untinged with sorrow. For this reason the blessed Paul also said to the Corinthians: "But we pray that you may do no evil

---

[114] The horse was a popular comparison in sophistic rhetoric. Paul Gallay, *Langue et style de saint Grégoire de Nazianze* (Paris 1933) 86. Cf. *Bab.* 60.

[115] Cf. Mt 14.1–11.

[116] Citing *Hom. 8 in Eph.* 4.1, Vandenberghe calls Chrysostom the poet of the "hymn of the chains," which proclaims the ecstasy of martyrdom. Bruno H. Vandenberghe, *John of the Golden Mouth* (London 1958) 73 f.

at all, not wishing ourselves to appear approved, but that you
may do what is good, and we ourselves pass as reprobate."[117]
At this time, to be sure, that marvelous man did not desire the
rewards of imprisonment but the salvation of his disciple, and
that he come to his senses and deprive him of this praise, or
rather that he had never fallen into this aberration.

(58) For the saints do not want their crowns to come from
others' misfortunes; and if not from others' misfortunes,
much less from the disasters which befall their own. On account of this, blessed David lamented and wept over the
trophies and the victory which were the occasion of his child's
downfall. The departing commanders he strictly charged to
protect the rebel, and restrained their eagerness to kill him,
saying: "Save the boy Absalom."[118] When he died, he lamented him, and although he was his enemy, he called him by
name with groanings and bitter tears.[119] If, therefore, the
physical father is so affectionate, how much more the spiritual father? Listen to Paul affirming that parents according to
the spirit are more solicitous than parents according to the
flesh: "Who is weak, and I am not weak? Who is made to
stumble, and I am not inflamed?"[120]

(59) This shows us their parity (although earthly fathers
hardly utter such words, we shall nevertheless concede that
they attain this much); it remains to exhibit their superiority.
Whence shall we exhibit this? From the same entrails of char-
ity[121] again and from the words of the lawgiver.[122] What does
the latter say? "Either forgive them this trespass, or if thou do
not, strike me out of the book that thou hast written."[123] Is
there a father who would choose to be punished with his
chidren rather than to enjoy unlimited prosperity? But the

---

[117] 2 Cor 13.7.
[118] 2 Sm (2 Kgs) 18.5.
[119] 2 Sm (2 Kgs) 18.33.
[120] 2 Cor 11.29.
[121] Paul.
[122] Moses.
[123] Ex 32.32. In *Stat.* 3.1 (PG 49.48) Chrysostom alludes to this verse and
says: "For such are the bowels of the saints, that they think death with their
children sweeter than life without them" (trans. C. Marriott and revised by
W.R.W. Stephens NPNF 9 [1889]: 355).

Apostle, inasmuch as he abided in grace, augmented this affectionateness on account of Christ. He did not choose to be punished together with them like the lawgiver, but prayed for his own destruction so that it might be well with others, saying: "I could wish to be anathema from Christ for the sake of my kinsmen, who are my brethren according to the flesh."[124] Such is the compassion and mercy in the souls of the saints.

(60) Whence he too became more and more tormented, seeing the destruction of the emperor progress further. What he did, he did not only from anger on account of the sanctuary, but also moved by goodwill towards the emperor, whose outrage against the divine liturgy did not harm it at all but pierced him with innumerable evils. Thus, observing the violator being thrust over a precipice by his anger, the philoprogenitive father tried to restrain this irrational movement as one would restrain a refractory horse, hastily stopping him short and drawing him backwards by means of a reproach. But that miserable man did not allow it; taking the bit between his teeth, resisting, and abandoning himself to rage and madness in place of straight thinking, he flung himself into the abyss of utter destruction and ordered the saint to be fetched from prison and led away to execution in chains.

(61) What actually happened was the opposite of what appeared. The bound man was freed from all bonds at once, both those of iron and those still stronger—I mean worry, pain, and all the rest that befalls our mortal life. On the other hand, the one who seemed to be free of both iron and steel was encircled by other more oppressive bonds, "the ropes of sins with which he was bound fast."[125] Accordingly, on the point of being executed the blessed man gave instructions that his body be buried together with the iron fetters, showing that what seems to be ignominious, when it occurs on account of Christ, is respectable and glorious, and that he who suffers

---

[124] Rom 9.3.
[125] Cf. Prv 5.22, also quoted by Chrysostom in *Hom.* 8.4 *in Eph.* (PG 62.60): "For every one is shackled with the chains of his own sins; and those bonds are accursed, whereas these for Christ's sake are blessed and worth many an earnest prayer" (trans. W.J. Copeland and revised by G. Alexander, NPNF 13 [1890]: 88).

should not be ashamed but be proud of it.[126] And in this he imitated the blessed Paul, who advertised his scars, bonds, and chain, boasting and glorying in what put others to shame.[127]

(62) That they were ashamed he himself made clear to us in his defense before Agrippa. When the latter said, "You risk making a Christian of me in a short time," he replied: "I would to God that, whether it be short or long, not only you but also all who are standing around might become Christians, except for these chains"[128]—which he would not have added if most people did not consider the thing disgraceful. But the saints, who love their Master, accepted sufferings for the Master with great eagerness and became happier because of them. The one says: "I rejoice in my sufferings."[129] Another, Luke, makes the same utterance concerning the remaining members of the chorus of apostles: after many lashes they withdrew, "rejoicing that they had been counted worthy to suffer disgrace for the name."[130]

(63) Therefore, lest any unbeliever think that his exploits were the outcome of necessity and dejection, he ordered that together with his body should be buried the distinguishing marks of the contest, showing that these were pleasant and lovely to him because of his strong attachment to the love of Christ.[131] These fetters are now lying with his ashes and admonish all who preside over the churches that they must receive chains, death, and all sorts of sufferings eagerly and

---

[126] Cf. *Bab.* 63 and the corroborative statement of Chrysostom, *Hom.* 9.2 *in Eph.* (PG 62.71): "This man [Babylas] when he was dying gave charge that his bonds should be laid with his body, and that the body should be buried bound; and to this day the fetters lie mingled with his ashes, so devoted was his affection for the bonds he had worn for Christ's sake. 'He was laid in chains of iron' as the Prophet saith of Joseph (Ps. cv:18)" (trans. W.J. Copeland and revised by G. Alexander, NPNF 13 [1890]: 96).

[127] Cf. Gal 6.17. Col. 4.18. Phlm 10. Eph 6.20. Acts 28.20. 2 Tm 1.16.

[128] Acts 26.28 f.

[129] Col 1.24.

[130] Acts 5.41.

[131] Cf. notes 116, 126 above. In Christian antiquity the bonds of the martyrs were considered "beautiful ornaments," and were kissed by the faithful. Eusebius, H.e. 5.1.35 (trans. NPNF 1:215). Tertullian, *Ux.* 2.4 (ANF 4:46). Ignatius, *Polyc.* 2.3 (FOTC 1.125).

with great pleasure rather than betray and dishonor even the least part of the liberty confided to us.

PROEM TO MODERN HISTORY OF BABYLAS: SIGNIFICANCE OF RELICS

(64) The blessed man thus gloriously ended his life; perhaps someone thinks that we shall also end our discourse here, because after the termination of life there is no opportunity for well–doing and valor, just as athletes cannot win crowns when the games are over. But Greeks naturally think this way since they have limited their hope to the present life; we, however, for whom the end here is the beginning of another, more luminous existence, are far from this supposition and opinion.[132] And that we are right I shall show more clearly in another discourse.[133] Meanwhile, the accomplishments of the noble Babylas after his death suffice to settle the question in great measure.

(65) When he had contended for the truth unto death and spilled his blood in the battle against sin and, so as not to relinquish the post[134] which the great King[135] himself had assigned, had relinquished his life and died most gloriously in combat, he was received by heaven henceforward; the earth has his body which served in the combat, and thus the crea-

---

[132] Whereas pagans believed in one life only (e.g., Euripides, *El.* 956), early Christians posited the existence of two lives or ages: death was viewed as a birth, and the day of death as a birthday characterized by radiance. See Alfred C. Rush, *Death and Burial in Christian Antiquity*, The Catholic University of America Studies in Christian Antiquity 1 (Washington, D.C. 1941) 72–87.

[133] Chrysostom believes that the existence of another life is easy to prove from scripture and reason (*Laz.* 4.3–4; PG 48.1011). The promised treatise, however, seems not to exist among Chrysostom's extant works.

[134] Cf. 4 Mc 9.23. The military metaphor of not abandoning one's station is used in reference to the office of bishop also at *Bab.* 51. Elsewhere Chrysostom uses the image to describe the duty of virgins and of the preacher. *Fem. reg.* 9 (*Saint Jean Chrysostome: Les cohabitations suspectes, comment observer la virginité*, ed. and trans. J. Dumortier [Paris 1955] 126). *Hom. in Ac.* 5.3 (PG 60.53 f.); trans. NPNF 11:35.

[135] Cf. Pss 46(47).3; 47(48).3; 94(95).3. Mal 1.14. Mt 5.35.

tion divided the athlete.[136] And yet he could have been translated like Enoch and snatched up like Elijah,[137] whom he emulated. But God, who is philanthropic and provides us with countless opportunities to be saved, in addition to other ways also prepared for us this way which is a powerful inducement to virtue, by leaving the relics of the saints in our midst for the time being.[138] In fact, the tombs of the saints occupy second place after the word in the power that they have to excite a similar zeal in the souls of those who behold them.[139] And if anyone approaches such a tomb, he immediately receives a distinct impression of this energy.[140] For the sight of the coffin, entering the soul, acts upon it and affects it in such a way that it feels as if it sees the one who lies there joining in prayer and drawing nigh. Afterwards, one who has had this experience returns from there filled with great zeal and a changed person.[141]

(66) That the vision of the dead enters the souls of the living at their burial sites[142] becomes clear if one considers

---

[136] Cf. Eccl 12.7.

[137] Cf. Gn 5.24. 2 Kgs (4 Kgs) 2.11.

[138] The fourth century was the decisive period in the development of the early Christian veneration of relics. See Hippolyte Delehaye, *Les origines du culte des martyrs*[2] (Brussels 1933) 24–99, Ernst Lucius, *Die Anfänge des Heiligenkults in der christlichen Kirche* (Tübingen 1904), Peter Brown, *The Cult of Saints* (Chicago 1980).

[139] "The word": possibly the formal encomia, which were delivered annually at the tombs of the martyrs. These encomia, many of which were spoken by Chrysostom, are analyzed by Hippolyte Delehaye, *Les passions des martyrs et les genres littéraires*[2] (Brussels 1966).

[140] According to F. Pfister, the essence of the Christian veneration of relics was that the power of the living person remained in the relics. *Der Reliquienkult im Altertum* (Giessen 1912) 1,2: 613, 615. Chrysostom frequently alludes to the power of Babylas's relics in this discourse (*Bab.* 75, 90, 93, 99, 109).

[141] Elsewhere Chrysostom writes of the impression produced by the sepulcher of the martyr Ignatius of Antioch (*Pan. Ign.* 5; PG 50.595 f.): "Thence on this account God allowed us the remains of the saints, wishing to lead us by them to the same emulation, and to afford us a kind of haven, and a secure consolation for the evils which are ever overtaking us. Wherefore I beseech you all, if any is in despondency, if in disease, if under insult, if in any other circumstances of this life, if in the depth of sins, let him come hither with faith, and he will lay aside all those things, and will return with much joy, having procured a lighter conscience from the sight alone" (trans. T.P. Brandram, NPNF 9 [1889]: 140).

[142] Cf. Origen, *Cels.* 2.60 (Origen, *Contra Celsum*, trans. Chadwick 112).

mourners, who as soon as they approach the grave of the dead, immediately address them from the threshold, as if they saw instead of the tomb those who lie in the tomb standing up. Many of those who are inconsolable in their sorrow have settled themselves for all time beside the monuments of the dead; they would not have done so, if they did not receive some consolation from the sight of the place. And why speak of the location of a grave? Many times, in fact, the sight of a garment alone and the recollection of a word of the dead move the soul and restore the failing memory. For this reason God has left us the relics of the saints.

GALLUS TRANSFERS THE RELICS OF BABYLAS TO DAPHNE

(67) The miracles performed by martyrs every day, and the multitude of men who are thereby converted,[143] and, no less than all this, the accomplishments of this blessed man after his death, attest that my present words are not bragging, but that this phenomenon has occurred for our benefit. Thus, when he had been buried according to his instructions, and a great amount of time had elapsed after the burial, so that only bones and dust remained in the sarcophagus, one of the subsequent emperors decided to transfer the coffin into this suburb of Daphne;[144] it was God who inspired the emperor with this plan. For, upon seeing the district under the tyranny of

---

[143] Jerome states that miracles occurring at the tombs of martyrs are for the sake of unbelievers (*Vigil.* 10; PL 23.363). Chrysostom frequently mentions the power of martyrs' relics to cast out demons, to cure mental and physical diseases, and to give spiritual tranquillity. *Pan. Aeg.* 1 (PG 50.695). *Laud. Paul.* 4 (PG 50.490). *Catech.* 7.8 f. (SC 50bis: 232 f.). *Delic.* 2 (PG 51.348). *Pan. Juln.* 1 (PG 50.665 f.).

[144] Gallus, nephew of Constantine and step-brother of emperor Julian, was made Caesar of the orient by Constantius in 351 and resided at Antioch from 351–54. At some point during this period Gallus transferred the relics of Babylas from the common Christian cemetery of Antioch (cf. *Bab.* 90, 93, 96) to Daphne, suburb of Antioch (Sozomen, H.e. 5.19; trans. NPNF 2,2: 341). Daphne was a pleasure resort with a flourishing cult of Apollo (cf. I. Benzinger, "Daphne," RE 4:2136–38). Rivalry between pagan and Christian worship at a single spot was not infrequent at this time (Delehaye, *Origines* 409).

profligate youths, and in danger of becoming inaccessible to people who desired to live respectably and decently,[145] he took pity on the ill-treatment of the spot and sent someone to restrain the debauchery.

(68) In reality, God made the suburb fair and lovely by the abundance [and beauty] of its waters, the properties of its soil, and the possession of an equitable climate, not simply to refresh us but also that we might praise the "best of artificers"[146] for it. But the enemy of our salvation, who always perverts the gifts of God, occupied the site beforehand with a crowd of dissolute youths and the abodes of the demons,[147] and then bestowed upon it a certain shameful myth, by means of which he dedicated the graceful suburb to the demon. The myth is as follows.[148] Daphne, he says, was a maiden and daughter of the river Ladon. (And in fact his wont is always to represent rivers giving birth, to transform their progeny into insensible objects, and to proclaim many such monstrosities.) This comely maiden Apollo once espied, he says, and at first sight was enamored of her, and enamored pursued her so as to possess her. But she fled and in her flight arrived at the suburb, where her mother protected her from this outrage. For she immediately opened to receive the maid and in place of the child yielded a plant named after the child. When the rash paramour lost the object of his affection, he embraced the tree, appropriated both the plant and the place, and hence-

---

[145] Emperor Marcus Aurelius refers to soldiers "living in luxury and conducting themselves in the morals of Daphne." Church historian Sozomen says that "men of grave temperament considered it disgraceful to approach this suburb and anyone who dwelt at Daphne without a mistress was regarded as ungracious and was shunned as an abominable and abhorrent thing." These and other ancient allusions to the dissoluteness of Daphne are quoted by George Haddad, *Aspects of Social Life in Antioch in the Hellenistic-Roman Period* (Ph.D. diss. University of Chicago 1949) 175–77.

[146] "Best of artificers": said of Zeus by Pindar, frag 48 in *Pindari carmina cum fragmentis*, ed. C.M. Bowra, 2nd ed. (Oxford 1947).

[147] Pagan gods are demons, as in Ps 95 (96):5. 1 Cor 10:20. Justin, 1 *Apol.* 5. Tatian, *Orat.* 8. Clement of Alexandria, *Prot.* 2.40–41. There were temples of Apollo, Nemesis, and Zeus, among others, at Daphne. Glanville Downey, *Antioch in the Age of Theodosius the Great* (Norman, Oklahoma 1962) 34–37.

[148] Chrysostom may have based his narration of the myth of Daphne on Libanius' monody (cf. *Bab.* 98). Consult Downey, *History* 82–84, on the legendary origin of the suburb Daphne.

forth resided at the site, to which he clung and which he
preferred to all the rest of the earth. The reigning monarch
then ordered the construction of a temple and an altar for
him,[149] so that the demon might be able to assuage his
madness by the consolation of the place. This is the myth; but
the evil which followed from the myth was no longer a myth.

(69) Since young libertines from the first, as I said, had
defiled the beauty of the suburb in the course of their debauchery and drunkenness there, the devil, wishing to inten-
sify this evil, invented the myth and installed the demon, so
that this history would be greater fuel for their licentiousness
and impiety.[150] For the purpose of deliverance from such
great evil the emperor conceived this very wise plan: the
transfer of the saint and the conveyance of the physician to
the ailing. Doubtless, a blockade of the road to the suburb by
imperial edict and authority would have seemed to the inhabitants of the empire rather the work of tyranny, cruelty,
and great incivility; and if he added that "the more respectable and balanced may go up,[151] but the licentious and dissolute are to be prevented," the edict would have been impracti-
cable, and daily tribunals would have been necessary to
examine each person's life. The only satisfactory way out of
such difficulties was the presence of the blessed one; for the
martyr was able to destroy the power of the demon and to
restrain the merriment of the youths. And the emperor was
not deceived in his hope.

SOBRIETY

(70) Just as a youth at a party, who observes his pedagogue
nearby exhorting him by look to drink, eat, speak, and laugh

[149] The temple of Apollo at Daphne was built by Seleucus I (ca. 358–280
B.C.). Benzinger, "Daphne," RE 4:2137.
[150] The argument that the mythical crimes of the gods may influence human conduct is found in Plato and the Greek apologists. See the excellent
discussion in A.J. Festugière, *Antioche païenne et chrétienne: Libanius, Chrysostome et les moines de Syrie* (Paris 1959) 225–27.
[151] The plateau of Daphne is situated on a higher level than the city of
Antioch, and so Chrysostom says that one "goes up" to Daphne and "goes

with proper decorum is prevented from overstepping measure and thus injuring his reputation,[152] likewise as soon as one arrives at Daphne and sees the martyr's shrine from the entrance of the suburb,[153] he is chastened and, becoming more pious by the sight and imagining the blessed one, immediately hastens to the coffin; and when he comes there, he is affected with greater fear, renounces all cynicism, and departs on wings. Those who ascend from the city he receives en route and escorts to the relaxation of Daphne; to them he all but cries out: "Rejoice unto the Lord with trembling,"[154] and adds the apostolic: "whether you eat or drink or do anything else, do all for the glory of God."[155] Those who descend to the city after the revelry—if by chance they heedlessly threw aside the bit, and were carried away into a bout of drunkenness and debauchery—he again receives, drunk, into his inn, and does not let them return home injured by strong drink, but disciplines them with fear and restores them to the same sobriety which they maintained before their inebriation. And indeed like a faint breeze there blows all round those within the martyr's shrine an imperceptible breeze,[156] which does not affect bodies but penetrates the soul itself; and, ordering it decorously in all respects and removing every terrestrial weight,[157] refreshes and lightens the heavy-laden and downcast soul.

(71) The beauty of Daphne draws the more sluggish to herself; the martyr, as if sitting in a cave and laying a trap for

---

down" to Antioch. The ancient geographer Strabo gives the distance between Antioch and Daphne as about five miles. Downey, *History* 19.

[152] The moral influence of the pedagogue is discussed by Marrou, *History of Education* 201 f., 301.

[153] Evidently, Gallus had built a shrine at Daphne to house the coffin of Babylas. Gibbon, *The Decline and Fall of the Roman Empire*, chap. 23 (2:467, note 113) evidently confuses this martyrium at Daphne built by the order of Gallus (351–54) with the church erected in honor of Babylas by bishop Meletius outside the city in 379–80. See Introduction 1.

[154] Ps 2.11.

[155] 1 Cor 10.31.

[156] Cf. 1 Kgs (3 Kgs) 19.12.

[157] Cf. the cherubic hymn in the liturgy of St. James. F.E. Brightman and C.E. Hammond, eds., *Liturgies Eastern and Western*, Vol. 1 (Oxford 1896; reprint ed., Oxford, 1965) 41, line 25.

those who enter, detains them and only releases them after teaching them henceforth to treat the beloved not wantonly but with respect. Since some people do not wish to have recourse to the tombs of the martyrs either because of laziness or because of wordly cares, God arranged for them to be caught in this net and to receive spiritual healing. It is much as if someone should outwit a sick person who refuses to take beneficial medicines, by disguising the medicine with something sweet to the taste.[158]

(72) At any rate, in the process of time they were healed, and it reached the point that for most people revelry alone was no longer the reason for their ascent to the suburb, but also desire for the saint. Or rather, the more decent folks came there for this reason alone; the ones inferior to them for both reasons. The ones who were disposed still less perfectly than these went up only on account of the revelry, but when they arrived, the martyr invited them to feast on his goods and provided them with excellent armor, which did not allow them to suffer any evil. What happened there, namely, a dissolute and licentious person becoming temperate, is as miraculous as recovery from total madness or immunity from the fire, if one falls into a furnace.[159] For, while youth, recklessness, unreason, wine, and surfeit envelop the thoughts worse than a flame, the dew of the blessed one, descending through the eyes into the soul of those who see him, put the flame to sleep, halted the conflagration, and instilled in the mind great godly fear.

SILENCE OF THE ORACLE OF APOLLO

(73) Thus the blessed one put an end to the tyranny of debauchery; but how did he also annul the power of the demon? First, as mentioned above, by rendering ineffective

---

[158] A proverbial expression; e.g., Plato, *Leg.* 659e–60a, Lucretius 1.936–42, Gregory of Nazianzus, *Or.* 31.25.

[159] Possibly an allusion to the three holy children (Dn 3.13 ff.). The miraculous nature of conversion and moral regeneration is emphasized by Origen (*Cels.* 1.43, 64, 68; 2.48,51).

both his presence and the harm caused by the myth, and later by also driving away the demon himself. But before stating the manner of the eviction, I ask you to note that he did not expel him as soon as he went up but while he remained he (Babylas) rendered him ineffective, curbed him, and made him more silent than the stones—and to overcome him while remaining was no less difficult than to drive him away. And the one who previously deceived everyone everywhere did not even dare to face the dust of the blessed Babylas. So great is the power of the saints that while they live the demons cannot endure even their shadows and clothing;[160] and when they die these also tremble at their coffins. If, therefore, one doubts the works accomplished by the apostles, let him consider the present events and desist from his impudence forever. For he who had formerly been victorious in all the affairs of the Greeks when reproached by his master, the martyr, stopped barking and did not utter a sound.[161]

(74) At first he seemed to do this because he did not share in sacrifices and the rest of the cult.[162] Such in fact is the character of the demons: when they honor them with savor, smoke, and blood, they come to lap it up like blood-thirsty and voracious dogs; but when there is no one to supply this, they are destroyed by hunger, as it were.[163] As long as the sacrifices and shameful rituals are carried out—for their mysteries are nothing else but sexual immorality, child molestation, violations of marriages, and upsettings of families (for I disregard at this point the perverse methods of murder and

---

[160] Cf. *Bab.* 9 and notes.

[161] The oracle of Apollo had been silenced by the transfer to Daphne of the remains of Babylas: Socrates, H.e. 3.18 (trans. NPNF 2,2: 88 f.). Sozomen, H.e. 5.19 (trans. NPNF 2,2: 341). Theodoret, H.e. 3.6 (trans. NPNF 2,3: 98).

[162] Cf. Sozomen, H.e. 5.19 (trans. C.D. Hartranft, NPNF 2,2 [1890]: 341): "This silence was at first attributed to the neglect into which his service was allowed to fall and to the omission of the former cult," i.e., under emperor Constantius (337–61). Cf. *Bab.* 98.

[163] Animal sacrifices are made to feed hungry demons. This was also the view of the pagan philosopher, Porphyry. See J. Geffcken, *Zwei griechische Apologeten* (Leipzig 1907) 219 f. J. Bidez, *Vie de Porphyre: Le philosophe néoplatonicien* (Gent and Leipzig 1913; reprint ed., Hildesheim 1964) 100.

the banquets more lawless than the murders)[164]—but in any case as long as these rites are carried out, they are present and rejoice,[165] even if the persons in charge are malefactors, charlatans, and scoundrels; or rather, no other kind of person renders these services. Indeed, the temperate, moderate, and honorable man does not put up with revelry and drunkenness, and does not utter shameless speech, or listen to another behaving in an unseemly manner. And yet, if he[166] were concerned about human virtue and paid the least attention to the well-being of his adherents, he ought to have required nothing more than an excellent life and moral rectitude, and to have entirely dispensed with that unseemly repast.[167] But since they are committed above all to the destruction of the human race, they both delight in and say that they are honored by that which tends to subvert our life and tear up from their foundations all good things.

(75) At first this appeared to be the reason why he too was silent; but it was proved later that he was bound by the shackles of strong necessity. Compelling fear, instead of a bridle, lay upon him and prevented him from using his customary deceit against humanity. How did this become clear? Hold your peace, for I shall proceed to the proof itself, after which it will not be possible even for the most impudent to contradict either the ancient miracles,[168] the power of the martyr, or the weakness of the demon. I do not need conjectures or probabilities to make this plain, but will employ the evidence of the demon himself in this matter: for he dealt you a fatal blow and undermined all your confidence. But do not be angry at him; he did not willingly subvert his own cause, but was compelled by a superior power to do this.

---

[164] Chrysostom's brief contemptuous reference to the mystery religions, which he associates with immorality, may have been occasioned by the fact that the apostate emperor Julian had been initiated into the mysteries of Cybele, Eleusis, and Mithra. See below note 175.

[165] Viz., the demons.

[166] I.e., Apollo.

[167] I.e., animal sacrifices.

[168] The miracles of the apostles.

JULIAN BECOMES EMPEROR AND
RESTORES PAGANISM

(76) How did this happen and in what way? When the emperor died who had carried up the martyr,[169] the one who had earlier invested him with the honor also appointed his brother to succeed in the rule; and he assumed power except for the crown—for such was also the measure of authority of his dead brother.[170] A foul imposter, he at first played the role of a partisan of the Lord on account of the one who had bestowed the rule.[171] When, however, the latter also had departed this life, he tore off the mask for good, and with a bare face published and made manifest to all the superstition which he had been concealing for a long time. Orders were dispatched all over the world to repair the temples of the idols, to set up their altars, to render the ancient honors to the demons, and to enrich them with tribute from many sources.[172]

(77) Whereupon, magicians, sorcerers, soothsayers, augurs, mendicant priests, and entire workshops of the occult assembled from all quarters of the world;[173] and one could see the imperial court filled with felons and fugitives. Some long since consumed by hunger,[174] others inhabiting prisons and working mines because of drugs and witchcraft, and others hardly able to sustain life from their disgraceful occupations

[169] Gallus, executed at the behest of Constantius in 354 (Gibbon, *Decline and Fall*, chap. 19, 2:252–54). *Bab.* 67.

[170] Constantius appointed Julian "caesar" in 355. "Power except for the crown" is a description of the office of "caesar" in the tetrarchic imperial system created by Diocletian.

[171] As a youth Julian was Christian. Gibbon, *Decline and Fall*, chap. 23, 2:433–35. On the religious dissimulation of Julian see Gibbon, *Decline and Fall*, chap. 23, 2:441–43.

[172] Upon the death of Constantius (361), Julian decreed that the pagan cults be reestablished and the temples reopened.

[173] Many magicians and theurgists were in the entourage of emperor Julian, including the Neoplatonic Maximus of Ephesus, to whom Julian was especially attached. F.E. Peters, *The Harvest of Hellenism* (New York 1970) 705.

[174] This statement reflects the economic straits into which the practitioners of pagan religion had fallen due to the repressive legislation of Constantius. J.F. D'Alton, *Selections from St. John Chrysostom* (London 1940) 67.

were suddenly proclaimed priests and hierophants[175] and held in great honor. And the emperor dismissed generals and governors with contempt, but male and female prostitutes he made rise from the brothels in which they were prostituting themselves and form a cortege which he himself led around the streets of the entire city. And the royal cavalry and all the bodyguards followed behind at a great distance, while brothel-keepers, procuresses, and the entire company of prostitutes formed a circle with the emperor in the middle, promenading through the agora and speaking and laughing in the manner of people of that occupation.[176]

(78) We know that to those who come after us these things will seem unbelievable because of their excessive irregularity: no ordinary person who leads a servile and ignominious existence would choose to act so unseemly in public. But I need not address myself to those who are still alive: they were present and observed these events taking place and now hear them also in narrative form. For this reason I am writing while there are still witnesses who survive; so that no one thinks that I am free to lie because I am recounting events of the past to people who are unfamiliar with them.[177] For among the spectators of these events there still remain old men and youths, all of whom I request to come forward and prove that I have added anything. But they cannot convict me of adding but only of omitting some details, since it is impossible to represent in discourse the totality of the excess of his indecorum. To incredulous posterity I would say that your demon, whom you call Aphrodite, is not ashamed to have such worshipers.

(79) It is no wonder then that this miserable man, who had once given himself over to the ridicule of demons, was not ashamed of what the gods whom he worshiped were proud

---

[175] The hierophant of Eleusis personally explained to Julian the symbolism of the Eleusinian mysteries.

[176] Is Chrysostom describing a festival of Aphrodite (cf. *Bab.* 78)?

[177] Here Chrysostom gives a reason for writing this discourse when he did (approximately the year 378): the presence of eyewitnesses to Julian's visit to Antioch in 362–63, who would give credibility to his narrative. On the evidentiary value of eyewitnesses in antiquity see note 49 above.

of. How can one describe the necromancy,[178] the infanticide? These sacrifices, which were ventured before the coming of Christ and after his appearance were halted, were again ventured—no longer openly (although he was an emperor and did everything with impunity, nevertheless the excessive impiety of these actions would have confuted the magnitude of his power)—but they were ventured nevertheless.[179]

JULIAN CONSULTS APOLLO AND DISCOVERS THE ORACLE'S SILENCE

(80) Thus the emperor often went up to Daphne with large quantities of offerings and sacrificial victims, and caused torrents of blood to flow from the slaughter of cattle.[180] He vigorously pressed the demon in his demand for an oracle and asked him to respond concerning matters of interest to him. But that noble personage, who (as they say)

counts the sand and measures the sea, hears the mute and gives ear to the silent,[181]

fearing to incur the ridicule of his worshipers refused to state explicitly and clearly: "I am unable to utter a sound because holy Babylas and the power in the neighborhood have muzzled me." Instead, wishing to conceal his defeat, he gave a pretext for his silence, which made him appear more ridiculous than the silence. For, in the one case he would only have revealed his own weakness; but now, in an attempt to hide what was not to be hidden, he showed not only weakness but indecorum and shamelessness.

(81) What was the pretext? "Corpses," he says, "fill the area of Daphne and hinder the oracle." How much better would it

---

[178] On necromancy cf. note 5 above.

[179] Cf. Theodoret, H.e. 3.26 f. (GCS 44:205; trans. NPNF 2,3: 106).

[180] Chrysostom again notes the lavish way Julian offered animal sacrifices at Bab. 89, 103 and Pan. Juv. 2 (PG 50.574).

[181] Chrysostom ironically quotes the first two lines of the Delphic oracle given to the ambassadors of king Croesus of Lydia. His source was probably Eusebius, P.e. 5.34.2 (GCS 43,1: 284; Preparation for the Gospel: Eusebius, trans. Gifford 248). Eusebius also ironically quotes the second line of this oracle at Hierocl. 14 in reference to Apollonius of Tyana.

have been, O wretched one, to confess the power of the martyr than to allege this impudent pretext? Thus far the demon; and the madcap emperor, as if acting on a stage and playing a part in a drama, immediately went after the blessed Babylas. O abominable and all abominable rascals! Did you not purposely deceive each other and play tricks in order to destroy the rest of mankind? Why did you speak of nameless, unspecified corpses, while you heard a certain specific name and, neglecting the rest, moved only the holy one? Indeed, according to the assertion of the demon, it was necessary to dig up all the graves in Daphne and to remove the bugbear as far as possible from the sight of the gods.[182]

APOLLO REQUESTS THE REMOVAL OF BABYLAS'S RELICS

(82) "But he did not mean all the corpses." Then why didn't he admit this openly? Truly, you played a part in the drama of error and to you he uttered this conundrum: "I shall say 'corpses,'" he said, "so that my defeat does not become plain; and besides I am afraid to mention the saint by name. But you interpret what is said and instead of all corpses move the martyr, for he silenced us."[183] Such madness he imputed to his worshipers as to be unable to recognize so manifest a deception. In fact, not even if all people had lost their minds and

---

[182] Cf. Theodoret, H.e. 3.6: "Julian, wishing to make a campaign against the Persians, dispatched the trustiest of his officers throughout the Roman Empire, while he himself went as a suppliant to implore the Pythian oracle of Daphne to make known to him the future. The oracle responded that the corpses lying hard by were becoming an obstacle to divination; that they must first be removed to another spot; and that then he would utter his prophecy, for, said he, 'I could say nothing, if the grove be not purified.' Now at that time there were lying there the relics of the victorious martyr Babylas and the lads who had gloriously suffered with him, and the lying prophet was plainly stopped from uttering his wonted lies by the holy influence of Babylas. Julian was aware of this, for his ancient piety had taught him the power of victorious martyrs, and so he removed no other body from the spot, but only ordered the worshipers of Christ to translate the relics of the victorious martyrs" (trans. B. Jackson, NPNF 2,3 [1892]: 98). On the three children martyred with Babylas see Introduction 66–69. Cf. Amm. Marc. 22.12.8: Julian ordered "bodies" to be removed.

[183] This statement is confirmed by Julian himself, who says that he removed "the corpse" (i.e., the remains of Babylas) from Daphne (Mis. 361b).

become insane, could he have escaped the obloquy of a defeat, which was so manifest and clear to everyone. If, as you say, human cadavers are really some kind of pollution and defilement,[184] animal carcasses are much more so, inasmuch as their race is less honorable than ours. Near the temple are buried many dogs, apes, and asses, whose bones you should rather have removed, unless you consider men less honorable than apes.

(83) Where are now those who insult the sun, that beautiful creation of God which exists to serve us, and dedicate it to the demon and identify him with it?[185] Although numerous cadavers lie embedded in the soil, the sun pours down upon the world and nowhere withdraws its rays or their energy by reason of defilement.[186] Your god, on the contrary, does not turn away from or hate profligacy, sorcery, and murder but even accepts, pursues, and sanctions these actions—while recoiling from our bodies. And yet, evil seems to deserve rich condemnation even among those who do it; whereas the dead and motionless body has no share in blame or guilt. The policy of your demons, however, is to loathe what is not loathsome and to honor and approve what is altogether worthy of hatred and aversion.

(84) The good man will not be prevented from useful deliberation or necessary action by a dead body, but if he has health of soul, although dwelling alongside graves, he will exhibit temperance, justice, and all virtue. And each artisan also will produce unimpeded all the works of his own craft and will supply them to those in need of him, not only when he is located near corpses but even if he must build the very monuments of the departed: and the painter, the stone ma-

---

[184] Cf. Introduction 32.

[185] "They say that Apollo is the Sun himself, which goes round the heaven" (*Clem. recogn.* 10.34; trans. T. Smith, ANF 8 [1886]: 201). The sun (Helios) was identified with Apollo since the middle of the fifth century B.C. H.J. Rose, *A Handbook of Greek Mythology* (New York 1959) 33 f., 134.

[186] Cf. Athanasius, *Inc.* 17.7: "For if the sun too, which was made by Him, and which we see, as it revolves in the heaven, is not defiled by touching the bodies upon earth, nor is it put out by darkness, but on the contrary itself illuminates and cleanses them also . . ." (trans. A. Robertson, NPNF 2,4 [1892]: 45). Additional parallel texts on the undefiled sun: J. Bücher, *Kommentar, Tertullian De spectaculis* (Würzburg 1935) 137. FOTC 10.390. G.W. Clarke, ed., *Minucius Felix: Octavius* 32.8 (ACW 39: 346).

son, the carpenter, the smith, and all artisans contribute their own part. One only of all, Apollo, says that he is hindered by cadavers from foreseeing the future.

(85) And in fact we also have great and wondrous men, who prophesied events fourteen hundred years in advance.[187] In the course of prophesying they did not question, find fault, or give orders to dig up the graves of the departed, throw away their bodies, and instigate a new and shameless form of tomb robbery. Though some of them dwelt among godless and unclean nations, and others were in the midst of barbarians, where deeds truly involving pollution and defilement were all perpetrated, they prophesied truthfully and the defilement of others did not hinder them from prophesying. Why? Because they were truly energized by divine power to say what they said, whereas the demon, who was void and bereft of that energy, was not able to prophesy but, in order not to seem at a loss, was constrained to allege merely plausible and ludicrous excuses.

(86) Explain to me why he never spoke this way in the past. Because then he had the excuse of not being worshiped, but when he was stripped of this defense he fled to the cadavers, anxious that no ill befall him. He did not wish to disgrace himself; you forced him, cutting off his defense by assiduous worship and not allowing him to take refuge in the dearth of sacrifices.

JULIAN MOVES THE COFFIN OF BABYLAS BACK TO THE CITY

(87) When the hypocrite heard this, he ordered the coffin to be brought down,[188] so that the defeat might be clear and evident to all. If he had said:[189] "I am unable to speak on account of the saint, but do not move anything and make no further disturbance," it would only have been manifest to his

---

[187] The Old Testament prophets. On Chrysostom's use of round numbers see Introduction 3 (with note 5).

[188] I.e., Julian ordered the removal of Babylas from Daphne (see note 182 above).

[189] Viz., Apollo.

own; for they would not have disclosed it to others out of shame. But now, as if eager to publicize his own weakness, he forced everything to be done which made it impossible—even for those who desired—to conceal the event. For it was no longer possible even to maintain the hypocrisy because no other cadaver but only the martyr was dislodged from there. And not only the residents of the city, the suburb, and the countryside, but also people far removed from the locality, when they did not see the coffin in place and then investigated the cause, immediately learned that the demon had been asked by the emperor to deliver an oracle, and had said that he could not do it until someone moved blessed Babylas away from him.

(88) And yet, O ridiculous fellow, you could have taken refuge in other pretexts, as you often do, using numerous subterfuges in your perpetual difficulties.[190] Thus to the Lydian you said that when he crossed the Halys river he would destroy a great empire, and you exhibited him upon the pyre.[191] In the case of Salamis you employed this same stratagem and added the ridiculous "knot." In fact, to say: "you will destroy the children of women," was similar to the response given to the Lydian; but to add: "when Demeter is either being scattered or coming together,"[192] is an occasion for more laughter and resembles the sayings of vagabonds at the crossroads. But you did not wish to resort to this. And it was possible to hide your discourse in obscurity (for this also is a constant feature of your art), but everyone would have pressed you anew, ignorantly seeking for a solution. And you

[190] Direct address to Apollo, which cites notoriously ambiguous oracles of Delphi. Chrysostom's source is evidently Eusebius, P.e. 5.20.10 (GCS 43,1: 260; Preparation for the Gospel: Eusebius, trans. Gifford 229). P.e. 5.24.2 (GCS 43,1: 267 f.; Preparation for the Gospel: Eusebius, trans. Gifford 235).

[191] The Lydian king Croesus consulted the Delphic oracle as to whether he should attack the Persians, and, having received this ambiguous reply, initiated a war, was defeated, placed on a burning pyre, and then rescued by Apollo (Herodotus 1.53, 86–87). Earlier pagan authors commented unfavorably upon this oracle: Aristotle quotes it as an example of fallacious ambiguity; Lucian mentions it repeatedly with sarcasm; and Dio Chrysostom interprets it as an example of the danger inherent in commerce between man and the gods. H. Parke and D. Wormell, The Delphic Oracle (Oxford 1956) 1:134.

[192] Oracle concerning the battle of Salamis (Herodotus 7.141.4). Cf. Parke and Wormell, Delphic Oracle 1:177.

could have taken refuge in the stars, as you do often without shame or embarrassment.[193]

(89) Your discourse is not directed to intelligent men but to dumb animals and creatures more stupid than dumb animals. Among the Greeks were there none more clever than those who heard the oracle and did not shrink from the deceit? "But they discerned the lie." Then it was necessary to tell the truth to the priest alone,[194] and he would have found how to conceal your defeat better than you. But now, O wretch, who persuaded you to throw yourself into impudence so manifest? But perhaps you did not err but the emperor played his role badly when he heard about indiscriminate cadavers and proceeded only against the saint: he confuted you and exposed the fraud. But he did it unwillingly. For one and the same person would not honor you with great offerings[195] and then abuse you; but the power of the martyr blinded them all at the same time and did not allow them to comprehend the situation. Thus, while everything was done as if against Christians, ridicule devolved not upon the victims but upon the perpetrators. After this fashion madmen always imagine that they are repelling those who approach them by kicking against the walls and cursing and swearing at those in attendance; but, in acting this way, they dishonor not others but themselves—which is just what happened then.

(90) The coffin was dragged all along the road,[196] and the martyr returned, like an athlete, carrying a second crown into his own city where he had received the first.[197] Therefore, if someone denies the resurrection, let him henceforth be ashamed, observing the more brilliant works of the martyr

[193] According to Porphyry, Apollo once blamed his ignorance on the surrounding (astrological) environment. Eusebius, P.e. 6.5-6 (*Preparation for the Gospel: Eusebius*, trans. Gifford 258 f.).
[194] I.e., the priest of Apollo. Cf. *Bab.* 95, 96, 107.
[195] Cf. note 180 above.   [196] Cf. note 151 above.
[197] The sources have left the narrative of the triumphal removal from Daphne in which the entire populace took part. Probably the body of Babylas was newly located in its original resting place (cf. *Bab.* 93), the great cemetery outside the Daphne gate, usually called "the cemetery" of Christian Antioch. This cemetery was surrounded by a fence, and in the center was located the edifice (martyrium) with the remains of the martyrs, including the alleged remains of Ignatius of Antioch. See Pietro Rentinck, *La cura pastorale in Antiochia nel IV secolo* (Roma 1970) 128–30.

after his decease. Like some champion he joined great and wonderful triumphs to greater and more wonderful triumphs. Then he contended only against an emperor, but now against both an emperor and a demon; then he drove the ruler from the sacred precinct, but now he removed the corrupter from the entire area of Daphne, not using a hand as before but by invisible power prevailing against the invisible power. While alive, his freedom of speech was not tolerated by the murderer; after death, neither the emperor nor the demon, who moved the emperor to perform these acts, could endure his dust.

(91) That he inspired these two individuals with greater fear than the first person is clear from this fact. The one seized, bound, and executed him, but the others only changed his location. Why didn't he order or he require the coffin to be drowned in the sea?[198] Why didn't he smash it and burn it up?[199] Why didn't he order it to be carried away to a deserted and uninhabited place? For, if it was really an accursed and defiled thing, which he moved from there out of revulsion and not from fear, he should not have introduced the abomination into the city, but should have banished it to the recesses of the mountains. But no less than Apollo himself the wretch knew the strength of the blessed one and his relationship to God, and he feared that if he did this he would call forth a thunderbolt or some other disease upon himself.

(92) And in fact he had many examples of the power of Christ exhibited in the rulers before him and in those who together with him administered the empire in his time.[200] Past emperors who dared to commit such deeds ended their life in a shameful and pitiable condition after many unbearable calamities: the pupils of one (Maximinus) spontaneously burst out of his eyes while he was still alive;[201] a second went

---

[198] Apollo and emperor Julian, resp.

[199] The relics of the Lyons martyrs were burned up and thrown into the Rhône river. Eusebius, H.e. 5.1.62 (NPNF 2,1: 217).

[200] A traditional theme of Christian apologetics and application of the doctrine of providence. The power of Christ manifests itself empirically in the punishment of persecutors. See the discussion by J. Moreau, ed., *Lactance: De la mort des persécuteurs* (SC 39: 57–64).

[201] Cf. Eusebius, H.e. 9.10.15 (trans. NPNF 2,1: 367).

mad,[202] and a third experienced some other such calamity when he died. Of those who were with him at the time, his paternal uncle, who engaged in the madness against us with a vengeance, had dared to touch the sacred vessels with his defiled hands; and, not content with this, had gone further in his outrage: he had turned them over, placed them upon the ground, and sat upon them. Immediately, he paid the penalty for this unlawful session: his genitals became putrified and generated worms. That the disease was sent by God is shown by this fact: when physicians killed luscious rare birds and placed them next to the putrified members to elicit the worms, these did not emerge but clung tenaciously to the rotten parts, and he perished consumed after many days.[203] Another one, who was in charge of the imperial treasury, suddenly burst in the middle before crossing the threshold of the palace; he too paid the penalty for another such transgression.[204] Bearing in mind these facts and more than these (for now is not the time to recount them all),[205] the disgusting fellow was afraid to carry his boldness further.

OWING TO THE POWER OF BABYLAS'S RELICS, THE TEMPLE OF APOLLO PARTIALLY BURNS DOWN; THE STATUE OF APOLLO IS DESTROYED

(93) That I am not now uttering an unfounded opinion will be clear to us from what he did afterwards; but meanwhile let us stick to the sequence of events. What happened next? This is the miracle, which displayed not only the power but also the ineffable philanthropy of God. The holy martyr was within the sacred precincts, where he had also been before coming to

---

[202] Perhaps Diocletian (Eusebius, H.e. 8.13.11; trans. NPNF 2,1: 335).

[203] Cf. Acts 12:23. The sacrilege and punishment of Julius Julianus, *maternal* uncle of emperor Julian, whom he appointed *comes orientis*, is elsewhere mentioned by Chrysostom. *Laud. Paul.* 4 (PG 50.489). *Exp. in Ps.* 110.4 (PG 55.285). *Hom.* 4.1 *in Mt.* (PG 57.41).

[204] Amm. Marc. states that Felix died of a hemorrhage (23.1.5). Cf. Acts 1:18 and F.H. Ely, "On *prēnēs genomenos* in Acts 1:18," *Journal of Theological Studies* 13 (1912): 278–85, 415.

[205] Cf. *Bab.* 118.

Daphne;[206] the evil demon realized immediately that his deception had been contrived in vain, and that he was contending not with a cadaver but with a living and energetic being, not only stronger than he but stronger than all demons. For, having beseeched God to release fire onto the temple, he burned down the entire roof and, after demolishing the idol to the soles of its feet and rendering it ashes and dust,[207] left all the walls standing.

(94) One who visits the place today will deny that what happened was the work of fire. For the destruction wrought by the fire was neither disorderly nor such as inanimate matter could produce; but the temple was uncovered in a symmetrical and workmanlike manner, as if a hand led the flame around and pointed out what it ought to spare and what it ought to consume. It resembles not simply the ruins from a fire, but an edifice which has its sides intact and lacks only a roof: besides the rest, all the columns which uphold the roof and which uphold the entrance remain standing except for one of those around the back vestibule; and even this was not allowed to be broken at random, but for a reason which we shall give later on.[208]

(95) After this happened, the priest of the demon was immediately brought into court and required to name the person responsible. When he could not, although they bound his hands behind his back and beat him unmercifully, and then hoisted him in the air and lacerated his sides, they learned nothing more. Nearly the same thing occurred as at the resur-

---

[206] Cf. note 197 above.

[207] Cf. Chrysostom, *Pan. Bab.* 1.3 (PG 50,532): "For as soon as the coffin was drawn into the city, a thunderbolt came from above upon the head of the wooden statue and burnt it all up." Theodoret, H.e. 3.11.4 (GCS 44: 188): "for a thunderbolt sent down from heaven burnt the whole shrine and turned the very statue of the Pythian into fine dust, for it was made of wood and gilded on the surface." (trans. B. Jackson, NPNF 2,3 [1892]: 99) The statue of Apollo, described by Libanius below (*Bab.* 105, 112), was evidently an acrolith, i.e., "a statue, with the head and extremities of stone, the trunk being usually made of wood, either gilt or draped" (OED s.v.). Arnobius describes acroliths as "being in one part made of wood, but in the other of stone" (6.16; trans. H. Bryce and H. Campbell, ANF 6 [1886]: 513). This type of statue was liable to destruction by fire (cf. *Epistula Ieremiae* 6:54).

[208] Cf. *Bab.* 117.

rection of Christ. For then too, soldiers were assigned to guard the body of Jesus lest, as they said, the disciples steal it and falsify the theft.[209] But the result was that not even a shameless pretext remained for those wanting to falsify resurrection faith. In this case the priest was dragged into court in order to testify that what happened was the work not of divine anger but of human wickedness. Tortured and tormented but unable to disclose anyone, he testified that the fire was of divine origin, so that even those wanting to be impudent had nothing left to say.[210]

(96) But now is the time to say what I deliberately postponed saying a little earlier. What is it? That he did not progress further in audacity because the martyr struck fear into his soul. It is a fact that on account of the roof he maltreated the priest, whom he earlier held in such high honor, and rent him asunder worse than a carnivore, and probably would have eaten his flesh if the act were not loathsome to all.[211] And it is a fact that he brought back the saint, who had closed the mouth of the demon, into the city so as to be in greater honor. If not earlier, when the demon confessed defeat, then after the conflagration, he would have overturned, destroyed, and burned down everything [the coffin, the two shrines of the martyr in Daphne and in the city],[212] if fright were not greater than anger and fear did not prevail over despair. For, most people overcome by anger and distress, if they do not apprehend the ones responsible for their sufferings, usually

---

[209] Cf. Mt 27.64.

[210] Cf. Bab. 107. Theodoret, H.e. 3.11.5 (GCS 44:188): "[Julius Julianus] scourged the officers in charge of the temple, for he conjectured that the conflagration was due to some Christian. But they, maltreated as they were, could not endure to utter a lie, and persisted in saying that the fire had started not from below but from above" (trans. B. Jackson, NPNF 2,3 [1892]: 99).

[211] The threat to taste human flesh as an expression of extreme anger occurs again in Hom. Clem. 20.13, 18 (trans. J. Donaldson, ANF 8 [1886]: 343, 345).

[212] The words in brackets are probably an interpolation because they disrupt the sentence and seemingly contradict what Chrysostom states elsewhere in the discourse, namely, that only one martyrium of Babylas existed at the time of writing, i.e., the martyrium in Daphne (Bab. 70, 97, 126). Cf. Introduction 1.

vent their anger on those who are at hand and under suspicion. And the martyr was very much under suspicion:[213] for as
soon as he arrived in the city, fire came upon the temple.

(97) But, as I said, emotion combated emotion and cowardice prevailed over anger. Pray imagine that good fellow going
up to the suburb, seeing the martyr's shrine intact, but the
temple burnt, the idol destroyed, the offerings consumed,
and every memorial of his own prodigality and of the satanic
pomp obliterated. If neither anger nor despair had entered
his mind when he saw this, he certainly would not have endured the shame and scurrilous laughter,[214] but would have
extended his lawless hands even to the shrine of the blessed
one, if what I said had not restrained him. And indeed the
event was not inconsequential but undermined all the
confidence of the Greeks, quenched all their merriment, and
poured over them a mist of despair as thick as if all the temples had perished.

PROOF OF THE OCCURRENCE: QUOTATIONS FROM THE LAMENT OF LIBANIUS

(98) And that I am not bragging when I say this, I shall
quote the very words of the lamentations and of the monody,
which the sophist of the city performed in honor of this demon.[215] The beginning of the dirge goes like this:

> Gentlemen, over whose eyes, as over mine, a mist is
> poured, let us no longer call this city beautiful or great![216]

Having brought up the myth of Daphne and discussed it[217]—
to avoid excessive length it is expedient not to include the
entire discourse here—he then says that the Persian king who

---

[213] Cf. Downey, *History* 388 on the repression of Christians which followed
the conflagration.

[214] Emperor Julian was an object of public derision in Antioch. Downey,
History 393–94.

[215] See Introduction 24–26 on Libanius's lament over the destruction of the
temple of Apollo at Daphne.

[216] Libanius, *Or.* 60, frag. 1 *Libanii opera*, ed. Foerster.

[217] Cf. *Bab.* 68.

once took the city spared the temple.[218] His words are as follows:

> He who led an army against us deemed it better for himself that the temple be saved; and the beauty of the figure prevailed over barbaric anger. But now, sun and earth, who or whence is this enemy, who without the aid of hoplites, cavalry, or light troops, consumed everything with a small spark?[219]

Next, to show that the blessed one prevailed over him while the religion of the Greeks abounded the most in sacrifices and mystic rites of initiation, he says:

> And what is more, that great deluge did not sweep away our temple, but it was brought down in clear weather and when the cloud had passed by,[220]

calling the period of the earlier emperor[221] a "cloud" and a "deluge." And again a little further on he deplores this fact more bitterly and says:

> Then, Apollo, when your altars were thirsting after blood, you remained a scrupulous guard of Daphne, even though neglected, and however you were abused and despoiled of your outward honor, you tolerated it. But now, after many sheep and many oxen, having received the lips of a pious emperor on your foot; seeing the one whom you predicted; seen by the one announced by you,[222] rid of a bad neighbor, a certain troublesome cadaver nearby, you leaped away from the midst of your worshipers. How shall we still aspire to honor among men who are mindful of temples and images?[223]

(99) What are you saying, O mourner? Dishonored and abused, he remained the scrupulous guard of Daphne; honored and worshiped, he was unable to defend even his own

---

[218] Sapor I (240–72?): Downey, *History* 589. Cf. *Bab.* 106.
[219] Libanius, *Or.* 60, frag. 3 *Libanii opera*, ed. Foerster.
[220] Libanius, *Or.* 60, frag. 4 *Libanii opera*, ed. Foerster.
[221] Constantius (337–61). Cf. *Bab.* 74 with note 162.
[222] Cf. *Bab.* 108.
[223] Libanius, *Or.* 60, frag. 5 *Libanii opera*, ed. Foerster.

temple, though he knew that if it fell he would be in greater disgrace than before.[224] And who is the cadaver, O sophist, which troubled your god? What sort of bad neighbor? Here, after touching upon the bravery of the blessed Babylas and being unable to weather the shame, he simply hid his face and treated the subject in a cursory way, by saying that the demon was troubled and oppressed by the martyr, but not adding how, in an attempt to cover up his defeat, the demon further revealed it. But he says simply: "rid of a bad neighbor." Why don't you identify the cadaver? Why does he alone trouble your god? Why was he alone removed? And why do you call him a bad neighbor? Tell me. Because he confuted the deceit of the demon? In truth this was not the work of someone bad, just as it was not the work of a corpse, but of a living, acting,[225] good patron and protector,[226] who would do everything for your salvation if you wanted it.

(100) He utterly expelled him from this site, which was dearest to him of all places and which he preferred to other spots to the point that he remained there even when dishonored (as you said earlier), and at the time when the emperor was slaughtering many sheep and many oxen to him. This was so that it would be impossible for you further to beguile yourselves and say that he withdrew of his own accord, because he was angry and charged you regarding sacrifices and blamed you regarding the rest of his cult. Thus it is proved in every way that he abandoned Daphne under compulsion and forced by a greater power. He could have been banished while his statue remained, but you would not have been convinced; just as in the past you were not convinced that he had been shackled by him but persisted in worshiping him. This is why, after having first allowed the statue to stand, he brought it down when the flame of impiety rose especially high—to show that the conqueror should conquer and be superior to his enemies not when they are humbled but when they are exalted and vigorous.

---

[224] Cf. *Bab.* 111.

[225] Cf. Heb 4.12.

[226] On patron saints see Peter Brown, "The Rise and Function of the Holy Man in Late Antiquity," in *Society and the Holy in Late Antiquity* (Berkeley 1982).

(101) At that time why didn't he order the prince, who had brought him up to Daphne,[227] to demolish the temple and transfer the statue, as he had the coffin? Because he was not hurt by him and did not need human collaboration but both then and now overthrew him without the instrumentality of a human hand. The first victory he did not make public to us, but silenced him only and kept still.

(102) Such are the saints: they only desire the success of what tends toward human salvation, not that it also be exhibited to the multitude that the success is theirs, except if some need requires it, and by need I again mean concern for those who are being saved. Exactly this happened then. The evil deception intensified, whereupon our victory was disclosed; and it was disclosed not by the conqueror but by the one who had been conquered. Thus the evidence was not suspected even by enemies, while the saint escaped speaking about himself though there was a necessity. But when, nevertheless, error did not cease but they again, more insensibly than stones, insisted on invoking the defeated one and being blind to so manifest a truth, at that point he was forced to release fire onto the statue to extinguish with this conflagration the other conflagration of idolatry.

(103) Why then do you blame the demon, saying: "You leaped away from the midst of your worshipers." He did not leap away of his own accord but was driven away and cast out against his will by force, at the time when he especially wished to remain because of the nidor and the sacrifices. It is as if the ruler reigned at that time for the express purpose of consuming all the beasts of the inhabited world—so lavishly did he slay sheep and oxen upon his altars; and he reached such a pitch of madness that many of those in their midst still considered philosophers called him "cook," "butcher," and all such names.[228] From so plentiful a table, nidor, smoke, and torrents of blood, the demon would not have withdrawn of his own accord, since he remained even without these, as you said, due to madness for his beloved.

---

[227] Viz., Gallus. See above *Bab.* 67, 69.
[228] Cf. *Bab.* 80 with note 180.

(104) But let us suspend our discourse for the time being to listen to the lamentations of the sophist again. Quitting Apollo, he addresses his complaint anew to Zeus, saying:

O Zeus, what a resting place for a weary mind has been taken away from us! How devoid of turmoil the site of Daphne and the temple more so, like a harbor built by nature itself behind a harbor, both sheltered from the waves, but the second offering more tranquillity. Who would not have put off disease here? Fear? Sorrow? Who would have longed for the islands of the blest?[229]

What sort of resting place has been taken away from us, scoundrel? How is the temple more devoid of turmoil and a harbor sheltered from the waves, where there are flutes, kettledrums, headaches, revelry, and drunkenness? "Who would not have put off disease here?" he says. Actually, which of your sympathizers, even if he happened to be healthy before, would not have contracted a disease here and the most dire disease? What passion? Is this what you call a resting-place for the soul and a harbor sheltered from the waves? A deliver-still remains by this place and this tree even after his beloved has been devoured—what scorching flame of madness will he not receive therefrom? What storm? What confusion? What disease? What passion? Is this what you call a resting place for the soul and a harbor sheltered from the waves? A deliverance from diseases? And is it amazing that you juxtapose opposites? For madmen do not perceive the true nature of anything but decide contrary to the realities.

(105) "The Olympics are not too far off"[230]—again I shall return to the lament and show what a great blow was dealt to all the Greeks who then resided in the city, and that the emperor would not have meekly put up with it, but would have vented all his anger on the coffin of the martyr, if he were not restrained by a greater fear. What does he say?

---

[229] Libanius, Or. 60, frag. 6 Libanii opera, ed. Foerster. The islands of the blessed are the abode of heroes (Hesiod, Op. 171) and of just and holy men (Plato, Grg. 523b) after death.

[230] The Olympic festival at Antioch would take place in summer 364.

The Olympics are not too far off, and the festival will convene the cities, and they will come bringing oxen as a sacrifice to Apollo. What shall we do? Whither shall we go? Which god will open the earth for us? What herald, what trumpet will not induce tears? Who will call the Olympics a holiday, when the nearby ruins impel lamentation. "Give me my bow drawn by the horns" (says the tragedy)[231] and a little divination (I say), so that with one I may catch and with the other I may shoot the person who did this. O impious boldness, O defiled soul, O rash hand! He is another Tityus or Idas, the brother of Lynceus; not a giant like the one, or an archer like the other, but knowing this one thing: to rage against the gods.[232] When the sons of Aloeus were yet hatching plots against the gods, you stopped them by death, Apollo;[233] but the one who brought fire from afar encountered no arrow flying into his heart. O spiteful hand, O unjust fire! Where did it fall at first? What was the preamble of the evil? Did it begin from the roof and proceed to the rest: head, face, bowl, zither, and robe falling over the feet?[234] Hephaestus, dispenser of fire, did not admonish the destructive fire though he was indebted to the god in the past for a piece of information.[235] But even Zeus, who controls the rain, did not release water onto the flame though he extinguished the pyre of the unfortunate Lydian king of old.[236] What did he first say to him when he declared war? Whence his boldness? How did he carry out the attack? Why didn't he change his mind out of respect for the beauty of the god?[237]

G. Sievers, *Das Leben des Libanius* (Berlin 1868) 207 f. There was an Olympic stadium at Daphne (Downey, *History* 325 f., 649 f., 660).

[231] Euripides, *Or.* 268. Libanius was familiar with Euripides, and shows special fondness for the *Orestes*. Cf. E. Richtsteig, *Index nominum propriorum, Libanii opera*, rec. R. Foerster 12 (Leipzig 1923) 33.

[232] Tityus tried to rape Leto; Idas shot his bow at Apollo. H.J. Rose, *A Handbook of Greek Mythology* (New York 1959) 81, 142.

[233] The giant Aloadai threatened to topple Olympus. Rose, *A Handbook of Greek Mythology* 60 f.

[234] Cf. *Bab.* 112 for Libanius's description of the statue of Apollo. For representations of the statue on coins see Downey, *History* 85 note 143. D. Brinkerhoff, *A Collection of Sculpture in Classical and Early Christian Antioch* (New York 1970) 33 f. and illustrations 44 and 45.

[235] Cf. *Bab.* 110; cf. Homer, *Od.* 8.270–71, 302.

[236] Cf. note 191 above.

[237] Libanius, *Or.* 60, frags. 7–10 *Libanii opera*, ed. Foerster.

How long, wretched and miserable man, will you close your eyes and say that a human hand was responsible, contradicting and quarreling with yourself like an insane person? (106) Indeed, if the Persian king, who had captured the city at the head of so great an army and set fire to the other shrines, holding the torch in his hand and already about to apply it to this temple, was turned aside by the demon—for this is what you said in the beginning of the monody, lamenting with these words:[238]

> When the Persian king, ancestor of the one now at war,[239] after having captured the city by treachery and set it on fire, went to Daphne to do the same thing, the god turned him aside; and he threw away the torch and worshiped Apollo. In such wise did he appease and reconcile him at first sight.[240]

The one who prevailed over barbaric anger and so great an army, as you say, and was then able to escape danger—and you say that "he stopped the children of Aloeus hatching plots against the gods by death"—how is it that the one able to do such great things did nothing of the sort in this case?

(107) And yet, if nothing else, certainly when the priest was wrongly tortured,[241] he should have taken pity and exposed the conspirator. Even if he escaped during the conflagration,[242] at the point when the wretched man was being hung, ribs gouged, and interrogated, but could not say who did it—at that point at least he should have assisted and delivered the perpetrator, or simply identified him, if he was really unable to deliver him. But now the unfeeling ingrate allows his own worshiper brutally to be flayed, and the emperor after so many sacrifices to be ridiculed. In fact, he was universally derided as a raving madman, when he let loose his anger on that unfortunate fellow.

---

[238] Cf. Bab. 98 and note 218.
[239] Sapor II (309–79). On the Persian campaign of emperor Julian see Bab. 122 f.
[240] Libanius, Or. 60, frag. 2 Libanii opera, ed. Foerster.
[241] Cf. note 194 above.
[242] Julian says that Apollo left the temple before it burned. See note 85 to Introduction.

(108) And how did the one who had predicted the arrival of the emperor so far in advance (as you stated above in your lament)[243] fail to see the person nearby who burned him down? And yet, you people[244] say that he is oracular and, assigning various activities to your gods as if to men, assigned the faculty of divination to him; and you[245] ask him to share the faculty with you. Then how was he ignorant of his own misfortune? After all, even a man would have noticed it. But was he asleep when the fire was set? No one, however, is so insensitive that he will not immediately awaken, when a flame is applied to himself, and stop the incendiary. Truly, "Greeks are always children and no Greek is an old man."[246] For you sit mourning the destruction of statues, when you ought to be lamenting your own folly; because, although the facts proclaim demonic deceit, you do not swerve, but having given yourselves up to destruction and having relinquished your salvation, you are led like cattle wherever they[247] order you to follow.

(109) And you also demand a bow, the same as the person in the tragedy who says this.[248] Is it not manifest and clear madness to expect to accomplish anything with the weapons which did not benefit their owner at all? If you say that you have greater skill and experience than the demon, there is no need to honor him when he is ignorant and weak in matters in which you say that he altogether excels. But if you concede the first prize in archery and divination to him, how did you with a portion of the art expect to do what he who possessed all of it could not do? It is to laugh! What drivel! For he neither partook of the faculty of divination nor, even if he had, would he have accomplished anything. No; for it is not a man who did this but divine power.

(110) And I shall state the cause after this;[249] but meantime

---

[243] See note 222 above.
[244] I.e., pagans.
[245] I.e., Libanius.
[246] Dictum of a priest of (Egyptian) Sais to Solon, recorded by Plato (*Ti.* 22b).
[247] I.e., the demons.
[248] See above note 231.
[249] See *Bab.* 114, 124.

it is worthwhile to learn why he charges Hephaestus with ingratitude, speaking this way: "Hephaestus, dispenser of fire, did not admonish the destructive fire, though he was indebted to the god in the past for a piece of information."[250] Indebted in the past? For what piece of information? Say! Why do you hide the grand accomplishments of your god? Because if you had told the indebtedness, you would have further displayed the ingratitude of Hephaestus. But you are blushing with shame; well then, we shall state your case with frankness. What was the indebtedness? They say that Ares was once enamored of Aphrodite and, afraid of Hephaestus (her husband), watched for his absence to approach her. Apollo beheld them copulating and went to Hephaestus to report the adultery. When he came and found them both in bed, he threw chains around them in that very position and, summoning the gods to the unseemly spectacle, exacted this penalty for their adultery. Such is the favor which Hephaestus owed; and when the time came to repay it, he says that he acted ungratefully.

(111) And what about Zeus? Fine fellow! You even accuse him in turn of cruelty, saying: "But even Zeus, who controls the rain, did not release water onto the flame, though he extinguished the pyre of the unfortunate Lydian king of old."[251] But in fact you did well to remind us of the Lydian. For he too was deceived by this foul demon, who inflated him with vain hopes and thrust him into impending evil; and if Cyrus had not been humane, Zeus would not have helped him at all. Therefore, you unfairly accuse Zeus of having preferred the Lydian to his child; for he did not even defend himself when struck by a thunderbolt in the city which honored him more than all others—I mean the city of Romulus.[252]

---

[250] See above *Bab.* 105 (note 235).   [251] See above *Bab.* 105 (note 236).

[252] Eusebius, P.e. 4.2.8 mentions two destructions of the temple of Jupiter Capitolinus, apparently in 83 B.C. and A.D. 69 (GCS 43,1: 167 f.; *Preparation for the Gospel: Eusebius* trans. Gifford 147). Cf. also Arnobius 6.23: "When the greedy flames so often consumed the Capitol, and had destroyed the Capitoline Jupiter himself with his wife and his daughter, where was the Thunderer at that time to avert that calamitous fire, and preserve from destruction his property, and himself, and all his family?" (trans. H. Bryce and H. Campbell ANF 6 [1886]: 516).

(112) Let us listen to the remainder of the lament; for in this way we shall fully grasp the sorrow which overwhelmed their souls:

Gentlemen, I am drawn towards the form of the god and imagination sets his image before my eyes: his elegant outline and smooth skin (this even in stone),[253] the sash round his breast which gathers the folds of a golden tunic[254] so that part of it settles and part rises. His whole appearance would have calmed the most seething anger. He seemed to be singing a song:[255] and someone somewhere even heard him, as they say, playing the zither at noon. Happy ears! The ode was a commendation of the earth to whom he is also pouring a libation from the golden cup, I believe, because it broke open and reclosed to conceal the maiden.[256]

Then, groaning a little about the conflagration, he says:

When the glow arose a traveler cried out; and the priestess of the god, who dwelt in the forest of Daphne, was panic-stricken. The beating of breasts and a sharp groan, traversing the well-wooded territory, reached the town with a terrible and dreadful noise; and the magistrate, who had just tasted sleep, was aroused from bed by the bitter news. He was frantic: seeking the wings of Hermes, he went to inquire into the root of the evil, inwardly no less inflamed than the temple.[257] Beams collapsed, carrying fire which destroyed whatever it approached: Apollo, instantaneously, since he was close to the roof, and then the other beautiful objects: images of the founding muses, gleaming stones,[258] lovely pillars. The groaning throng stood round at a loss how to help, as happens to those who see a ship-

---

[253] The statue was an acrolith (note 207 above).

[254] Philostorgius corroborates the fact that the tunic was gilded (H.e. 7.8a; GCS 21:87).

[255] Cf. Tacitus, *Ann.* 14.14.2. See the replica of the head of Apollo reproduced by Brinkerhoff, *Collection of Sculpture* plate 41, and remarks on p. 36.

[256] Libanius, *Or.* 60, frag. 11 *Libanii opera*, ed. Foerster.

[257] Cf. Theodoret, H.e. 3.11.5 (GCS 44: 188): "Julianus the uncle of Julian, prefect of the East, learnt this by night, and riding at full speed came to Daphne, eager to bring succour to the deity whom he worshiped" (trans. B. Jackson NPNF 2,3 [1892]: 99).

[258] Mosaics?

wreck from the shore, whose help consists in deploring the
occurrence. Great was the wail raised by the nymphs, leaping from their fountains;[259] and by Zeus, situated nearby, at
the destruction of his son's honors;[260] and by a throng of
countless demons residing in the grove. No less a lament
was raised by Calliope from the middle of the city,[261] when
the gladdener of the muses was injured by fire.[262]

Then he says at the end:

> Become for me now, Apollo, such as Chryses made you
> when he cursed the Achaeans: filled with anger and resem-
> bling night;[263] because, as we were in the act of restoring
> your pomp and reinstating everything that had been taken
> away, the object of this honor was carried off beforehand,
> like a bridegroom who leaves when the nuptial crowns are
> already woven.[264]

(113) This is the lament, or rather small parts of the lament.
To me it is amazing that he thinks to exalt him by things which
he ought to blush at; as when he makes him no better than a
licentious and shameful youth playing the zither at noon, and
says that his beloved is the subject of the ode, and calls the
ears happy which listened to the shameful ditty. That certain
inhabitants of Daphne and its outskirts wept, and that the
magistrate of the city was inflamed and did nothing but lament, is not surprising. That the gods were equally helpless
and only wept like them; and that neither Zeus nor Calliope
nor the great throng of demons nor even the nymphs themselves were sufficient for the blaze, but that all raised shriek-
ings and wailings only—this is total absurdity. They therefore
received a great blow, as I have amply demonstrated from his
words; in fact, somewhere in the middle of the monody he
distinctly confessed that they were struck in a vital part. Ac-

---

[259] The springs of Daphne which supplied Antioch with water. See Introduction 21.

[260] A temple of Zeus was located near that of Apollo. Downey, *History* 214.

[261] The muse Calliope was a patron deity of Antioch; her statue was located
in the city theater. Downey, *History* 216f.

[262] Libanius, *Or.* 60, frags. 12–13 *Libanii opera,* ed., Foerster.

[263] Hom. *Il.* 1.47.

[264] Libanius, *Or.* 60, frag. 14 *Libanii opera,* ed. Foerster.

cordingly, the emperor would not have patiently endured it, if he had not been restrained by greater fear and trembling.

WHY DID GOD STRIKE THE TEMPLE?

(114) It is time at last to set forth the reason why God loosed his anger not on the emperor but on the demon; and also why the fire did not destroy the entire temple but stopped after demolishing the roof and the idol simultaneously. It did not simply happen without a reason but everything was done by the philanthropy of God for the sake of those in error. For, he who knows all things before they come into existence, knew this besides: if the thunderbolt hit the emperor, those who were present and beheld the stroke would be afraid momentarily, but after two or three years the memory of the event would perish and there would be many who would not accept the prodigy; if, however, the temple receives the flame, it will proclaim the anger of God more clearly than any herald not only to contemporaries but also to all posterity. Therefore every pretext has been taken away from those wishing impudently to throw a veil over the occurrence. For everyone who arrives at this place receives the impression that the conflagration has just occurred; a certain dread enters his mind and, facing heaven, he immediately glorifies the strength of the one who wrought this.

(115) Just as if someone from above breaking into the cavernous lair of a robber chief should lead out the inhabitant in chains[265] and, having taken all his things, should leave the place as a refuge for wild beasts and jackdaws; then every visitor to the lair, as soon as he sees the place, pictures in his imagination the raids, the thefts, and the features of the earlier inhabitant—so it happens here. For, seeing the columns from a distance, then coming and crossing the threshold, he pictures to himself the malignity, deceit, and intrigues of the demon and departs in amazement at the strength of God's anger. Thus the house (earlier) of error and blasphemy has

---

[265] Cf. Mt 12.29 (Mk 3.27).

become now the subject of praise. Such is the ingenuity of our God.

(116) And now is not the first time, but he has performed these amazing marvels from time immemorial. It is not pertinent to enumerate them all; I shall mention what seems to resemble these events most closely. Once when the Jews waged war in Palestine with certain foreigners, and the enemy was victorious and took the ark of God, they dedicated it as the choice part of the spoils to one of their local idols named Dagon; and, as soon as the ark was brought in, the statue fell down and lay on its face. Since they did not comprehend God's mighty power from this fall, but set it up and again placed it on its pedestal, when they appeared the next day at dawn they observed that it was no longer simply fallen but also quite broken. The arms, detached from the shoulders, were flung onto the threshold of the temple, with the feet; and the rest of the statue was scattered in another place in pieces.[266] And, to compare small with great, the land of Sodom together with its inhabitants was destroyed by fire and became infertile so that not only contemporaries but also all their successors might learn self–control from the spot.[267] For if the punishment extended only to men, the occurrence would be doubted later on. Therefore the place, which is able to exist for a long time, receives the blow and reminds each succeeding generation that those who do such things are or-

[266] Cf. 1 Sm (1 Kgs) 5.1–4.
[267] Cf. Chrysostom, *Stat.* 19.2 (PG 49,191): "This also happened at Sodom. For when they burned in their lust one towards another, then too the very earth itself was burned up, being kindled by the fire from above. For He designed that the vengeance of this sin should permanently remain. . . . And now the sight of the land, through all the generations since, hath given an admonition beyond all powers of speech, crying out, as it were, and saying, 'Dare not to do the deeds of Sodom, lest ye suffer the lot of Sodom!' For precept commonly makes not so deep an impression upon the mind as a fearful spectacle does, which bears upon it the vestiges of calamity through all time. And persons that have visited these places bear witness, who often when they hear the Scripture discoursing of these things are not much terrified; but when they have gone and stood upon the site, and see the whole surface of it disfigured, and have witnessed the effects of the fire, with soil nowhere visible, but everything dust and ashes, they come away astonished with the sight, and taking with them a strong lesson of chastity" (trans. C. Marriott and revised by W.R.W. Stephens, NPNF 9 [1889]: 466–67).

dained by law to suffer such things even if they do not pay the penalty at once; which is exactly what happened in the case of this temple.

(117) See: it is twenty years after the event[268] and none of the edifice left behind by the fire has perished in addition; but the parts which escaped the fire remain solid and firm, and are so strong as to suffice for a hundred years and for another two times as much and again much more time than this.[269] And why is it amazing that none of the columns separated from the others and fell to the ground? Only one of the columns around the back vestibule was broken in two at the time, and it did not even fall down but was detached from its own base and fell back towards the wall, where it remained. The part from the foundation to the break leans sideways towards the wall, while the part from the break to the capital is on its back, supported by the lower part. Although violent winds assailed the place many times and earthquakes occurred and the earth was shaken,[270] the remains of the fire were not even shaken but stand firmly, all but shouting that they have been preserved for the chastisement of future generations.

WHY DIDN'T GOD STRIKE EMPEROR JULIAN?

(118) And one could say that this is the reason why the temple was not entirely consumed by fire; as to why the thunderbolt did not come for the emperor, one could search and find another cause stemming from the same source, i.e., the goodness and philanthropy of Christ. He held back the fire from the emperor's head and threw it against the roof so that

---

[268] See Introduction 3.

[269] Philostorgius (ca. 368–430/40) says remains of the temple were still standing in his day (H.e. 7.8; GCS 21: 94). Evagrius (ca. 536–ca.600), who lived in Antioch, does not mention the temple of Apollo (H.e. 1.16; PG 86². 2468). Modern archaeologists have not yet discovered any trace of the temple. See P. Canivet, *Histoire d'une entreprise apologétique au ve siècle* (Paris 1957) 14 and note 4.

[270] Earthquakes occurred at Antioch in 365 and during the reign of Theodosius (379–95). See Downey, *History* 400, 435 note 137, 438.

he might be instructed in the misfortunes of others and escape the punishment in store for him by changing his purpose and ceasing from error. Nor was this the only or the first sign which Christ gave to him of his personal power, but there were many others in addition equally great: the manner in which his uncle and his treasurer died; a famine which accompanied his arrival in the city; and the water shortage which never happened prior to the sacrifices which he offered at the springs.[271] And in the army and in the cities there were many other additional events able to bend a heart of stone not only because of their quantity and their occurrence all together in succession on the heels of his escapades—as in the case of the Egyptian king of old[272]—but because each of the miracles displayed was such as not to need another to effect the conversion of those who saw them, but each of them sufficed by itself to do this.

(119) Not to mention the others—wouldn't the sign which was exhibited round about the foundations of the ancient temple of Jerusalem have astounded anyone of ordinary sensitivity?[273] What was it? When the tyrant saw that the Christian faith had spread into the entire realm under his authority, and already touched that of the Persians and other barbarians beyond them, and in turn was progressing within them, and so to speak covered all the land under the sun—he was vexed and pained and prepared for war against the churches; the wretch did not realize, however, that he was kicking against

[271] This is a continuation of *Bab.* 92 concerning the various signs worked by Christ in order to warn Julian. On the famine and drought in Antioch see Downey, *History* 383, 386, 388–89.

[272] Cf. Ex 7.3 f.

[273] Chrysostom discusses Julian's unsuccessful attempt to rebuild the temple in Jerusalem again in *Jud.* 5.11 (PG 49.900 f.; trans. FOTC 68.137–40) and *Jud. et gent.* 16 (PG 48.835) translated in this volume. One may still consult with profit William Warburton, *Julian, or a Discourse concerning the earthquake and fiery eruption which defeated that emperor's attempt to rebuild the temple at Jerusalem, in which the reality of a divine interposition is shown, the objections to it answered, and the nature of that evidence which demands the assent of every reasonable man to a miraculous fact is considered and explained,* 2nd ed., with additions (London 1751). See also David B. Levenson, *A Source and Tradition Critical Study of the Stories of Julian's Attempt to Rebuild the Jerusalem Temple* (Ph.D. diss., Harvard University 1980).

the goad.[274] First of all he attempted to build the temple in Jerusalem, which the power of Christ had razed to the ground; and he courted the Jews, though a Greek, desiring thereby to test the power of Christ. And having summoned certain of the Jews and bid them sacrifice, saying that their ancestors worshiped in this manner—when they took refuge in the excuse that they were not permitted to do this after the fall of the temple outside of their ancient capital,[275] he ordered them to take money from the royal treasury and all the other supplies necessary for the construction, and to go away and build the temple and return to their ancient custom of sacrifices. And the imbeciles, misled from the womb and immature till old age,[276] went away to collaborate with the emperor; and as soon as they began to clear away the mound for him, fire suddenly leaped from the foundations and devoured them all. When these events were reported to the emperor, he neither pursued the audacious enterprise further (henceforth restrained by fear); nor did he wish to be freed from the error of the demons now that he was once and for all under their control.

(120) For a while, however, he kept quiet; but when a little time passed, he engaged in the same vain labor: no longer daring to build the temple but hurling his missiles against us from another side. Hitherto he hesitated to declare war openly; first and foremost because he was utterly convinced that he would be undertaking an impossibility, and secondly so as not to provide us with any opportunity to weave a crown of martyrdom. For he considered it unbearable and the worst of all calamities for someone to be brought before the tribunal and endure torture unto death in behalf of the truth: he thus displayed his deep-seated hostility towards us. A clever rascal, he released all those everywhere whom the rulers of the church had punished on account of certain sins and

---

[274] A Greek proverb. Cf. Acts 26.14. *Corpus Paroemiographorum Graecorum*, ed. E.L. von Leutsch and F.G. Schneidewin (Göttingen 1839; reprint ed., Hildesheim 1958) 1:ZV 70, DVI 84. 2:GCM IV 100, Ap VI 57, XIV 100.

[275] Chrysostom explains why a Jew cannot sacrifice outside Jerusalem in *Jud.* 4.6 (PG 48. 879 f.; trans. FOTC 68.88–91).

[276] Cf. Is 46.3 f. Note 246 above.

had deposed from office, so as to bestow authority on the most worthless, upset the ordinances of the church, and cause dissension among all: for we could easily be subdued in the future if previously devoured by internecine strife. A certain person, who had been deposed from ecclesiastical office on account of the perversity of his doctrine and the depravity of his life—Stephen by name—acquired the bishop's throne again at his behest.[277] Meanwhile, he strove to extinguish the dominical name as much as he could, calling us Galileans instead of Christians in his decrees and urging his officials to do this.[278]

(121) Amidst the occurrence of the signs, which I mentioned, appearing in the famine and the drought, he persisted in the same impudence and inflexibility. On the eve of his Persian campaign he descended so vaingloriously as if he were about to exterminate the entire race of barbarians; he directed innumerable threats to us, saying that after his return from there he would destroy us completely: for this war was more difficult in his opinion than the Persian and he ought to accomplish the easier first and then proceed to the harder. And this was told us by those who were privy to his plans.[279] Nonetheless, seething with anger against us and each day aroused to greater madness, he never stayed with the same plan but retracted his earlier intention and again threatened us with persecution. But God, wishing to check him and keep down his fever, brought about this new sign in Daphne, releasing fire onto the temple. Yet even that being so, he did not renounce his anger; on the contrary, bursting with the desire to plunder us, he did not wait for the time which he had threatened but, as he was about to cross the Euphrates, he put his soldiers to the test; and, although he corrupted some few with flattery, he did not discharge the recalcitrant

---

[277] Stephen of Antioch, who led the Arianizing eastern bishops at the synod of Serdica (342 or 343). See CMH 1:126, 130.

[278] Julian's religious policy steered a hypocritical course between persecution and toleration. See Philip Schaff, *History of the Christian Church* 3 (New York 1910; reprint ed., Grand Rapids, Mich., 1964), pp. 50–54. Jedin, ed., *History of the Church* 2: 54–57.

[279] Cf. Jedin, ed., *History of the Church* 2:58.

from the expedition because he feared that by their dismissal he might render the army weaker against the Persians.[280]

(122) Who will recount for us the subsequent events, which were much more terrible than those which occurred on the desert, by sea, and in Egypt when that insensible Pharoah was punished and all were drowned?[281] At that time, since the Egyptian did not yield to any of these calamities and wish to become better thereby, God finally destroyed him together with his army; likewise at this time since he shamelessly withstood every divine portent and did not wish to profit from them but remained incorrigible, he henceforth involved him in the worst evils in order that others might become better by the sufferings of him who was not to be chastened by the sufferings of others. For he who led down a greater number of soldiers than any previous emperor ever and expected at one fell swoop effortlessly to capture all of Persia, fared as wretchedly and pitiably as if his army were composed of women and small children rather than men. First of all by his own negligence he drove them to such dire necessity that they were eating horseflesh, and some wasted by hunger and others by thirst died. As if commanding in behalf of the Persians and striving not to capture them but to betray his own over to them, he shut them up in the wilderness and all but handed them over in chains.

(123) No one, even if he saw and experienced what happened there, will be able to recount all the misfortunes, which so exceeded all measure.[282] To be brief: when he had fallen shamefully and pitiably—some say that he died after being hit by a certain porter, who was dissatisfied with the state of affairs; others say that they do not know the identity of his murderer but only that he was struck and asked to be buried in the land of Cilicia, where he lies now. In any case, when he

---

[280] Christians regularly served in the armies of pagan and Christian Roman emperors. Cf. Eusebius, H.e. 5.5 (trans. NPNF 2,1: 219). H.e. 6.5.5 f. (p. 253). H.e. 7.11.21 (p. 301). H.e. 7.15 (p. 303). H.e. 8.1.8 (p. 323). H.e. 8.4.2 (p. 326). H.e. 8 App. 1 (p. 340). M.P. 11.20 f. (p. 353). H.e. 10.8.10 (p. 385). Chrysostom, *Educ. lib.* 89 (SC 188: 196).

[281] Cf. Ex 14.27–28, 15.4.

[282] Norman H. Baynes narrates the "riddle" of Julian's Persian expedition and death in CMH 1:81–84.

had fallen in this shameful manner, the soldiers, seeing that they were in a critical situation, bowed in submission to the enemy; and, upon oath that they would withdraw from altogether the most secure position, which was like an impregnable wall of our civilization, and finding the barbarians humane, they thus escaped and a few of the many returned, after they too had endured physical hardship: ashamed of the treaty, but compelled by the oath to yield their paternal property to them. And a spectacle more pitiful than the worst captivity met the eye. The inhabitants of that city[283] expected to receive thanks because they had served as a barrier to harbor all those within and in place of all were continually exposed to all the dangers; instead they were treated as enemies: displaced to a foreign land, relinquishing houses and fields, separated from all their ancestral possessions— they endured this from their own. Such are the benefits we have obtained from the good emperor.[284]

(124) These facts were stated not for their own sake but to solve the difficulty of those who enquire as to why God did not punish the emperor. Many times, in fact, he wanted to impede the further progress of his lunacy and correct him by the mishaps of others; but when he resisted, he delivered him up to the worst evils, reserving the true recompense of his audacious deeds for the great day[285] and through the present punishment arousing the more remiss and making them saner. For God's long-suffering is such that it brings crueler punishment on those who misuse it; and just as it is beneficial to those who repent, likewise is it the occasion for greater punishments to the obstinate and impenitent.

(125) If someone asks: "Why didn't God foreknow that the tyrant would be incorrigible?," we shall say that he foreknew

---

[283] I.e., the city of Nisibis, "the firmest bulwark of the provinces of the East" (Gibbon, *Decline and Fall* 2:525). Quotations from Gibbon are reprinted here and in the next note with the permission of Methuen & Co., London.

[284] In fact, it was Jovian, Julian's successor, who made the disadvantageous treaty of peace with Persia. Gibbon states that "this ignominious peace has justly been considered as a memorable aera *(sic)* in th[e] decline and fall of the Roman empire" (*Decline and Fall* 2:527).

[285] Cf. Jude 6, Rv 6.17.

but never, in consequence of the foreknowledge of our evil, ceases to do his part. But even if we do not accept the admonition, he exhibits his own philanthropy. If we involve ourselves in greater evils it is not His fault: he is long-suffering not in order that we may perish but in order that we may be saved;[286] but it is our fault for abusing his ineffable forbearance. Thus his infinite philanthropy is manifested. When we ourselves do not wish to benefit from his great long-suffering, then he turns it to the profit of others, everywhere exhibiting philanthropy and resourcefulness at the same time.

(126) Thus the tyrant ended his life; his madness, however, and the power of the blessed Babylas are memorialized by the temple and the martyr's shrine:[287] the one is desolate and the other has the same energy which it had before. The coffin has not yet been brought up again,[288] and God arranged this too in order that passersby might have more definite knowledge of the accomplishments of the saint. For every foreign visitor who arrives at the place seeks for the martyr and then, when he does not see him there, immediately goes to enquire the cause; and, having heard the whole history, departs with greater profit than before. Thus he[289] confers the greatest benefits by having been located at Daphne and again by having vacated it.

CONCLUSION

(127) Such is the power of the martyrs during life, after death, when they are present in a place, and again when they leave it behind. The fact is that from beginning to end his accomplishments were joined together in a continuous sequence. Observe: he defended the outraged laws of God; exacted proper punishment in behalf of the deceased; showed the great gulf between priesthood and kingly office;

---

[286] Cf. 2 Pt 3.9, 15; Jn 3.17; 1 Tm 2.4.
[287] I.e., the martyrium built by Gallus at Daphne. See note 153 above and Introduction 1.
[288] Cf. note 151 above.
[289] Viz., Babylas.

put an end to all mundane vanity and trampled under foot
the fantasy of existence; taught emperors not to carry their
authority beyond the measure given them by God; and
showed bishops how they ought to exercise this office. These
accomplishments and more than these were his when he was
in the flesh; when he died and departed, he put an end to the
strength of the demon; utterly refuted the deceit of the
Greeks; exposed the nonsense of divination, shattered its
mask, and displayed all its hypocrisy laid bare, having
silenced and defeated by main force the one who seemed to
be its master. Even now the walls of the temple are standing,
proclaiming to all the shame, ridicule, and weakness of the
demon; the crowns, victory, and strength of the martyr. So
great is the power of the saints, so invincible and fearsome,
both to emperors, and to demons, and to the chief of the
demons himself.[290]

---

[290] See Introduction 29. In a like manner Chrysostom ends his treatise on
the priesthood with a description of the spiritual battle between the bishop/
priest and the devil (*Sac.* 6.13; SC 272:356–60; trans. NPNF 9:82 f.).

DEMONSTRATION AGAINST THE PAGANS THAT CHRIST IS GOD

(Pros Hellēnas apodeixis hoti theos estin ho khristos)

Translated by

PAUL W. HARKINS

Professor Emeritus

Xavier University

Cincinnati, Ohio

CONTENTS

SELECT BIBLIOGRAPHY

Texts and Translations of the Demonstration (see below, *Introduction* Sects. 71–73)

Savile, Henry. *S. Johannis Chrysostomi opera omnia*. 8 vols. Eton 1612.
Duc, Fronton du (Fronto Ducaeus). *S. Johannis Chrysostomi opera omnia*. 12 vols. Paris 1636–42.
Montfaucon, Bernard de. *S. Iohannis Chrysostomi opera omnia*. 13 vols. Paris 1718–38 and Venice 1734–41. 2nd ed. by T. Fix. Paris 1834–39. Reprint of 2nd edition by J.-P. Migne. PG 47–61. Paris 1863. Earlier printing of vol. 48: 1859.
Bareille, J. *Oeuvres complètes de S. Jean Chrysostome*. Montfaucon's text with French translation. 19 vols. Paris 1865–73.
McKendrick, Norman G. *"Quod Christus sit Deus* of John Chrysostom." Edited for Ph.D. dissertation, Fordham University 1966. Used as the basis for the present translation.

Other Patristic Texts and Translations

Cyril of Jerusalem, St. *The Works of Saint Cyril of Jerusalem*. Vol. 2. Trans. L. McCauley and A. Stevenson. FOTC 64. Washington, D.C. 1970.
Eusebius of Caesarea. *Vita Constantini*. PG 20.905–1316.
Gregory of Nyssa. St. *Gregory of Nyssa: The Lord's Prayer; The Beatitudes*. Trans. H. Graef, ACW 18. Westminster, Md. 1954.
John Chrysostom, St. *Adversus Judaeos orationes*. PG 48.839–942.
―――― *De incomprehensibili dei natura contra Anomoeos*. PG 48.701–812.
―――― *De s. Babyla contra Julianum et gentiles*. PG 50.533–72. Ed. and trans. Margaret A. Schatkin. Ph.D. dissertation, Fordham University, 1967. See Part I of present volume.
―――― *Commentary on St. John the Apostle and Evangelist*. Trans. Sr. Thomas Aquinas Goggin. FOTC 33 and 41. New York 1957, 1960.
―――― *Huit catéchèses baptismales*. Ed. and trans. A. Wenger SC 50bis. Paris 1957. 2nd ed. 1970.
―――― *St. John Chrysostom: Baptismal Instructions*. Trans. P.W. Harkins, ACW 31. Westminster, Md. 1963.
―――― *St. John Chrysostom: Discourses against Judaizing Christians*. Trans. P.W. Harkins. FOTC 68. Washington 1979.
―――― *St. John Chrysostom: On the Incomprehensible Nature of God*. Trans. P.W. Harkins. FOTC 72. Washington 1984.
―――― *Sur l'incompréhensibilité de Dieu*. Vol. 1, *Homélies I–V*. 2nd ed., introd. J. Daniélou. Text ed. A.M. Malingrey. Trans. R. Flacelière. SC 28bis. Paris 1970.
Pseudo-Gregory of Nyssa. *Testimonia adversus Judaeos*, PG 46.193–234.
Socrates, Scholasticus. *Ecclesiastica Historia*. Ed. R. Hussey. Oxford 1853. Also in PG 67.

158   ST. JOHN CHRYSOSTOM

Bible

The Septuagint Version of the Old Testament and the Apocrypha. London n.d.

Septuaginta. Ed. A. Rahlfs. 2 vols. Stuttgart 1935.

The Greek New Testament. Eds. K. Aland, M. Black, B. Metzger, A. Wilgren. London 1966.

The Jerusalem Bible. Ed. A. Jones. Garden City, N.Y. 1966.

The New American Bible. Trans. Members of the Catholic Biblical Association of America, sponsored by the Bishops' Committee of the Confraternity of Christian Doctrine. Paterson, N.J. 1970.

Brown, R.E., Fitzmyer, J.A., Murphy, R.E., eds. *The Jerome Biblical Commentary* Englewood Cliffs, N.J. 1968.

McKenzie, J.L. *Dictionary of the Bible.* Milwaukee 1965.

Orchard, B., Sutcliffe, E., eds. *A Catholic Commentary on Holy Scripture.* London 1953.

Other Works

Armstrong, A. *An Introduction to Ancient Philosophy.* Boston 1965.

Bardenhewer, O. *Patrology.* Trans. T. Shahan. St. Louis 1908.

Baur, Chrysostom. *John Chrysostom and his Time.* Vol. 1, *Antioch*, Vol. 2, *Constantinople.* Trans. M. Gonzaga Westminster, Md. 1960–61.

———— *S. Jean Chrysostome et ses oeuvres dans l'histoire littéraire* Louvain 1907.

Benzinger, I. "Daphne." *Paulys Real-Encyclopädie der classischen Altertumswissenschaft.* Vol. 4. Ed. G. Wissowa (1901): 2136–38.

Bidez, J. *La vie de l'empereur Julien.* Paris 1930.

Campenhausen, H. von. *Fathers of the Greek Church.* Trans. S. Godman. New York 1959.

Cataudella. Q. "Giovanni Crisostomo." *Enciclopedia Cattolica* 6 (1951): 534–43.

Carter, R.E. "The Chronology of St. John Chrysostom's Early Life." *Traditio* 18 (1962): 357–64.

Chapman, J. "St. John Chrysostom on St. Peter." *Dublin Review* 132 (1903): 1–27.

Cumont, F. *Oriental Religions in Roman Paganism.* New York 1956.

Dölger, F.J. "Das Segnen der Sinne mit der Eucharistie." *Antike und Christentum* 3 (1932): 231–44.

Downey, G.A. *A History of Antioch in Syria.* Princeton 1961.

———— *Antioch in the Age of Theodosius the Great* Norman, Okla. 1962.

Duchesne, L. *The Early History of the Christian Church.* Vol. 3. Trans. Claude Jenkins. New York 1924.

Finegan, J. *Light from the Ancient Past.* 2nd ed. Princeton 1959.

Graetz, H. *History of the Jews* Vol. 2. Philadelphia 1967.

Grant, F.C. "Astral Religion." NCE 1 985–86.

Harkins, P.W. "Chrysostom the Apologist: On the Divinity of Christ." *Kyriakon. Festschrift Johannes Quasten.* Vol. 1. (Münster 1970) 441–51.

Humbert, A. "Docetism." NCE 4 934–35.

Jugie, M. "Saint Jean Chrysostome et la primauté de Saint Pierre." *Echos d'Orient* 11 (1908): 5–15.

Leclercq, H. "Hélène, Impératrice." DACL 6.2 (1925): 2126–46.

Lietzmann, H. *History of the Early Church.* Vol. 4. Trans. B. Woolf. New York 1952.

———— "Ioannes." *Paulys Real-Encyclopädie der classischen Altertumswissenschaft.* Vol. 12.2. Ed. G. Wissowa and W. Kroll (1916): 1811–28.

Long, H.S. "Astrology." NCE 1 986–88.

———— "Horoscopes." NCE 7 151–52.

MacRae, G.W. "Gnosticism." NCE 6 525.

Meeks, W. and Wilken, R. *Jews and Christians in Antioch in the First Four Centuries of the Common Era.* Missoula, Mont. 1978.

Pistorius, P.V. *Plotinus and Neoplatonism.* Cambridge 1952.

Puech, A. *Histoire de la littérature grecque chrétienne.* Vol. 3. Paris 1930.

Quasten, J. *Patrology.* 3 vols. Utrecht 1950–60. Spanish edition, Madrid 1977).

Racle, G. "A la source d'un passage de la VIIe catéchèse baptismale de S. Jean Chrysostome." *Vigiliae Christianae* 15 (1961): 46–53.

Simon, M. "La polémique antijuive de S. Jean Chrysostome et le mouvement judaïsant d'Antioche." *Annuaire de l'Institut de Philologie et d'Histoire Orientales et Slaves* 4 (1936): 140–53.

Wilken, R. *John Chrysostom and the Jews.* Berkeley, Calif. 1983.

Williams, A.L. *Adversus Judaeos.* Cambridge 1935.

Williams, G.H. "Christology and church-state relations in the fourth century." *Church History* 20 (1951) n.3, 3–33; n.4, 3–26.

ABBREVIATIONS

ACW	*Ancient Christian Writers.* Westminster, Md. and London (later Ramsey, N.J.) 1946–.
Adv. Iud.	John Chrysostom. *Discourses against Judaizing Christians.*
Baur	Baur C. *John Chrysostom and His Time.* Vol 1, *Antioch,* Vol 2, *Constantinople.* Trans. M. Gonzaga. Westminster, Md. 1960–61.
CCHS	Orchard B., Sutcliffe E., eds. *A Catholic Commentary on Holy Scripture.* London 1953.
DACL	*Dictionnaire d'archéologie chrétienne et de liturgie.* Paris 1907–53.
DB	McKenzie, J.L. *Dictionary of the Bible.* Milwaukee 1965.
De incomp.	John Chrysostom. *De incomprehensibili Dei natura.* PG 48.701–812. Homilies 1–5 also SC 28bis.
Demonstration	John Chrysostom. *Demonstration against the Pagans that Christ is God.* PG 48.813–38.
Downey	Downey, G. *A History of Antioch in Syria.* Princeton 1961.
DTC	*Dictionnaire de théologie catholique.* Paris 1903–50.
FOTC	*The Fathers of the Church: A New Translation.* New York (later Washington, D.C.) 1947–.
FOTC 68	Harkins, P.W. *St. John Chrysostom: Discourses against Judaizing Christians.* Washington, D.C. 1979.
FOTC 72	Harkins, P.W. *St. John Chrysostom: On the Incomprehensible Nature of God.* Washington, D.C. 1984.
Graetz	Graetz, H. *History of the Jews.* Philadelphia 1967.
JB	Jones, A., ed. *The Jerusalem Bible.* Garden City, N.Y. 1966.
JBC	Brown, R.E., Fitzmyer, J.A., Murphy, R.E., eds. *The Jerome Biblical Commentary.* Englewood Cliffs, N.J. 1968.
LXX	Rahlfs, A. *Septuaginta.* 2 vols. Stuttgart 1935.
NAB	*The New American Bible.* Trans. Members of the Catholic Biblical Association of America. New York 1970.
NCE	*New Catholic Encyclopedia.* New York 1967.
NT	New Testament.
OT	Old Testament.
PG	Migne, J.P., ed. *Patrologiae cursus completus: Series Graeca.* 161 vols. Paris 1857–66.
Quasten	Quasten J. *Patrology.* 3 vols. Utrecht 1950–60. Spanish edition, Madrid 1977.

SC   *Sources chrétiennes.* Paris 1942–.
Wilken   Wilken, R. *John Chrysostom and the Jews.* Berkeley 1983.
Williams   Williams, A.L. *Adversus Judaeos.* Cambridge 1935.

INTRODUCTION[1]

HE FIRST PORTION OF THIS VOLUME deals with an apologetic treatise of St. John Chrysostom, *De s. Babyla contra Julianum et gentiles,* which presents an encomium on the triumph of Christianity and the downfall of paganism. In this second part we offer a second apologetic treatise of Chrysostom on the divinity of Christ, and again the principal targets are the pagans.

(2) However, both its genre and addressees leave the door of doubt ajar. The title calls it an *apodeixis* (or "demonstration"), but in the very first paragraph the author himself refers to the work as a *logos* (or "discourse"), a word he often uses in referring to his homilies.[2] In the second paragraph he speaks of those with a strong distaste for reading and of his intention to make his audience listen to the topic he proposes to discuss.[3] Even though many of Chrysostom's sermons are inordinately long by today's standards, the very length of this work seems to preclude any possibility that it was orally delivered—especially to a hostile audience.

(3) Secondly, there is the question of the audience to which the work is addressed. All the printed editions entitle it: *Demonstration against Jews and Pagans that Christ is God,* but the whole trend of argument is against the pagans.

---

[1] A large portion of what is said in this introduction stems from my article "Chrysostom the Apologist: On the Divinity of Christ," which appeared in *Kyriakon, Festschrift Johannes Quasten,* vol. 1 (Münster 1970): 441–51. Rev. Patrick Granfield, the American editor of *Kyriakon,* graciously arranged with Verlag Aschendorf that permission to reuse the material be given to me. This permission was granted on condition that full acknowledgment be given to Verlag Aschendorf. This acknowledgment I hereby gratefully give.

[2] See below Chap. I.1. References to the *Demonstration* will be made by chapter (Roman numerals) and paragraph (Arabic numerals). Bracketed numbers in the translation refer to approximate sections in PG 48.

[3] Ibid. Chap. I.2.

(4) Rev. Norman McKendrick, S.J., prepared a stemma of the MSS of the treatise for his doctoral dissertation presented to Fordham University in 1966. His research showed that the MSS fall into two families in the text tradition, and that the first characteristic for distinguishing between the two groups is to be found in the different titles given to the treatise in each group. The one group names both Jews and pagans as addressees; the other (and older) omits any mention of the Jews. Both titles, however, point to the main purpose of the treatise: a proof of the divinity of Christ.[4]

(5) Neither group of MSS presents any series of arguments specifically aimed against the Jews; both families show an abrupt ending which strongly suggests that the treatise has come down to us in an incomplete state. In fact, in both groups, Chrysostom starts his argument by saying: "First, I shall do battle with the pagans."[5] Since all the printed editions include the Jews in the title, they must be primarily based on the group of MSS which names both Jews and pagans as addressees. These printed editions may well explain why the treatise is commonly known by the longer title: *Demonstratio contra Iudaeos et gentiles quod Christus sit deus.*

(6) How, then, can we explain the two different titles? There can be no sure answer, but several are possible. Perhaps, it was Chrysostom's original plan to engage two opponents; perhaps, too, he felt that his frequent use of Scripture and of prophecies fulfilled was argument enough against the Jews; perhaps, the incomplete state of the text and the abruptness with which it ends may be indicative of a lost segment or an unfulfilled intention. In any event, the text as we have it would be more aptly entitled *A Demonstration against the Pagans that Christ is God.*

(7) In Dom Baur's monumental *John Chrysostom and His*

---

[4] Although it is as yet unpublished, McKendrick's work is summarized in *Dissertation Abstracts* 27, number 8 (Ann Arbor 1967): 2512 A. The most important contribution which McKendrick makes is the new critical text of the *Demonstration* which he presents in his dissertation and on which, with his kind permission, I shall base my translation.

[5] See below Chap. I.4.

Time, a chapter is devoted to Chrysostom as an apologist.[6] Baur admits here that Chrysostom's basic contributions to apologetics are found in his *Demonstration Against the Jews and Pagans on the Divinity of Christ.*[7] But he does not discuss the treatise for two reasons: first, the remaining works of Chrysostom offer enough material for learning his apologetic view; second, there are doubts about the authenticity of the *Demonstration.*[8]

(8) One hesitates to argue with Dom Baur about his first reason because his treatment of Chrysostom's apologetic against heretics is more than adequate. As evidence for his second reason, however, Baur merely cites, in a footnote, Chapters I and XII–XIII of the *Demonstration.* But as one reads these and other chapters he is sure to find the unflagging eloquence which marks the treatise as a bona fide work of the Mouth of Gold. And in this he will not stand alone.[9]

(9) Of course, in the works of a man like Chrysostom, there is always some room for doubt about authenticity, because so many spurious works have been circulated in his name.[10] Perhaps, in the present *Demonstratio contra Iudaeos et gentiles quod Christus sit deus* we find more grounds for suspicion because it is not always clear whether it be sermon or treatise, because the style of the second half is, in places, excessively redundant, and because, despite its length, it is almost certainly incomplete and ends abruptly.[11] Furthermore, this demonstration of Christ's divinity breathes a quite different spirit

---

[6] C. Baur, *John Chrysostom and His Time,* vol. 1, *Antioch,* vol. 2, *Constantinople,* trans. M. Gonzaga (Westminster, Md. 1960–61) 1.337–54. Hereafter cited as Baur.

[7] Baur 1.337. The Greek text of the *Demonstration* is most readily available in PG 48.813–38.

[8] Baur, ibid.

[9] J. Quasten, in his *Patrology,* 3 vols. (Utrecht 1950–60) 3.467–68, admits its authenticity (hereinafter cited as Quasten). Bernard de Montfaucon, in his *Notice* (PG 48.811–12), never questions that Chrysostom wrote it (hereinafter cited as *Notice*). A. Williams in his *Adversus Judaeos* (Cambridge 1935) 136, positively affirms it as authentic (hereinafter cited as Williams).

[10] On the problem of spurious Chrysostomica both in printed works and in MSS see Quasten 3.470–73 with bibliographies on the subject.

[11] See *Notice* (PG 48.811–12); Quasten 3.468; Williams 135–36.

from Chrysostom's eight homilies *Adversus Iudaeos* and shows little of their anti-Semitic rancor.[12] The reason for this may be found in the incomplete condition of the treatise. He begins by addressing himself to the pagans and, throughout the work, he seems to have the pagans chiefly in mind despite his frequent references to the Jews and their sacred writings. Perhaps, if the work did not end so abruptly, if Chrysostom had kept his promise to speak against the Jews more fully and clearly, we might have had a polemic to match his *Adversus Iudaeos*. Or the eight homilies *Adversus Iudaeos* may be the promised polemic.[13]

(10) There is little, if anything, to be gained in arguing the authenticity of the *Demonstration*. It would be more profitable to accept it as bona fide and then pursue Baur's statement that this work contains Chrysostom's basic contributions to apologetics. A scrutiny of its methods and arguments may reveal these contributions and thus fill in a lacuna left by Baur in his treatment of Chrysostom as an apologist.

(11) The *Demonstration*, despite its shortcomings, should be ideal for this purpose. Since it does not attack such heretics as the Arian Anomoeans,[14] it will not address itself to the usual Christological or Trinitarian problems; since it professedly aims at proving the divinity of Christ to an audience of pa-

---

[12] On Chrysostom's *Adv. Iud.* see Williams 132–35; Quasten 3.452–53; M. Simon, "La polémique antijuive de S. Jean Chrysostome et le mouvement judaïsant d'Antioche," *Annuaire de l'Institut de philologie et d'histoire orientales et slaves* 4 (1936): 140–53. The text of the eight homilies is found in PG 48.843–942. P. Harkins has published a translation with commentary of these homilies in The Fathers of the Church series (FOTC 68), under the title of *St. John Chrysostom: Discourses against Judaizing Christians* (Washington 1979). R. Wilken, in his *John Chrysostom and the Jews* (Berkeley, Calif. 1983), gives us a most valuable study of the caustic rhetoric of the late fourth century (hereinafter cited as Wilken). See especially his chapter four on the rhetoric of abuse (95–127).

[13] Montfaucon, in his *Notice* (PG 48.811), thinks that the promise (made below XVII.7) is fulfilled in Chrysostom's *Adv. Iud.*, especially in homilies 4–8, which treat at length the abrogation of the Jewish worship. Cf. FOTC 68.1, li, and 72–241. See also n. 37 to this introduction.

[14] There are twelve homilies, in two series, *De incomprehensibili dei natura (On the Incomprehensible Nature of God)* against the Anomoeans (PG 48.701–812; translated by P. Harkins under the title of *St. John Chrysostom: On the Incomprehensible Nature of God*, FOTC 72 [Washington, D.C. 1984]). Quasten 3.451, states that only homilies of the first series (1–5), which were delivered

gans and Jews, it should show Chrysostom arguing on much
the same level as the disciples did in spreading the kerygma to
Jews and gentiles.[15]

(12) Shortly after a typical exordium Chrysostom says that,
first, he must do battle with the pagans;[16] in fact, the main
thrust of his argument is against them throughout the work.
He realizes that any pagan will scornfully reject any proof for
Christ's divinity if that proof starts out with Christ's miracles
and promises. He must find as a foundation for argument
something which even the pagan admits that Christ has done.
What is this?

(13) "The pagan must admit that from Christ came the
family of Christians. He must admit that Christ founded the
Churches everywhere throughout the world. From these facts
I will furnish proof of his power; I shall show that Christ is
God; I shall maintain that it is not the mark of a mere man to
bring under his sway so much land and sea in so short a time;
I shall make clear that it is not the mark of a mere human to

---

at Antioch, attack the Anomoeans; he says that the second series (6–12) was
given at Constantinople, but that these homilies are not directed against the
Anomoeans, who were the most radical Arian sect. It is true that homily 6 is
an interruption of his attack as Chrysostom praises St. Philogonius on his
feast day, speaks of the approaching celebration of Christ's birthday in the
flesh and the need to cleanse our consciences before receiving him in the
mysteries. But homilies 7–10 all stress the glory and power of the only begotten and reply to the objections of the Anomoeans of Antioch. Homily 11
clearly affirms that it is only the second sermon he delivered to his new
congregation in Constantinople. Both homilies 11 and 12 return to the
themes of the glory of the only begotten, Christ's divinity, and his equality
with the Father—all doctrines which the Anomoeans would deny. So it would
seem that there are two series divided by both time and place. The first series
(1–5 and 7–10) was delivered at Antioch about A.D. 386–87; the second (11–12)
belongs to Constantinople about 398. However, all but homily 6 clearly attack
the tenets of the Anomoean Arians. See FOTC 72.22–35.

[15] It must not be forgotten that the work is incomplete and is addressed
chiefly to the pagans, even though such frequent reference is made to the
Jews and their sacred writings. Chrysostom's apologetic against the Jews
might better be sought in the series Adv. Iud., although there he speaks chiefly
to Judaizing Christians and only incidentally to the Jews. Cf. FOTC 68.x;
xxxi–xlii.

[16] See below Chap. I.4. Paganism, always strong at Antioch, had enjoyed a
revival under Emperor Julian and was still strong in Chrysostom's day. See
G. Downey, Antioch in the Age of Theodosius the Great (Norman, Ok. 1962) 85–
102. See also Baur 1.330.

call men to lofty deeds, especially men who were preoccupied with such strange customs or, rather, men who were caught in the trap of such an evil way of life."[17]

(14) The historical facts give the start. The Church has spread over the world. Only a person of power could have done what Christ did. Only a person of divine power—no mere man— could have wrought such a change in man's evil ways. Only a person who is God could have gotten men to root out their ancestral ways, laws, and customs and plant another way in their place, the way which led them from an easygoing life to his own program of austerity. And when did Christ's success begin? At the hour of his shame, when the whole world waged war on him, when men jeered him and forced him to endure shameful death on the cross.

(15) His success continues, even in the face of current and past persecutions. It has spread from cities to deserts, villages, fields, islands, ship basins, and harbors. Now not only ordinary men but rulers and emperors serve him. These are facts, but they did not merely happen; they had been predicted long before.

(16) At this point Chrysostom does what at first sight seems a strange thing. He says: "I do not wish you to suspect that what I say had not been foretold. Therefore, I must bring forward as evidence the books of the Jews, who crucified him. I must go through the Scriptures, over which the Jews have kept such careful guard, and set before the eyes of those who are still unbelieving the predictions and testimonies about Christ which these books contain."[18]

(17) Strange as this may seem, it may have been more clever and forceful than we suspect. First, Chrysostom is going to take his arguments from Christ's archenemies, the Jews, who crucified him. The force of favorable testimony from one's foes is not small nor would it be lost on the pagans. Secondly, the pagans had great respect for any oracle, prophet, or seer, and we know that this respect extended itself to the sacred books of the Jews.[19] Anything which had been predicted and

---

[17] See below Chap. I.6.
[18] See below Chap. II.2; cf. also Chap. XI.5.
[19] In *Adv. Iud.* 1.6 (FOTC 68.21–22) Chrysostom tells how Ptolemy

then came to pass would be a forceful argument to the pagan mind.

(18) And here we can see the whole pattern of Chrysostom's apologetic: a fulfilled prediction is a proof of power; the fulfillment of the predictions concerning Christ gives proof of a power which can only be divine. In Chapters II–XI he takes the predictions of the prophets about Christ; in Chapters XII–XVII he takes, chiefly, two predictions of Christ himself, which are sometimes elaborated by reference to the Old Testament. All the predictions point to a power that is more than human; all the fulfillments prove that Christ was no mere man.

PREDICTIONS OF THE PROPHETS

(19) Once Chrysostom has established this pattern, he is on a favorite battlefield. Now he can use the Scriptures of the Jews to prove that many facts about Christ and his Church had been foretold. He begins by proving that it had been predicted that Christ, still remaining God, became man, moved among men, and is himself the lawgiver. Even before his coming in the flesh, he arranged and disposed all things by the Law he gave and by his providence and care.[20]

(20) Drawing his texts chiefly from Isaiah and the psalms, Chrysostom then shows that Christ's career from birth to death had been predicted. He would be born of a virgin; he would be of Jesse's tribe and the house of David; he would come quietly, as the Prince of Peace, to be born in Bethlehem at the predicted time, when Jewish princes were subject to Roman rule. He would come up from Egypt; he would cure the lame, make the blind to see, publish his glad tidings to the poor. His betrayal, passion, death on the cross, burial, descent

---

Philadelphus deposited the books of the Septuagint in the temple of Serapis, although there the point is that the presence of the holy books does not make the pagan temple a holy place.

[20] The text adduced (below Chap. II.2) is Bar 3.36–38, which Chrysostom attributes to Jeremiah, whose secretary Baruch had been. See Chap. II, n. 2.

into hell, and resurrection had all been foretold.[21] Such things could not have been predicted and then have come true in the case of any mere man.

(21) As proofs of Christ's divinity the passion and crucifixion would naturally be a stumbling block for any pagan. But if all this had been foretold and then came to pass, if, as predicted, he was handed over for the evils of the world, if the slaying of Christ was the ransom paid for man's sins, if by his bruises we are all healed, perhaps the pagan could see divinity in the Man of Sorrows who, like a lamb led to slaughter, was silent and opened not his mouth.

(22) Chrysostom continues to draw his predictions from the prophets as he shows that they had foretold the mission of the apostles and how they had conquered the world. They won their victory by the word the Lord had given them to preach. But that word had great power and was proved by signs and wonders.[22] It made Peter and Paul mightier than kings and, long after they had died, the Church they spread in Christ's name remains firm and indestructible and brings peace over the world. Not only the meek and mild but the savage Scythians, Thracians, Mauretanians, Indians, Sarmatians, and Persians serve him under one yoke and each one adores him from his own place. No longer must men go up to Jerusalem to offer worship to God.[23]

(23) As was predicted, the Jews rejected the faith because they, themselves, are rejected and a new covenant and ritual has supplanted theirs. But even this had its salutary side for the Jews because they are so stung by rivalry and jealousy that they have become better men. No longer do they sacrifice their children to pagan gods; no longer do they rush off to worship idols or a golden calf.[24]

(24) Furthermore, it was foretold that Christ would come

---

[21] See Chaps. II–IV. The texts are cited in their proper places in the translation.

[22] Chap. V.

[23] Chap. VI. Chrysostom was convinced there could be no true official worship for the Jews apart from the sacrifices and worship in the temple of Jerusalem. Cf., e.g., FOTC 68.109 n.; 138–39; 143–44.

[24] Chap. VII.

again in power and majesty to judge the living and the dead. On his first coming, it was predicted that he would be the prophet to whom all men must hearken or be destroyed. The Jews would not hearken, so they have been destroyed or exiled. The Jews rejected him and inflicted on him the ignominy of the cross. But this shameful death proved to be more glorious than a crown. Before his death, he had been betrayed, denied, and deserted. After his death, all is changed. Among every race and in every land we hear his name and find him worshipped. From this you may understand that the Crucified was no mere man. The cross had been a symbol of shame and a curse. Now no man shudders at it but all vie to have a representation of it. We see the cross everywhere in public places and in private homes. How is it that men are eager to have and wear this symbol of an accursed death? The reason must be the great power of him who was crucified.[25]

(25) Men had loathed the cross but now they love it; they encase relics of it in gold to be worn around their necks. This sign of death has destroyed death, cut the sinews of sin, and rescued the whole world from the calamity to which it had been condemned. The world was a desert void of virtue; the cross made it into a fruitful garden. The cross is the symbol of the new covenant with men by which Christ has taken away man's transgressions, no more remembers man's sins, and will, on Judgment Day, reward the just with his kingdom.[26]

(26) At this juncture Chrysostom crystallizes his pattern of argument. "Do you not see how precisely the prophets took up each point and predicted what was going to happen? How, then, can you have the boldness to refuse to believe, even though you have been given such proofs of his power, even though you hear the words which foretold it so long beforehand, even though you see that events did occur to match the predictions and that everything which the prophets foretold has been fulfilled to the last detail?"[27] Fulfilled predictions are a proof of power and demand our belief in Christ as

[25] Chaps. VII–IX.
[26] Chaps. X–XI.
[27] Chap. XI.4.

more than mere man. And the predictions have been preserved by his enemies.

CHRIST'S OWN PREDICTIONS

(27) Now Chrysostom is ready to turn to Christ's own predictions and to show that their fulfillment is proof of his divine power. Christ came down to earth to achieve salvation
both for men of his own day and for men of future ages. To
accomplish this he worked miracles and predicted things that
would come to pass long after. His miracles guaranteed to
men who heard him in his own day that his predictions of
what would happen long after were true. The fulfillment of
his predictions proved to men of future ages that the miracles
he worked in his own day were worthy of their belief.

(28) His predictions were of two kinds. Some are to be
fulfilled in the present life; others will come true after the
consummation of the world. But the first kind, when fulfilled,
confirms the second and gives abundant proof that the
prophecies about the world to come are also true. Miracles
and predictions together prove his divine power and guarantee that his kingdom, the kingdom of God, will surely come.

(29) Chrysostom takes two of Christ's predictions to prove
these points: (1) his prediction concerning the Church (Chapters XII–XV), and (2) his prediction concerning the temple
(Chapters XVI–XVII). He made his prediction about the
Church at a time when neither the name nor the reality of a
Church had occurred to anyone. He had only twelve followers, the synagogue was flourishing, the rest of the world was
sunk in godlessness, when he said: "Upon this rock I will
build my Church, and the gates of hell shall not prevail
against it."[28]

---

[28] Mt 16.18. See NAB note ad loc. Chrysostom omits the first part of the
verse: "And I say to you, you are Peter." Of course, when we consider his
purpose and audience, Chrysostom had no need to defend the primacy of
Peter, much less of Peter's See. He does seem to have upheld the primacy of
Peter but he never clearly upholds the primacy of Rome. See J. Chapman,
"St. John Chrysostom on St. Peter," *Dublin Review* 132 (1903): 1–27 and

(30) How miraculously this prediction has come true! Old altars, temples, idols, rites, and festivals are gone. They have disappeared like the smoke of unclean victims. New altars have been raised all over the world, even in the British Isles beyond the seas. Men's souls were like fields of thorns, but they have been cleansed and cleared to receive the seeds of godliness. All this surpasses greatness and provides a proof of his divine power.

(31) Even under ideal circumstances such a change in so many souls would have been a marvel. But the new way was narrow, straight, and steep; it had to oust long-standing habits and a love of pleasure and win men over to embrace a program of austerity. Yet it did win them over by the thousands through the help of eleven men who were unlettered, ignorant, and poor, who spoke a strange and foreign language.[29]

(32) And these apostles and their disciples faced persecution on every side, in every nation, in every city, in every home. Their teaching opposed imperial edicts and ancestral ways and customs. Even though their doctrine was difficult, they did spread the Church over the world because they did it through the power of him who commanded them to do it. He made the hard things easy. If there were not a divine power working in this, the Church would never have had a foreword, much less a first chapter. But just as God created the world by his divine word, so Christ created the Church by his divine word: "I will build my Church." And this is the power of the words of God. They create works beyond our expectation.

(33) The more the Church was persecuted, the more it grew in numbers and courage. Many died, were imprisoned, were exiled. But many more came forward, even rushed to meet their captors. When blood gushed from those who had embraced the faith, other disciples came in greater numbers and with deeper fervor and joy to take their place. The apostles did not build Christ's Church in stones but in men's souls.

M. Jugie, "Saint Jean Chrysostome et la primauté de Saint Pierre," *Echos d'Orient* 11 (1908): 5–15.

[29] Chap. XII.

They succeeded because they worked through the invincible power of him who said: "Upon this rock I will build my Church, and the gates of hell shall not prevail against it."[30]

(34) The pagan emperors persecuted the Church. Some were less harsh, others more severe. Even those who seemed to let the Church alone were still a constant threat because their officers would try to prove their loyalty to the pagan emperor by waging a war against the Church. These persecutions produced whole choirs of martyrs and left to the Church treasures that will never perish, columns that will always stand, towers that no foe can take by storm.

(35) The power of Christ's prediction was seen in the days of persecution, when the Church was small, when the seed of its teaching was newly planted. Even then nothing could overcome the Church. We see this power all the more now that the Church is spread over the world. Pagans there still are, but their altars and idols are gone. How did the Church overcome so many obstacles? How did it arrive at the glorious growth it enjoys today? Only through the divine and invincible power of Christ who foretold it and then brought it to accomplishment. And this is most reasonable. His words are not mere words; they are the words of God, and God's words create works.[31]

(36) Christ's prediction about the Church has stood and will stand firm and unshaken from the day it was spoken until the day when the world will end. Men of Chrysostom's day, men of an age before that, and men of still earlier times knew the power of that prediction. They saw the troubles, tumults, waves, and storms which came upon the Church; they also saw that the Church was not drowned, conquered, or consumed. They saw it flourish and prosper. So, too, men of future generations will see the power and truth of Christ's prediction right up to the consummation of the world.

(37) Such, too, is the second prediction, which Chrysostom now introduces. It, too, has been fulfilled and will continue in fulfillment till the end of time. And this proves the divine

---

[30] Chaps. XIII–XIV and Mt 16.18.
[31] Chap. XV.

power of him who made the prediction and then brought to pass what he had foretold. What is this second prediction? (38) One day he entered the temple area of the Jews. On every side its magnificent structures shone with gold and beauty. No expense had been spared on its workmanship or materials. His disciples marvelled at what they saw. But what did Christ say to them? "Do you see all these things? Amen I say to you, there will not be left here one stone upon another."[32] By these words he foretold the future destruction of the temple, the utter ruin, the desolation, the wreckage which now exists in Jerusalem. For all those glorious and splendid buildings are now destroyed.

(39) Such is the power of his word. By his first word he built up and exalted those who paid him worship; by his second word, he humiliated, destroyed, and uprooted those who had offended him. A single word from his lips destroyed the magnificence of the temple, obliterated it, and swept it from sight like so much dust. Where before only the high priest could enter once a year, now the harlot and whore-chaser can walk wherever they want. Only enough of the temple remains to point out where it once stood.

(40) No one has destroyed the Church which Christ built; no one has rebuilt the temple which Christ destroyed. Before Christ's prediction, the old temple had been destroyed and then, after the return from Babylon, it had been rebuilt. After Christ's prediction destroyed the new temple, even though the apostate Emperor Julian authorized its reconstruction and lent men and money to the project, no progress could be made because flames came leaping from the foundation stones and drove the workmen away.[33]

(41) Indeed, the Jews did try to rebuild it because the temple was essential to their ancestral worship. They had manpower, money, and material. You can see where they tried to dig a trench for the foundation, but they could not raise the structure because the power of Christ's prophecy was work-

---

[32] Mt 24.2.
[33] Chrysostom reports the same incident in *Adv. Iud.* 5. See FOTC 68.137–40. For the temple in Jerusalem and Christian apologetics see Wilken 128–60.

ing against them. Hundreds of years have now passed, but there is no thought, no expectation, no hope that anyone will ever see the temple again.[34]

(42) Without the temple there is no Jewish commonwealth or way of life; without it their sacrifices and the other religious rituals which the Law prescribed could not exist. Their own prophets made it clear that they could not sing their canticles, observe their fasts, celebrate their festivals, offer sacrifices, or even read their Law while they were exiles in Babylon and their temple in desolation. There was one proper place for such worship and that was the temple of Jerusalem.[35]

(43) After their captivity in Babylon, the Jews did rebuild their temple and restored the place where they were allowed to observe all these rituals according to the Law. But now the power of Christ, the power which founded the Church, has also destroyed their restored temple. And their prophets foretold this and showed that God would reject Judaism and introduce a new way of worship.[36] But Chrysostom will give a fuller and clearer explanation of this when he speaks against the Jews.[37]

(44) Chrysostom then returns to the pagans. He did not base his apologetic to them on signs and wonders, he did not speak of the dead who were brought back to life or of the lepers who were made clean. Yet the witnesses for these signs and wonders are the same evangelists who meticulously reported the shame and ignominy of Christ's passion and death. The pagans accept the evangelists as trustworthy wit-

---

[34] Chap. XVI.10.

[35] Chrysostom adduces as his proof for this Ps 136 (137).1–4; Dn 3.38; Am 4.5; Zec 7.5. The same texts are cited to the same purpose in *Adv. Iud.* Cf. FOTC 68.84–85; 179–80.

[36] Chrysostom adduces as his proof for this Am 5.1, 2; Zep 2.11 and 3.9; Mal 1.10, 11. He cites the same texts to the same purpose in *Adv. Iud.* Cf. FOTC 68.141–42.

[37] Chap. XVII.7. This last statement might mean that Chrysostom intended to speak against the Jews at greater length in the present *Demonstration*, and this would explain its abrupt ending. Williams would favor this explanation since he says that Chrysostom's promise to speak more fully is not fulfilled (cf. his *Adv. Iud.* 135–36). Montfaucon, in his *Notice* (PG 48.811), thinks that the promise is fulfilled in Chrysostom's homilies *Adv. Iud.*, espe-

nesses of the gloomy side. Why, then, do they regard them as imposters making idle and empty boasts for their Master's sake when they report his miracles?

(45) Since the pagans would scoff at the stories of miracles, Chrysostom had nothing to say about these signs and wonders. What did he do? "I took what you see today, what lies before your very eyes, what is clearer than sunlight, what has spread over the whole world and taken root in every land. I took a success which far surpasses any human power, a success which could only be the work of God, and I brought this forward as my proof."[38] The pagans cannot say that there are no churches throughout the world, they cannot say that the Church has not been persecuted, they cannot say that the followers of Christ have not prevailed and conquered their foes. To deny these facts would be the same as denying that the sun exists.

(46) They can also see the desolation of the Jewish temple. The pagan should reason this way with himself. "If Christ were not God, if he were not a mighty God, how could those who worship him have grown to such great numbers despite such suffering and persecution? And how could those who beat him and crucified him have been so humbled that they were driven from their whole commonwealth and way of life? Now they go about as vagabonds, wanderers, and exiles."[39]

(47) What Christ has built, no one can destroy. What Christ has destroyed, no one can rebuild. And no length of time has changed the status of either the Christians or the Jews.

(48) Such are the proofs we find for Christ's divinity in the *Demonstratio contra Iudaeos et gentiles*. The pattern of argument is that a fulfilled prediction is a proof of power; the fulfillment of the predictions concerning Christ is the proof of a power which can only be divine. This is true of the predictions made by the prophets about Christ; it is still more so of Christ's own predictions, because he not only foretold fu-

---

cially homilies 4–8, which treat at great length the abrogation of the Jewish worship. Cf. above n. 13 and FOTC 68.71–241.

[38] Chap. XVII.10.

[39] Chap. XVII.12.

ture events to his disciples but also brought them to pass by the power of his divine word.

(49) How does this pattern square with Baur's picture of Chrysostom's apologetic method? Before any attempt to answer this, I must point out that Baur rightly considers Chrysostom as an apologist against two sets of foes: the heretics and the unbelievers. We need not look for too many parallels between the *Demonstration* and Chrysostom's apologetic assaults against the heterodox and heretics. There the problems are quite different, and so, too, must be the method of attack. And, in the area of heterodoxy, Baur gives an adequate appraisal of Chrysostom's efforts as an apologist.[40]

(50) But there is a proper parallel between the *Demonstration* and Chrysostom's treatment of unbelievers. As Baur says, the unbelievers of Chrysostom's time were not atheists, with whom he apparently never had anything to do, but they were the pagans and Jews who rejected Christ and the Christians.[41] What is the method, as Baur sees it, by which Chrysostom brings the pagans and Jews from unbelief to belief?

(51) To answer this question, Baur cites Chrysostom's own words: "Only the miracles that Christ performed; because the miracles were not done for the believers but for the unbelievers."[42] Baur further says that Chrysostom takes the historical authenticity of the miracles of Christ as a matter of course, doubted by no one. The wonderful deeds that Christ did were a proof of his divine power and majesty. However, the miracle alone does not produce the faith; that belongs much more to the consent of the will and above all to the grace of God.[43]

(52) So, for Baur, the pattern seems to be: miracles prove divine power and dispose the will to receive the grace of faith. He then quotes several passages dealing with faith and its

[40] Baur 1.340–52.
[41] Ibid. 337.
[42] *In Iohannem homiliae* 35.2 (PG 59.201), trans. T. Goggin. *St. John Chrysostom: Commentary on St. John the Apostle and Evangelist,* FOTC 33 (New York 1957) 349.
[43] Baur 1.337–38.

superiority to reason. But all save one passage are from Chrysostom's commentaries on Scripture; the one exception is from his apologetic work *De incomprehensibili dei natura* (PG 48.710; FOTC 72.73), against the heterodox Anomoeans, who are not unbelievers in the same way that Jews and pagans are. In these passages Chrysostom can be called an apologist only in the sense that he is explicating the faith to those who already possess it, in whole or in part.

(53) In the *Demonstration* there is no such formal treatment of faith. Nor should we expect one in a treatise whose obvious thrust is to make pagans (and Jews) recognize Christ's power as more than human and, therefore, divine. The next step would be for them to accept him as God and, with God's grace, believe in him and serve him. To be sure, the *Demonstration* offers many motives to dispose their wills to receive the faith. But at this stage, Chrysostom's purpose is to have his audience grasp the arguments he presents. "Once they have these stored in their memories, they will reap great profit from them."[44] No doubt, this great profit would include conversion to Christ and faith in his divinity and promises. But this audience of unbelievers is not yet ready to make an act of faith in Christ as God because he worked miracles.

(54) It is true that just before he begins to discuss the power of Christ's own predictions, Chrysostom does say that Christ worked miracles and that they served to prove to men of his own day that his predictions about the distant future were true. And men of the future would see in the fulfillment of his predictions a proof that his miracles were worthy of belief. By this double proof, Christ gave a guarantee that all he had said about his kingdom was true. Chrysostom, however, does not press the point of miracles but returns immediately to the predictions as a proof of Christ's power.[45]

(55) At the very end, Chrysostom again says that he did not argue from Christ's miracles but points out how illogical the pagans are to accept the witness of the evangelists on Christ's

---

[44]Chap. I.3.
[45]Chap. XI.12–13.

shame and death but then to reject their testimony on his miracles. Since the pagans would scoff at miracles, Chrysostom has used as proof the surpassing success of the Church. "I took a success . . . which could only be the work of God and I brought this forward as my proof." And then he almost slyly adds: "What do you say now? Did he not bring the dead back to life?"[46]

(56) Chrysostom makes it quite clear that his pagan audience would not accept the historical authenticity of Christ's miracles as a matter of course, doubted by no one. He was keenly aware that any blatant use of miracles as a proof of Christ's divinity was foredoomed to failure. He uses his rhetoric as a mask of simplicity through which he subtly presents, first, the miracles of Christ's career as foretold by the prophets and, then, Christ's own predictions concerning the Church and the temple, which were so miraculously brought to pass because God's words create works. But he does not call them miracles.

(57) Since the main thrust of the treatise is against the pagans, one may well wonder why the Jews were named first in its traditional title, *Contra Judaeos et gentiles.* Admittedly, the *Demonstration* is incomplete and the promise to speak more fully and clearly against the Jews is not kept in the treatise as we have it. But the Jews are not ignored in the argument against the pagans. In fact they are mentioned specifically more than a score of times and much more often by implication.

(58) Perhaps we have here another mask of rhetorical simplicity by which Chrysostom subtly suggests that the same arguments are even more valid against the Jew than the gentile. After all, the prophecies are drawn from their own sacred books, and they would have heard the predictions against a far richer apperceptive mass than the pagans. If they would see that it was the will of their Lord God that the Old Covenant yield to the New, if they would recognize as fact that what Christ has destroyed no man can rebuild, if they

[46] Chap. XVII.10.

would realize that what Christ has built no man can destroy, they would then reject God's rejection of them and accept the salvation which comes to them through the divine power of Christ.

(59) We have spoken of the *Demonstration* as a treatise. It is true that at the outset Chrysostom speaks of getting those who have a strong distaste for reading to listen with full attention. Still its very length militates against considering it as a homily delivered in its entirety at one time. Furthermore, despite its length, it can scarcely be considered a complete whole because it ends so abruptly. And it is in this mutilated condition that the work is found in all the printed editions and in the MSS.

(60) It bears some similarity in its redundancy and excessively rhetorical style to Chrysostom's *De s. Babyla contra Julianum et gentiles* (ca. A.D. 376–79),[47] an encomium on the triumph of Christianity and the downfall of paganism. Montfaucon believes that both works represent rough drafts which were never properly revised.[48]

(61) The date of the *Demonstration* is far from certain. Williams places it at a time when Chrysostom had not yet found for himself an assured place in the Church at Antioch, probably at the beginning of his diaconate (A.D. 381) if, indeed, it had not been composed still earlier for the benefit of his fellow monks.[49] Bardenhewer places it somewhere about the year 387,[50] the year following Chrysostom's ordination to the priesthood.

(62) Montfaucon says it belongs to a time prior to September 387 because, in the *Demonstration,* Chrysostom promises to explain at greater length the abrogation of the Jewish cult.[51] And Montfaucon sees this promise as fulfilled in the homilies *Adversus Iudaeos,* especially Homilies 4–8, which were deliv-

---

[47] PG 50.533–72. M. Schatkin's translation of this treatise constitutes the first portion of this volume.
[48] *Notice* (PG 48.812).
[49] Williams 136.
[50] O. Bardenhewer, *Patrology,* trans. T. Shahan (St. Louis 1908) 333.
[51] Chap. XVII.7.

ered, according to Montfaucon, beginning in September 387.[52] But Williams maintains that the promise is not kept and sees this as evidence that the *Demonstration* is incomplete.[53]

(63) There are some other indications in the text of the *Demonstration*, which set limits before or after which it could not have been written. In Chapter IX,[54] Chrysostom speaks of the honors shown to the tombs of the apostles Andrew, Luke, and Timothy in the Church of the Holy Apostles at Constantinople. Montfaucon seems to be correct when he says that Chrysostom, who nowhere else mentions Constantinople in the *Demonstration*, here speaks as a nonresident. He, therefore, assigns this work to Chrysostom's period at Antioch and before he became Patriarch of Constantinople in 398.[55]

(64) In Chapter XVI,[56] Chrysostom says that four hundred years have passed since the temple was destroyed (by Titus in the year A.D. 70). This obviously erroneous statement would date the *Demonstration* as late as 470, some sixty-three years after Chrysostom's death in A.D. 407. Again, in the same context, Chrysostom speaks of Julian the Apostate as a contemporary;[57] this could place the *Demonstration* prior to or shortly after Julian's death in 363. The fact is that Chrysostom often uses extremely round figures for dating.[58]

(65) Both Williams and Montfaucon seem to have missed a small piece of internal evidence. In Chapter I Chrysostom says: "And the unexpected thing is that this message flourished not only here but also among the Persians, who even today are still waging war against him. For among the Persians, at this very hour, there are multitudes of martyrs."[59] The reign of terror to which Chrysostom is possibly here alluding lasted down to the death of King Sapor II in 379.[60]

[52] *Notice* (PG 48.811). See introduction to FOTC 68.lvii–lix.
[53] Williams 135–36. See Introduction to FOTC 68.l–li.
[54] See below Chap. IX.6 and n. ad loc. Cf. *Notice* (PG 48.811–12).
[55] Cf. *Notice*, ibid.
[56] See below Chap. XVI.10.
[57] See below Chap. XVI.9 and nn.
[58] See R. Carter, "The Chronology of St. John Chrysostom's Early Life" in *Traditio* 18 (1962): 360 (hereinafter cited as Carter).
[59] See below Chap I.9 and nn.
[60] See L. Duchesne, *The Early History of the Christian Church*, vol. 3, trans. C. Jenkins (New York 1924) 378–84.

From this internal evidence it would seem that the *Demonstration* belongs somewhere between 363 (or 379) and 397. The date of Julian's death (363) is highly improbable because Chrysostom was not baptized until 368.

(66) He became a lector in 371 but took up the monastic life the following year. Ill health forced him to return to Antioch in 378, where he resumed his service as lector.[61] This may lend some weight to a bit of external evidence found in Socrates' *Historia Ecclesiastica*. Socrates states that Chrysostom, as a lector, had already composed the "Logos" against the Jews.[62] By this "Logos" he probably means the *Demonstration against Jews and Pagans that Christ is God*,[63] and this would not contradict the date of 379.

(67) But Baur considers that the *Demonstration* marks a "bridge between the moral-ascetic tracts and the theological-homiletic writings," which would seem to date it during Chrysostom's diaconate (380/81–385/86).[64] Puech also places the *Demonstration* among the treatises and before Chrysostom's priesthood.[65]

(68) An interesting theory is advanced by Q. Cataudella,[66] who dates the *Demonstration* in the Antioch period and then suggests that it might mark the occasion of the twentieth anniversary of the burning of Apollo's temple in suburban Daphne. Julian the Apostate had visited Antioch in July 362 and wished to consult Apollo's oracle. He was told that this was impossible; the god was silent because of the presence of "bodies." This was clearly a reference to the relics of St. Babylas, and Julian had them removed. A large crowd of singing Christians escorted the relics back to Antioch.[67]

---

[61] The dates are those suggested as most probable by Carter, 364.

[62] Socrates, *H.E.* 8.22 (PG 67.667).

[63] Cf. Baur 1.99.

[64] Ibid. 173. See also Marcellinus Comes, who states in his *Chronicon ad Annum 398* (PL 51.921) that during the five years of his diaconate Chrysostom produced "many godly books."

[65] A. Puech, *Histoire de la littérature grecque chrétienne*, vol. 3 (Paris 1930) 479.

[66] "Giovanni Crisostomo" in *Enciclopedia Cattolica* 6 (Rome 1951): 539.

[67] See G. Downey, *A History of Antioch in Syria* (Princeton 1961) 387 (hereinafter referred to as Downey, *History of Antioch*) and I. Benzinger in RE 4.2136–38.

(69) On October 22, the temple caught fire and the huge statue of Apollo, which reached to the temple's roof, was burned. Although the Christians maintained that the temple had been struck by lightning, they were accused of setting it on fire in retaliation for the removal of the relics of St. Babylas. A persecution of the Christians immediately followed, their Great Church was closed, and the sacred vessels were confiscated.[68]

(70) Such events were likely to be commemorated for years afterward. If Cataudella's hypothesis regarding the twentieth anniversary is true, the Demonstration would belong to the year 382. In any event, that date, if not correct, cannot be far wrong.

(71) The Greek text found in Migne (PG 48.813–38) is by far the most readily available. Although this text was collated with Codex Colbertinus 3055, only twice are the readings of this MS mentioned in footnotes, and in both places the variants, which are insignificant, are rejected. In fact, the Migne text is no more than a reprint of Bernard de Montfaucon's second edition, which had been reedited by Theobald Fix (Paris 1834–39). Fix, however, seems only to have collated the first Montfaucon edition (Paris 1718–38) with that of Henry Savile (Eton 1613), and the text of Fix shows very few and insignifiant differences from Montfaucon's earlier edition.[69]

(72) Hence, the preparation in 1966 of a truly critical edition of the Demonstration by Rev. Norman G. McKendrick, S.J., is more than welcome.[70] This edition shows extreme care, a wide use of the MS materials, and was done under the exacting mentorship of my former professor, the late Rev. Rudolph Arbesmann, O.S.A., to whom the present volume is dedicated. Unfortunately the McKendrick text has not been published, but, fortunately for me, Fr. McKendrick has gener-

[68] Downey, ibid. 388.
[69] C. Baur discusses Montfaucon's text in his S. Jean Chrysostome et ses oeuvres dans l'histoire littéraire (Paris 1907) 132–33 (hereinafter cited as Baur, S. Jean Chrysostome). He also discusses Montfaucon's second edition edited by T. Fix (123), Migne's reissue of this same text (132), and Savile's Eton edition (106).
[70] See above, introduction, paragraph 4 and n.

ously given me his permission to use it as the basis for my translation. I hereby express to Fr. McKendrick my deepest gratitude for his kindness. It enables me to offer a translation which stems from a text which reflects the most modern methods of textual criticism and must supersede the work of the giant editors of the seventeenth and eighteenth centuries.

(73) Montfaucon had prepared a Latin translation to go with his edition of the Greek text of the *Demonstration;* this has been reprinted by Migne. In some places one finds in this translation slight additions which are attributed to some unknown earlier translator but must have been missing from any of the Greek MSS used by Montfaucon and Savile. Abbé J. Bareille has reprinted the second Montfaucon edition and has added his own French translation in parallel columns to the Greek text. The *Demonstration* appears in the second volume of this nineteen volume edition (Paris 1865–73).[71] My own translation is the first English version of the *Demonstration* to be published.

(74) I have translated all biblical texts directly from the Greek. Of course, for the Old Testament (OT), Chrysostom used some version of the Septuagint (LXX), and I have found it useful to compare his citations with the readings given in A. Rahlfs's sixth edition.[72] I have also compared the LXX readings of Chrysostom with renderings of OT texts as translated in the *New American Bible* and the *Jerusalem Bible*.[73] Where differences in the readings have been significant, these variations have been pointed out in the footnotes. Where possible and compatible, translations of NT texts are taken from NAB.

(75) I have availed myself of some devices I used in FOTC 68, *St. John Chrysostom: Discourses against Judaizing Christians (Adversus Judaeos)*. I have numbered the paragraphs in each

---

[71] Baur, *S. Jean Chrysostome,* 132–33, discusses this edition. In *Jews and Christians in Antioch* by W. Meeks and R. Wilken (Missoula, Mont. 1978) 84, Wilken points out that Bareille's French version was made not from the Greek text but from the Latin translations of Hoeschel, Fronton du Duc, and Erasmus.

[72] *Septuaginta,* 2 vols. (Stuttgart 1935).

[73] Members of the Catholic Biblical Association, *The New American Bible* (New York 1970) and A. Jones, ed., *The Jerusalem Bible* (New York 1966).

chapter of the translation (as well as in the introduction) to make cross-references more easy. The chapter numbers are taken from Migne's text and are given in Roman numerals. The paragraph numbers (in Arabic numerals) are my own. Wherever "cf." precedes a Scriptural citation in my notes, it means either that the reader is referred to the text for confirmation of Chrysostom's argument, or that Chrysostom has quoted the text in an abridged form, or that his quotation varies from Rahlfs's LXX.

(76) Biblical proper names generally appear in the form used in NAB, from which I have also drawn the abbreviations for the books of Scripture. Where a given book of the Bible is differently designated in NAB and in the LXX (Vulgate), both forms are given, that from NAB first. Thus I give, e.g., 2 Sm (2 Kgs), Sir (Ecclus), Rv (Apoc). In the enumeration of the psalms (or of verses thereof), however, the Septuagint number is given first, e.g., Ps 138 (139). 14.

(77) As for commentaries on the Bible, I have found two which are both succinct, scholarly, and readily available. These are *A Catholic Commentary on Holy Scripture* (CCHS) edited by B. Orchard *et al.* (London 1953) and *The Jerome Biblical Commentary* (JBC) edited by R. Brown, J. Fitzmyer, and R. Murphy (Englewood Cliffs, N.J. 1968). I have made extensive use of both in my notes. My notes have also profited much from J. McKenzie, *Dictionary of the Bible* (Milwaukee 1965).

A DEMONSTRATION AGAINST THE PAGANS THAT CHRIST IS GOD

FROM THE SAYINGS CONCERNING HIM IN MANY PLACES IN THE PROPHETS[1]

CHAPTER I

Argument Against the Pagans

HERE ARE FEW PEOPLE [813] who would find it an easy thing to sustain their interest throughout a lengthy argument. Some men are naturally indifferent or have devoted themselves and all their energy to worldly affairs; others lack education and have but little knowledge of letters. This is why I judged that I would have to do away with your hesitation and to cut down on the exertion that a lengthy discourse would demand of you.

(2) In this way I expect to achieve two results. If I keep my remarks brief, I hope to make the lazy and indifferent ones less lazy and indifferent. If I keep my argument simple, I hope to win over those who have a strong distaste for reading and to get them to listen with full attention to the topic I propose to discuss. I shall not present an explanation carefully embellished with words and phrases.[2] I shall speak in such a way that the house servant, the lady's maid, the widow, the peddler, the sailor, and the farmer will find my arguments simple and easy to understand.

---

[1] These words are added to the title in PG 48.813. Following McKendrick's text, I have omitted "Jews" from the title.

[2] The whole exordium shows Chrysostom's familiarity with the classical rhetoric. In this sentence we have an echo of Plato's *Apology of Socrates* (17 b). Notice that the words "distaste for reading" and "listen with full attention" leave it unclear whether the treatise was written to be read or spoken. See introduction, paragraphs 2 and 59.

(3) I shall strive in every way to present my instruction in a few words and to keep it as short as I can in an effort to rouse up both kinds of listless listeners to a desire to hear my words. If I can succeed in this, they will grasp easily and without effort the arguments I present. Once they have stored these in their memories, they will reap profit from them.

(4) First, I shall do battle with the pagans.[3] Suppose a pagan should say: "Where is your proof that Christ is God?" I must first lay this proof as a foundation since everything follows from it. But I shall not draw my demonstration from heaven or any such divine source. For if I say that God created heaven, earth and sea, no pagan will stand for this as proof nor will he believe me; if I say that Christ raised the dead, cured the blind, and drove out demons, no pagan will accept that either; if I say that he promised a kingdom and ineffable blessings,[4] if I talk about the resurrection, the pagan will not only reject my arguments but he will laugh at them as well.

(5) How shall I persuade him, especially if he is ignorant and ill-informed? What source of proof can I use other than one on which we both together agree, one which is undeniable and admits no doubt? If I base my argument on the fact that he created heaven and the other things of which I spoke, the pagan would not find it easy to believe me. What is there which even the pagan admits that Christ has done and which not even he would deny?[5]

(6) The pagan must admit that from Christ came the family of Christians. He must admit that Christ founded the Churches everywhere throughout the world. From these facts

---

[3] As noted in the introduction (paragraphs 3–6; 57), the main thrust of the entire treatise is against the pagans. It is true that Chapters XVI–XVII deal with Christ's prediction of the temple and the rejection of the Jews, but even there one feels the same pattern of argument: a fulfilled prediction is a proof of power. Of course that prediction was fulfilled against the Jews and may have been intended as proof to the Jews of Christ's power. See Wilken 128–60, esp. 153–58; FOTC 68.99–111.

[4] Ineffable blessings often mean blessings which should be kept secret from the uninitiated, e.g., the mysteries of the eucharist. Here, however, the context clearly points to the blessings of the heavenly kingdom.

[5] Chrysostom must start his argument on some common ground or it will be fruitless. The argument will be the miraculous spread of the Church and the changes it wrought in men by turning them from pagan practices.

I shall furnish proof of Christ's power; I shall show that Christ is God; [814] I shall maintain that it is not the mark of a mere man to bring under his sway so much land and sea in so short a time; I shall make clear that it is not the mark of a mere human to call men to such lofty deeds, especially men who were preoccupied with such strange customs or, rather, men who were caught in the trap of such an evil way of life.

(7) And still Christ had the power to set the human race free from all these evils—not only the Romans, but the Persians, and simply every race of barbarians. And he succeeded in doing this with no force of arms, nor expenditure of money, nor by starting wars of conquest, nor by inflaming men to battle. He had only eleven men to start with, men who were undistinguished, without learning, ill-informed, destitute, poorly clad, without weapons, or sandals, men who had but a single tunic to wear.[6]

(8) Why do I say that he succeeded in doing this? He was able to persuade so many nations of men to pursue the true doctrine,[7] not only in what concerns the present life but also the life hereafter. He succeeded in winning over these men to drag down their ancestral laws, to tear out their ancient customs, long and deeply rooted as they were, and to plant in their place other ways, which led them from the easygoing life to his own program of austerity. And he succeeded in doing this when the whole world was waging war against him, when they jeered at him and forced him to endure the most shameful death of the cross.

(9) The pagans will not deny that the Jews crucified him and subjected him to countless tortures; they will not deny that he still preaches his message every day. And this message flourishes not only here but also among the Persians,[8] who

---

[6] Cf. Mt 10.10; Mk 6.8; Lk 9.3, 10.4.

[7] The Greek word is *philosophia* and refers basically to the love and pursuit of wisdom. In the Christian context, wisdom is the true doctrine, the Christian way of life, and so I have translated it here. See H. Graef, *St. Gregory of Nyssa*, Ancient Christian Writers (hereinafter referred to as ACW), vol. 18 (Westminster, Md. 1954) 190, n. 93.

[8] Eusebius in his *Vita Constantini* 4.13 reports that Constantine wrote in 333 to the Persian King Sapor II, commending to him the Persian Christians who were of considerable numbers in the principal districts. But the Gospel came

even today are still waging war against him. For among the Persians, at this very hour, there are multitudes of martyrs.[9] Men who were more savage than wolves hear his message, become more gentle than sheep, and accept the true doctrine on immortality, the resurrection, and the ineffable blessings of the mysteries.[10]

into collision with the official Persian religion, Mandaeism. Christianity and nationalism failed to mix, hostilities turned into a reign of terror which lasted down to Sapor's death in 379. At least some 16,000 Christians perished in the persecutions. See L. Duchesne, *The Early History of the Christian Church*, vol. 3, tr. C. Jenkins (New York 1924) 378–84.

[9] If Sapor's death in 379 brought an end to the persecutions and if this treatise was composed in 378, Chrysostom's statement may be literally true.

[10] As above (n.4) the blessings are ineffable, but here the reference would seem to be to the eucharist.

CHAPTER II

It Was Foretold that Christ Would Be Both God and Man

(1) These successes are not confined to the cities. They have spread to the desert, the villages, the fields, the islands, the ship basins, and harbors. Not only simple citizens and petty rulers but even those who wear the imperial crown have shown great faith and served as subjects to him who was crucified.[1] I shall now try to prove that all this did not simply happen but that it had been predicted long beforehand.

(2) [815] I do not wish you to suspect that what I say had not been foretold. Therefore, I must bring forward as evidence the books of the Jews, who crucified him. I must go through the Scriptures, over which the Jews have kept such careful guard, and set before the eyes of those who are still unbelieving the predictions and testimonies about Christ these books contain. Jeremiah was the first to say that God would become man and still stay God. "This is our God; no other will be compared to him. He has discovered the whole way of understanding, and has given it to Jacob, his servant, and to Israel, his well-beloved. Since then he has appeared on earth and moved among men."[2]

---

[1] The reference would not be to all Constantine's successors but to such Christian emperors as Valentinian I and Theodosius I. Certainly Chrysostom would not have included Julian, the Apostate or the Arian Valens.

[2] Actually the text is not from Jeremiah but from his secretary, Baruch. Cf. Bar 3.36–38. A greater difficulty arises from the way Chrysostom uses the text, understanding "he" (i.e., God) as the subject of the verbs "has appeared" and "moved" whereas both NAB and JB give "she" (i.e., "understanding" or "knowledge") as subject of the verbs. Since the Greek text expresses no subject, Chrysostom's use of "he" in v. 38 is grammatically correct. He is also correct in pointing out that it is God who possesses understanding (or wisdom) and has communicated it to the Israelites in the Mosaic Law. This makes the meaning of the whole section clearer. The Law was given to Israel out of God's love. It could not be acquired by human means. But Israel transgressed the Law and, as a punishment, the Jews were given up into the

(3) Do you see how, in a few words, the prophet made it altogether clear that Christ, still remaining God, became man, that he moved among men, and that he is, himself, the Lawgiver of the Old Testament? For the prophet said: "He has discovered the whole way of understanding and has given it to Jacob, his servant, and to Israel, his well-beloved." For here the prophet shows that, before his coming in the flesh, he arranged and disposed all things, that he did all things by giving the Law, by exercising his providence, and by granting to men the blessings of his care.

(4) Listen again to another prophet and how he said not only that Christ would become man but also that he would be born of a virgin. "Behold the virgin shall be with child and bear a son, and they shall call his name Immanuel."[3] The name Immanuel is interpreted as meaning "with us is God." Then to show that this child, on his appearance, would not be

---

hands of their enemies. Even though both Greek and Latin Fathers have applied this verse to the Incarnation, the context requires "Wisdom" as subject of the two verbs. The personification of Wisdom and the idea of her dwelling among men occur also in Sir (Ecclus) 24 (see NAB n. ad loc.). But Bar 3.38 may refer in a fuller sense, as does Chrysostom, to the Messiah through whom revelation has been brought to perfection. See P. Saydon in *A Catholic Commentary on Holy Scripture*, ed. B. Orchard (London 1953) 598 (hereinafter referred to as CCHS under the contributor's name and page). Chrysostom subsequently again cites v. 38 (see below VIII.6) but there attributes it properly to Baruch. See J. McKenzie, *Dictionary of the Bible* (Milwaukee 1965) 81–82, who points out that the book is not found in the Hebrew Bible nor in the Protestant canon. McKenzie will hereinafter be referred to as DB.

[3] Is 7.14. Chrysostom, and the translators who produced the LXX, may be assumed to have been familiar with the meaning and usage of *parthenos* and its cognates. As early as the works of Homer, Hesiod and Pindar, the noun and its cognate adjectives refer to an unwed maiden or to something that belongs to such a person. More to the point, Hesiod (*Works and Days* 519) uses *parthenos* to designate a "tender maiden . . . unlearned as yet in the works of golden Aphrodite." Even more significantly, Plato (*Cratylus* 406 b) in speaking about Artemis refers to her *parthenia* ("virginity") and surmises that her very name means one who hates sexual intercourse of man and woman. Following such tradition, Chrysostom could readily see in this passage a prophecy referring to Christ's virgin birth. See Mt 1.22–23. For a different view based on the meaning of the Hebrew word—perhaps unfamiliar to Chrysostom— see F. Moriarty in R. Brown, J. Fitzmyer, R. Murphy (eds.), *The Jerome Biblical Commentary* (Englewood Cliffs, N.J. 1968) 16:18, hereinafter referred to as JBC; E. Power, CCHS 546–47; J. McKenzie, DB 234–35.

a mere phantom of a man[4] but truly a human being, the prophet went on to say: ["He shall eat butter and honey,"[5] because it was usual for children to be fed these foods shortly after their birth. To make it clear the child was no mere human, the prophet then went on to say:][6] "For before the child learns good or evil, he will not heed the evil so that he may choose the good."[7]

(5) We learn, too, that Christ is not only a man and born of a virgin, but also that he is of the house of David. Again listen to how Isaiah predicted this long beforehand, even though his prediction was couched in figurative and metaphorical terms: "But a rod shall come forth from the root of Jesse and from his root a flower shall arise. The spirit of the Lord shall rest upon him, a spirit of wisdom and understanding, a spirit of counsel and of strength, a spirit of knowledge and piety, a spirit of fear of the Lord shall fill him."[8] For this man Jesse

[4] Perhaps a reference to Docetism, a form of Gnosticism according to which Christ was only apparently endowed with human nature, and salvation was not to be obtained through his merits but through the *gnōsis* which was manifested in him. See A. Humbert, "Docetism" in *New Catholic Encyclopedia* (hereinafter referred to as NCE) (New York 1967) 4.934–35.

[5] Is 7.15. The NAB note ad loc. takes these words as referring to the restricted diet of those who remained after devastation changed the once fertile fields of Judah into grazing land. Cf. Moriarty, JBC 16:18. Power (CCHS 547) alludes to a custom whereby, for the purpose of conferring sound judgment, a mixture of butter and honey was rubbed on the soft palate of a new-born child. Chrysostom may be referring to some such custom. Certainly, if Immanuel receives from God at his birth the gift of sound judgment, he will rule justly in the messianic tradition (cf. Ps 71[72].1; Is 9.7; 16.5; 28.17; Jer 23.5) if he be not the Messiah himself.

[6] The words between brackets are not read in the Greek printed text as we have it in PG 48. However, they do follow the sequence because they give v. 15 between the citation of Is 7.14 and 16. The Old Latin translation, which Montfaucon rejected in favor of his own version, certainly read the words, and Montfaucon retains them in his own Latin translation. They are also read in two MSS basic to McKendrick's text.

[7] The LXX for Is 7.15–16 reads: "He eats butter and honey: before he learns to choose wicked things, he will choose the good. For before the child learns good or evil, he will not heed the evil so that he will choose the good." Montfaucon's reading in PG 48 ("Before the child learns to call his father good or evil, he will not heed, etc.") is certainly corrupt and is not found in Rahlfs's LXX.

[8] Cf. Is 11.1–3. Jesse, father of David, is the root from which the Davidic dynasty did spring. Both rod and flower are the Messiah, scion of the de-

was the father of David. And it is clear from this that David came from Jesse's tribe.[9]

(6) So Isaiah predicted that he who was to come will come not only from the tribe but even from the house of Jesse when he said: "A rod will come forth from Jesse's root."[10] For the prophet was not simply speaking of the rod but of Christ and his kingdom. The words which follow make it clear that Isaiah did not say this about the rod, for when Isaiah had said: "A rod shall come forth," he went on to add: "And there shall rest upon him a spirit of wisdom and understanding."[11]

(7) No man, even if he is extremely senseless, will say that the grace of the Spirit came down on a rod of wood. It is quite obvious that the grace of the Spirit came down on that spotless temple of the Spirit.[12] This is why Isaiah did not say: "It will come," but: "It will come to rest," because after the Spirit came, he did not depart but remained. This is what John the evangelist made clear when he quoted the words of the Baptist: "I saw the Spirit descend like a dove from the sky and it came to rest on him."[13]

(8) And the Gospels did not remain silent about the senti-

---

throned house of David, destined to bloom after the exile in Babylon. Notice that v. 2 gives the traditional names of the gifts of the Holy Spirit.

[9] The word tribe is strange here. Perhaps all Chrysostom means is that David belonged to the same tribe to which Jesse belonged. It is also true that the Hebrew words for "staff" and "rod" can refer to the tribe or tribal standard. See McKenzie, DB 898.

[10] Is 11.1. See NAB n. ad loc.

[11] Ibid. 2. This implies that God is operative as author of the gifts, whose permanence is expressed by "rest upon". The distinction between wisdom and understanding is not quite clear, but there may be some scriptural grounds for the explanation of wisdom as knowledge of things in their relation to God, their author and end, while understanding is knowledge of things in themselves and in their mutual relationships. Isaiah may here have meant only the kingly gifts of a "wise and understanding heart" such as that bestowed by God on Solomon (1 Kgs [3 Kgs] 3.12).

[12] The spotless temple of the Spirit is, of course, Christ, who shall have indwelling and operating in him the gifts of the Spirit mentioned in Is 11.2. See preceding note.

[13] Jn 1.32. This reference, which recalls the descent of the Holy Spirit on our Lord at his baptism, is quite apposite since we, too, at our baptism, become temples of the Spirit and receive his gifts. See P. Harkins, *St. John Chrysostom: Baptismal Instructions*, in ACW 31 (Westminster, Md. 1963) 57, 296–97 n. 67. See also B. Vawter, JBC 63:53.

ments which the Jews showed after the child had been born. Matthew said: "When Herod heard this, he was troubled, and so was all Jerusalem with him."[14] Listen to how Isaiah predicted this long beforehand when he said: "They shall be willing to do so if they were burnt in fire. For a child is born to us, and a son is given to us: and his name shall be called Messenger of Great [816] Counsel, Wonderful Counsellor, God the Strong, the Mighty One, the Prince of Peace, Father of the world to come."[15]

(9) No one could say this of a mere man, as is obvious even to those who are very eager to show how stubborn they can be. No man from the beginning of time has been called God the Mighty nor Father of the world to come nor the Prince of Peace. For Isaiah said: "There is no end of his peace."[16] And what did happen makes it clear that this peace has spread over the whole earth and sea, over the world where men dwell and where no man lives, over mountains, woodlands, and hills, starting from that day on which he was going to leave his disciples and said to them: "My peace I give to you; not as the world gives do I give to you."[17]

(10) Why did Christ speak in this way? Because the peace which comes from man is easily destroyed and subject to many changes. But Christ's peace is strong, unshaken, firm, fixed, steadfast, immune to death, and unending. No matter

[14] Cf. Mt 2.3.
[15] Cf., Is 9.4, 5, 6. Vv. 1–6 speak of the heir of David, the Messiah, who will bring light after darkness to Galilee, which was the first part of Palestine to suffer deportation and become an Assyrian province in 734 B.C. But here, in later days, a light shall shine, joy shall abound, oppression shall cease, for the Messiah shall come to rule in peace with justice and judgment an eternal kingdom. Chrysostom omits from v. 4: "For with a renewal of friendship they shall make compensation for every robe collected by deceit, and for every garment;" he then continues with the rest of v. 4. In v. 5 he omits: "whose government is on his own shoulder" after "a son is given to us." What follows "Messenger of Great Counsel" is not found in all MSS of the LXX, and Rahlfs omits it from his LXX text but includes it in his critical apparatus. The names given to the Messiah are difficult. For a discussion of them see Power, CCHS 549.
[11] Is 9.7. This text together with the name "Prince of Peace" implies a reign of peace and prosperity. It also shows the source from which that peace and prosperity must be sought.
[17] Jn 14.27.

how many wars assail it, no matter how many plots rise against it every passing day, his peace is always the same. And it was his word, which accomplishes all things, that accomplished this along with his other blessings.

CHAPTER III

The Prophets Foretold the Manner of His Coming

(1) The prophets foretold not only that he would become man but also they predicted the manner of his coming. He was not going to come in the midst of thunder, lightning, earthquake, or tumult from the heavens. He was not going to stir up any consternation. His birth struck no man with fear, for he was born with no one to witness it, without tumult or confusion, in the house of a carpenter, in an ordinary and undistinguished home.[1] And the prophet David did not remain silent on the manner of his birth when he said: "He shall come down like rain upon the fleece."[2] By this David showed how peaceful and quiet his coming would be.

(2) Not only did David say this, but another prophet revealed how mild and reasonable he would be in his dealings with all men. See how Isaiah spoke of this. Christ was insulted, spat upon, reviled, outraged, scourged, and finally nailed to a cross. Yet he took no vengeance against those who had done these things but he endured courageously and mildly all the dishonors and plots, all the madness and untimely anger, all the assaults of that mob. Isaiah revealed all this when he said: "A bruised reed he shall not break, and smoking flax he shall not quench, until he brings judgment to victory, and in him the nations will put their hope."[3]

[1] Of course Chrysostom does not mean that Christ was born at Nazareth (see below n. 4) but into the family of Joseph, the poor Nazarene carpenter.

[2] Ps 71(72).6 (LXX) and the NAB n. to Ps 72. The whole psalm is messianic. Some moderns render "upon the mown grass" but T. Bird (CCHS 461) thinks "upon the fleece" is the true meaning. There may be a reference to Jgs 6.37–40 and Gideon's fleece. In any event the Messiah's coming was to be mysterious, peaceful, and quiet. See Hos 6.3; Is 55.10–11.

[3] Cf. Is 42.3–4 (LXX) which Chrysostom quotes as in Mt 12.20–21. Vv. 1–4 of Is 42 present the servant of Yahweh and his mission. The servant is here represented not as king and conqueror but as worker and sufferer. God has endowed his servant with his Spirit and made him instructor of the gentiles. His mission will be characterized by meekness and sympathy, fidelity and

(3) It was another prophet, again, who pointed out the place where he would be born. For Micah said: "And you, . Bethlehem, the land of Judah, are by no means the least among the princes of Judah. For out of you will come the leader who will shepherd my people, Israel: and his going forth is from the beginning, from the days of eternity."[4] Micah was pointing out both the divinity and the humanity of Christ. When he said: "His going forth is from the beginning, from the days of eternity," he revealed his existence before all ages. When he said: "There will come the leader who will shepherd my people, Israel," he revealed Christ's birth in the flesh.

(4) And notice here that he makes clear another prophecy. Micah not only said where Christ would be born but also that the place would become well known even if it was a little town and little known. For he said: "You are by no means the least among the princes of Judah."[5] So it is that now the whole world rushes to see Bethlehem, where he was born and laid in a manger. The place became famous, and there is no other reason than this why people go there.

(5) Again, another prophet made clear the time of his coming, when he said [817]: "A chief shall not depart from Judah, nor a ruler from his loins till he come for whom it is reserved. Even he is the expectation of the nations, binding his colt to a vine and the foal of an ass to the young vine. He shall wash his

---

constancy, and will succeed. The procedure of the servant in his mission is contrasted with that of a military conqueror like Cyrus. He will be merciful to his foes but will also bring judgment and hope to those he overcomes. Obviously Chrysostom saw a merciful Christ in the servant of Yahweh. See Power, CCHS 562 and cf. 2 Tm 2.24–26.

[4] Cf. Mi 5.1. Chrysostom does not quote the LXX but Mt 2.6 as far as that text goes in its quotation of Mi 5.1. The LXX reads: "But as for you, Bethelehem, house of Ephratha, you are too little to be one of the thousands of Judah. Yet out of you one shall come forth for me to be the chief of Israel. His goings forth have been from the beginning, from the days of eternity." Chrysostom gives to the latter part of the text its literal sense of the eternal origin of the Son from the Father. Both Jewish and Christian tradition have understood the first part of the text as referring to the birth of the Messiah in Bethlehem. See K. Smyth, CCHS 674–75 and P. King, JBC 17:23.

[5] Again Chrysostom is giving the text of Mi 5.1 as quoted in Mt 2.6. At the time Matthew wrote, Bethlehem had lost the insignificance it had in the days of Micah, for the Messiah has already been born there.

robe in wine and his mantle in the blood of the grape. His eyes bring the exhilaration which comes from wine, and his teeth are whiter than milk."[6]

(6) See how this prophecy fits what happened, too. For Christ came at a time when the Jewish princes had already ceased to rule and were subject to the empire of the Romans. In this way was fulfilled the prophecy which said: "A chief shall not depart from Judah, nor a ruler from his loins till he come for whom it is reserved,"[7] meaning Christ. For the first registration was held just at the same time that he was born,[8] and this was after the Romans had conquered the Jewish nation and had brought them under the yoke of their empire. Something further is meant by the words: "Even he is the expectation of the nations."[9] For after he had come, he did draw all the nations to himself.

(7) Herod sought him after his birth; he was going to kill all the children in that place. And the prophet revealed this, too, foretelling it long beforehand when he said: "A voice was heard in Rama, lamentation, mourning, and much weeping, of Rachel weeping for her children and refusing to be comforted, because they are not."[10] The Scriptures also predicted that he would come to Egypt when they said: "Out of Egypt I called my son."[11]

(8) Christ would work miracles and teach as soon as he came to well-known sections of his own country, and this, too,

---

[6]Cf. Gn 49.10–12. The passage is taken from Jacob's prophecies to his sons. Supremacy is promised to Judah until, through David, the Messiah shall come and he will bring an eternal kingdom. Vv. 11–12 describe the peace and prosperity which will mark Judah's supremacy and the messianic kingdom, because a land so abounding in vines cannot have known the ravages of hostile armies. See E. Sutcliffe, CCHS 204 and E. Maly, JBC 2:182.

[7]Gn 49.10.

[8]This registration was the reason why Joseph and Mary went to Bethlehem, where Christ was born. Cf. Luke 2.1–6.

[9]Gn 49.10. NAB reads: "while tribute is brought to him." See n. ad loc. in NAB. The LXX makes the messianic sense of the passage explicit.

[10]Jer 31.15; cf. Mt 2.18 and NAB n. ad loc.

[11]Mt 2.15 also applies this text of Hos 11.1 to the return of the Christ Child from Egypt. Hos 11.1 reads: "When Israel was a child I loved him, out of Egypt I called my son," but Hosea means by this to date the real beginning of Israel from the time of Moses and the Exodus. But cf. NAB n. on Mt 2.15 and J. McKenzie, JBC 43;21.

had been foretold. Listen to the words of Isaiah when he said: "The district of Zabulun, the land of Napthali, a people who were sitting in darkness saw a great light; upon those sitting in darkness and the shadow of death a light arose."[12] In these words Isaiah revealed that Christ came to those places, that he taught in the lands of Zabulun and Napthali, and that he was recognized by the wonders he wrought.[13]

(9) And Isaiah went on to tell of other marvels and showed how Christ cured the lame, how he made the blind to see, and the mute to speak: "Then will the eyes of the blind be opened, then will the ears of the deaf hear."[14] And thereafter he spoke of the other marvels: "Then will the lame man leap like a stag, and the tongue of those with impediments of speech will be clear and distinct."[15] And this did not happen until his coming.

(10) And the Scriptures made mention of these marvels in a special way. Certainly, on one occasion, when he entered the temple, infants still at their mothers' breasts, whose tongues were not yet ready to speak clearly, sang sacred hymns to him and said: "Hosanna in the highest. Blessed is he who comes in the name of the Lord."[16] But the prophet had foretold this

[12] Cf. Is 8.23 which reads: "First he degraded the land of Zabulun and the land of Napthali, but in the end he has glorified the seaward road, the land west of the Jordan, the district of the gentiles." Zabulun and Napthali were in northern Palestine, which was first to be attacked by the Assyrians. But God redeems it as he redeemed all his people. The "seaward road" ran from Damascus, across southern Galilee, to the Mediterranean. The "district of the gentiles" was in northern Galilee and was inhabited by pagans. Mt 4.15–16 refers to this, since Jesus began his public mission in Galilee. Is 9.1 also refers to these pagans when he says: "The people who walked in darkness have seen a great light; upon those who dwelt in the land of gloom a light has shone." Mt 4.15–16 reads: "Land of Zabulun and land of Napthali, by the way to the sea, beyond the Jordan, Galilee of the gentiles: the people who sat in darkness have seen a great light; and upon those who sat in the region and shadow of death, a light has arisen." Chrysostom has here given an abridgment and conflation of Is 8.23, 9.1, and Mt 4.15–16. Again his quotation comes closer to the NT citation of an OT text.
[13] Cf. Mt 4.15–16 and the same application ibid. 23–25.
[14] Is 35.5. Cf. Mt 15.30–31.
[15] Is 35.6. This and the preceding verse foretell the healing miracles of Christ, e.g., Mt 11.5; Mk 7.37; Lk 7.22.
[16] Cf. Mt 21.9, where it is the crowds that went before him on his triumphal entry into Jerusalem who kept crying out these words. Cf. Ps 117(118).26. In

long before, when he said: "Out of the mouths of babes and sucklings you have fashioned praise to destroy your enemy and avenger."[17] Do you see how nature struggled to surpass itself by proclaiming its creator? Do you see how innocent infants, who could not yet use their tongues for speech, undertook to spread the message of the apostles?

Mt 21.15 we read: "But the chief priests and the Scribes, seeing the wonderful deeds that he did, and the children crying out in the temple and saying, 'Hosanna to the Son of David,' were indignant, etc." Chrysostom has confused the two similar verses.

[17] Ps 8.3 and cf. Mt 21.16, where Christ confutes the indignation of the high priests and Scribes by quoting this Psalm in defense of the children who cried out to him: "Hosanna to the Son of David."

CHAPTER IV

The Ingratitude of the Jews Foretold

(1) Christ had much to say in many places while talking with the Jews. However, because of the hardness of their hearts, he veiled his message in parables. This also had been foretold. "I will utter dark sayings from the foundation of the world. I will utter things hidden of old."[1] The psalmist also predicted his wisdom in speech long beforehand, [818] when he said: "Grace is poured out by your lips."[2] Again, another prophet said: "Behold, my servant shall understand, he shall be exalted, and raised exceeding high."[3] And this prophet gave, as it were, a summary account of the virtues of his coming, virtues accompanied by signs and marvels, when he said: "The spirit of the Lord is upon me for the business for which he anointed me; he has sent me to publish glad tidings to the poor, to proclaim deliverance to captives, and a recovery of sight to the blind."[4]

[1] Cf. Ps 77(78).2, which reads in the LXX: "I will open my mouth with parables, I will utter dark sayings of old." Chrysostom probably omits the first half of the verse because he has just said that Christ veiled his message in parables. Chrysostom's citation of the second half of Ps 77(78).2 seems conflated with its quotation in Mt 13.35, which reads: "I will open my mouth in parables; I will utter things hidden since the foundation of the world."

[2] Ps 44(45).3. Ps 44(45) is a nuptial ode for the messianic king, and the reference in v. 3 is surely to Christ because the psalmist sees a king fairer than any ordinary man and he addresses him as God in v. 8. Cf. T. Bird, CCHS 456 but also R. Murphy, JBC 35:61 and NAB n. on Ps 45.

[3] Cf. Is 52.13. The LXX reads "will understand" while the NAB reads "will prosper," as does the Jerusalem Bible.

[4] Cf. Is 61.1. Isaiah seems to be speaking of the restoration of Zion, but Christ quotes these lines as referring to his mission in Lk 4.18–19, which read: "The Spirit of the Lord is upon me because he has anointed me; to bring good news to the poor he has sent me, to proclaim to the captives release, and sight to the blind; to set at liberty the oppressed, to proclaim the acceptable year of the Lord and the day of recompense." Christ read this

(2) And Christ did heap his favors on the Jews. Yet they would be so silly and foolish as to turn away from him even though they could make no charge against him, either great or small. Hear the words which David spoke when he foretold this. He said: "I was for peace with those who hate peace. They attacked me without provocation."⁵ Christ would also enter the city riding on an ass. Zechariah foretold this, too, long beforehand, when he said: "Rejoice exceedingly, O daughter of Zion, make proclamation, O daughter of Jerusalem! Behold, your king is coming for you, meek and mounted on a beast of burden, even a young colt."⁶

(3) He cast out of the temple the money changers and those who were selling doves. But in doing so out of zeal for the temple, he showed that his will was conformed to the will of his Father and that he was in no wise hostile to the Father. He did what he did only to avenge the honor of God's house where such huckstering was going on. David both foretold it and gave Christ's motive for this act. For David said: "Zeal for your house has consumed me."⁷ What could be clearer than that?

(4) Christ was going to be betrayed, and the traitor would be one of those who shared his table with him. See how the prophet foretold this when he said: "He who ate of my bread

---

passage in the synagogue at Nazareth and then said: "Today this Scripture has been fulfilled in your hearing" (v. 21). Chrysostom here again seems to be quoting the NT citation of the OT text, since both Luke and Chrysostom omit from Isaiah's text the words: "to heal them that are broken hearted" before "to proclaim, etc."

⁵Cf. Ps119 (120).7. This psalm is the first of fifteen appointed to be sung by pilgrims going up to Jerusalem. In this verse the pilgrim laments that he has to live among godless barbarians who give him no peace. The application which makes Christ the pilgrim and the Jews the godless barbarians is certainly apologetic. T. Bird, CCHS 470.

⁶Cf. Zec 9.9 and NAB n. ad loc. Chrysostom omits "A just savior is he" after the words: "for you." Pseudo-Gregory of Nyssa (PG 46.201A), in his Book of Testimonies, shows the same omission. Mt 21.4–5 and Jn 12.14–15 see a literal fulfillment of this prophecy in Christ's triumphal entry into Jerusalem, and indeed the mystery of the combination of mightiness and lowliness foretold by Zechariah was not to be fulfilled until Christ. See S. Bullough, CCHS 696.

⁷Ps 68(69).10. The whole psalm is a cry of anguish of a distressed sufferer

has raised his heel against me."[8] Consider, then, how the words of the Gospel agree with this. "He who dips his hand into the dish with me, he will betray me."[9] The traitor was not simply going to betray him but would do it while selling his precious blood and taking money for it. The prophet did not remain silent on this but recounted the disgraceful pact between Judas and the Jews and the words they spoke to each other. [For Judas said: "What are you willing to give me and I will deliver him to you?" And they replied: "Thirty pieces of silver."][10] What the prophet said in veiled language was: "The mouth of the sinner and the mouth of the treacherous man have been opened against me."[11]

(5) The traitor himself repented of what he had dared to do, threw down the silver pieces, and, after running for a halter, he ended his life by hanging.[12] His betrayal made his wife a widow, left his children fatherless, and his house empty. See how the prophet spoke of this disaster in tragic terms, when he said: "Let his children be fatherless and his wife a widow. May his children be tossed about and leave their land, and let them be cast out of the house where they lived."[13]

(6) After Judas's death, another became an apostle in his place, namely, Matthias.[14] And this David had foretold when

---

who prays to God. Jn 2.17 sees the text as fulfilled in Christ's cleansing of the temple, although vv. 6–13 of the psalm show the distressed one suffering because of his sins and in God's cause, for which he is subjected to jibes. Obviously Chrysostom takes the position of Jn 2.17. Cf. NAB n. on Ps 69.10.

[8] Ps 40(41).10. At the last supper our Lord applies these words to Judas. See Jn 13.18.

[9] Mt 26.23.

[10] Cf. Mt 26.15. The words in brackets are not found in the Greek printed texts, but the old translator must have read them in his Greek text, and Montfaucon includes them in his Latin translation. They are also read in the MSS basic to McKendrick's text.

[11] Cf. Ps 108(109).1. The whole psalm is an appeal for God's help to the psalmist against enemies who have repaid his love with calumny and treachery. In Acts 1.20 Peter applies v. 8 of this psalm to Judas.

[12] See Mt 27.5 and Acts 1.18.

[13] Cf. Ps 108(109).9–10. Because v. 8 is applied to Judas in Acts 1.20, Chrysostom probably applies vv. 9–10 to him as well. But in the psalm the words are spoken against a slanderous enemy.

[14] See Acts 1.15–26.

he said: "Let another take his office."[15] After Jesus willingly let himself be betrayed and arrested, a court filled with wicked men was assembled, a court consisting of Jews and pagans. See how the prophet foretold this when he said: "Why did the nations rage and the people plan vain things? The kings of the earth stood up and the rulers gathered themselves together against the Lord and against his anointed one, saying: 'Let us break away from their bonds and cast away their yoke from us.'" This is what the Jews were shouting after Pilate asked: "Shall I crucify your king?" and they replied: "We have no king but Caesar."[16]

(7) Not only were these events foretold, but Isaiah also predicted Christ's silence when he stood and made no reply to their many accusations [819]. For Isaiah said: "Like a lamb led to the slaughter or a sheep before the shearer, he was silent and so he opened not his mouth."[17] Then, to show that the court was corrupt and the sentence unjust, he went on to say: "In his humiliation his legal trial was taken away,[18] that is, no one judged justly in his case.

(8) Next, Isaiah told why they slew him. He did not undergo his sufferings because of his sins, since he was without blame or guilt; he was handed over for the evils of the world. Isaiah hinted at both these things when he said: "He who has done no iniquity nor was deceit found in his mouth."[19] Why, then, was Christ slain? "For the sins of the people he came to his death."[20]

---

[15] Ps 108(109).8 is here applied to Judas. In Acts 1.20 "office" means the apostolic office. Challoner-Rheims translated it "bishopric," but surely the Psalmist could neither have foreseen nor intended to predict the establishment of the Church by Christ, much less the characteristic of that Church being hierarchically structured.

[16] Cf. Ps 2.1–3 and also Acts 4.25. The psalm is messianic, and its theme is the conflict between the forces of evil, on the one hand, and God and his anointed, on the other. Cf. NAB n. ad loc. See also Jn 19.15.

[17] Is 53.7. Cf. Mt 26.63 and Acts 8.32 where Philip applies this text to Christ when the Ethiopian eunuch questioned him about it.

[18] Is 53.8. Only the LXX version would allow the interpretation which Chrysostom gives to the text here. Cf. Acts 8.33. See also FOTC 68.162–63.

[19] Is 53.9. This text is cited in 1 Pt 2.22. The application there is about the same, as it is also in 1 Jn 3.5.

[20] Cf. Is 53.8. See 1 Cor 15.3.

(9) What profit came from that death on the cross? These are the blessings it achieved: evil was destroyed, the wounds of the soul were set right by a wondrous cure and a healing beyond belief. See how Isaiah foretold that when he said: "We had all gone astray like sheep. Man had wandered in his way. The chastisement of our peace was upon him. By his bruises we are all healed."[21] The same prophet revealed that the Jews would pay the penalty for these crimes of theirs when he said: "I shall give the ungodly for his burial and the rich for his death."[22]

(10) Again, it was David who said: "Let us cast away his yoke from us,"[23] and then added: "He who dwells in heaven will laugh at them. Then he will speak to them in his anger and trouble them in his rage."[24] By this he meant that the Jews would be scattered all over the world. Christ himself revealed this in the Gospels, when he said: "But as for those who did not want me to be king over them, bring them here and slay them."[25]

(11) Not only did the prophets say that Christ would be slain but they also spoke out on how he would be slain. David revealed this when he said of Christ's executioners: "They have dug my hands and feet. They have numbered all my bones."[26] Again he spoke of their sinfulness after the

---

[21] Cf. Is 53.5, 6. Although this doctrine of vicarious expiation is not found elsewhere in the OT, it was taught by Christ, the evangelists, and especially St. Paul. Cf. e.g., 1 Cor 15.3; 1 Pt 2.24–25.

[22] Is 53.9. Only the LXX text would allow this interpretation. The NAB reading: "A grave was assigned him among the wicked and a burial place with evildoers" is taken to mean that even in death Christ's corpse would not find honorable burial.

[23] Cf. Ps 2.3. See n. 16 above. These are the words of the rebels.

[24] Cf. ibid. 4–5. The scene shifts to heaven and God shows anger at the rebels. The notion of laughing at one's foes as a sign of anger is oriental. See T. Bird, CCHS 447.

[25] Cf. Lk 19.27. The verse comes from the parable of the gold pieces (Lk 19.11–27) which is like to and different from the parable of the talents in Mt 25.14–30. Lk 19.14 adds a detail not found in Matthew when Luke says: "But his citizens hated him; and they sent a delegation after him to say, 'We do not wish this man to be king over us.'" This makes it necessary for Luke to add v. 27. It is certainly a formidable lesson. For a comparison of the two parables see R. Ginns, CCHS 962.

[26] Cf. Ps 21(22).17–18. The Romans properly speaking carried out Christ's

crucifixion when he added: "They divided my garments among them: and upon my vesture they cast lots."[27]

Christ's Burial Predicted

(12) Next, David made it clear that Christ would be buried when he said: "They have put me in the lowest pit in the dark places and in the shadow of death." Nor was David silent about the spices used on his shroud. Since the women brought myrrh, spice, and cassia, hear what the prophet said: "Your garments breathed forth myrrh, spice, and cassia, and with them the daughters of kings gladdened you for your honor."[28] See how he also predicted that Christ would rise again. "You will not leave my soul in hell nor will you give your holy one to see corruption."[29] Isaiah expressed the same thing in a different way. For he said: "The Lord wishes to cleanse him from his wounds, to show him light, to justify the righteous one who has served many well."[30]

(13) Isaiah also established that the slaying of Christ was the ransom for man's sins by saying: "He has borne the sins of many."[31] And he freed mankind from demons for, as Isaiah said: "He will divide the spoils of the strong."[32] And the same prophet spoke out clearly that Christ did this through his death when he said: "Because his soul was delivered up to

---

execution, but Chrysostom would feel that they crucified Christ at the urging of the Jews. Christ, on the cross, recited the first verse of this psalm. See Mt 27.46.

[27] Ps 21(22).19. See also Jn 19.24, which quotes this verse but applies the action to the Roman soldiers.

[28] Ps 87(88).7. To the Hebrew the lowest pit would be Sheol. See McKenzie, DB 800–801. The detail about the spices is omitted in PG 48 but is found in the older MSS and in McKendrick's text. For the quotation cf. Ps 44(45).8–9.

[29] Ps 15(16).10. For "hell" LXX uses the Greek word *haidēs;* again it means Sheol. Peter quotes the passage in Acts 2.25–32 as does Paul, ibid. 13.35. Both apostles refer the verse to Christ's resurrection, just as Chrysostom does. See NAB n. on Ps. 16.10.

[30] Cf. Is 53.10–11. Chrysostom quotes the LXX text in an abbreviated form.

[31] Cf. ibid. 12.

[32] Cf. ibid.

death."[33] That Christ would be put in charge over the whole world he revealed by these words of his: "He shall inherit many."[34]

(14) After he descended into hell, he threw all things into an upheaval. He filled everything with tumult and confusion. He destroyed the citadel. The prophets did not remain silent on this, but David exclaimed and said: "Lift up your gates, [820] you who are rulers, reach up, you ancient portals, and the king of glory will come in. The Lord of hosts, he is this king of glory."[35] Isaiah put it another way. "Bronze doors I will shatter, and iron bars I will snap. I shall open up to you and show you treasures out of the darkness, hidden away, unseen."[36] This is the way he referred to hell.

(15) Even if it was hell, it still preserved the sacred souls and precious vessels, Abraham, Isaac, and Jacob. This is why Isaiah called it a place of treasures, even if in darkness, because the Sun of Justice had not yet penetrated there with its rays nor with any message on the resurrection.[37] But hear how David made it clear that, after Christ's resurrection, he would not remain on earth but would ascend into heaven: "God is

---

[33] Cf. ibid.

[34] Cf. ibid. Notice that Chrysostom understands Is 53.10–12 as proof that the death of Yahweh's servant (Christ) was successfully sacrificial and expiatory. See E. Power, CCHS 568.

[35] Cf, Ps 23(24).7. The psalm is actually a processional hymn celebrating the bringing of the Ark to Zion, but Chrysostom sees in it, apparently, Christ's descent into hell, which is conceived as a fortress with gates and bars. Cf. Is 38.10 where Sheol is so conceived. Christ's arrival there would cause tumult and confusion, because Sheol, the land of the dead, is basically a place of inactivity. See Is 14.9–11 and McKenzie, DB 800–801.

[36] Cf. Is 45.2–3. Actually, in Isaiah, the bronze doors are the gates of Babylon.

[37] Sheol was not necessarily a place of punishment. Here Chrysostom has the patriarchs waiting in Limbo for Christ to redeem them and release them. The Sun of Justice was a common symbol in the ancient Near East. Always one of the principal gods, the sun was thought among pagans to provide warmth and life, light and law. Cf. J. Finegan, *Light from the Ancient Past* (2nd ed., Princeton 1959) 96–97. The Bible uses the same symbolism but identifies the deity as the one true God. Cf. Ps 18(19).4–11. Here Chrysostom uses the Sun of Justice to mean Christ, as he does also in ACW 31.56, 166; FOTC 72.258; *De Lazaro* 7 (PG 48.1046). In FOTC 72.186 the Sun of Justice means the Holy Spirit and in FOTC 68.5 it means Yahweh.

gone up with a shout, the Lord with the sound of a trumpet."
By speaking of the shout and the trumpet, David showed how
manifest Christ's ascension would be. Christ would not stand
with the angels, nor with the archangels, nor with any other
ministering power, but would be seated on the royal throne.
Hear again what David said: "The Lord said to my Lord: Sit
you at my right hand until I make your enemies a footstool
for your feet."[38]

---

[38] Ps 46(47).5 and Ps 109(110).1. Cf. R. Murphy, JBC 35:126; also NAB nn.
on Ps 110. Notice that Chrysostom's thought has been following the sequence
of articles in the Apostles' Creed.

CHAPTER V

The Mission of the Apostles Foretold

(1) After these events, he would send forth his apostles, as Isaiah had foretold. "How beautiful are the feet of those who preach the gospel of peace, of those who bring glad tidings of good things,"[1] he said. Look what part of the body he praised. He lauded their feet, which took them everywhere they went. Furthermore, David showed the manner and source of their strength and success when he said: "The Lord shall give the word to them who preach the good tidings with great power."[2]

(2) It would not be by wielding weapons, nor by expenditure of money, nor by strength of body, nor by abundance of armies, nor by any other such means that the apostles would conquer the world. They would gain victory by a mere word, since that word had great power and was proved by signs and wonders. For they preached Christ crucified, they wrought miracles and, in this way, they conquered the world. It was on this account that David said: "The Lord shall give the word to them who preach the good tidings with great power,"[3] because this was his way of speaking of the miracles and wonders they worked.

(3) And it was the result of an ineffable power that the fisherman, the publican, and the tentmaker,[4] at their mere commands, raised the dead to life, drove out demons, drove off death, stopped the tongues of philosophers, stitched shut the mouths of rhetoricians, overcame kings and rulers, and were victorious over barbarians, pagans, and every nation.

[1] Cf. Is 52.7 but Chrysostom quotes Paul's version of the text as given in Rom 10.15.
[2] Cf. Ps 67(68).11 (LXX). This is not the usual sense given to the verse but it is clearly the sense which Chrysostom gives to it. Cf. NAB n. to Ps 68.
[3] Ibid.
[4] Peter is the fisherman, Matthew the publican, and Paul the tentmaker.

(4) Indeed, David described the situation well in that way. For it was by that word which God gave them that they accomplished all those things they did. And it was with God's great power that they brought the dead back to life, changed sinners into just men, restored sight to the blind, and drove out disease from the body and evil from the soul. And where did they get that power? That it came from the Holy Spirit is made quite clear from these words: "And they were filled with the Spirit,"[5] and both men and women prophesied.

(5) Tongues seen in the form of fire settled on each one of them,[6] as Joel had long before predicted when he said: "I shall pour out a portion of my spirit on all flesh, and your sons will prophesy and your daughters will see visions, and your young men will dream dreams before the coming of the great and illustrious day of the Lord."[7] [By "the great and illustrious day" he meant both the day of the Spirit and the day which would come at the consummation of the world.][8] This same prophet predicted salvation through faith—for he did not remain silent on this—when he said: "And it will be that whoever will call on the name of the Lord will be saved."[9]

---

[5] Cf. Acts 2.4.
[6] Ibid. 3.
[7] Cf. Joel 2.28–31 (LXX) or 3.1–4 (NAB). In the OT the spirit is the gift of God given to those acting as his agents. This promise of the spirit is quoted by Peter in Acts 2.17–21, who sees it as fulfilled in an eminent way by the gift of the Holy Spirit bestowed on the apostles at Pentecost.
[8] The day of the Spirit is Pentecost. See Acts 2. The bracketed words are omitted in McKendrick's text and in his primary MSS.
[9] Joel 2.32 (LXX) or 3.5 (NAB). Cf. Rom 10.13.

CHAPTER VI

Peter and Paul are Superior to Kings

(1) No part of the world will fail to hear his message. "To [821] every land their sound has gone forth, and their words to the limits of the world."[1] Furthermore, David showed that they preached with power and were stronger than those who wore the crown of royalty when he said again: "You shall make them princes in all the land."[2]

(2) The facts of history make it clear that Peter and Paul were mightier than kings and rulers. Certainly the laws of kings are destroyed and overthrown even while these kings are still alive. But long after those fishermen had died, their laws remain fast-fixed and firm. They stand fast-fixed even though many kings, armed avengers, punishments, even though many a skilled and clever speaker, many a kinsman and friend may try to overthrow them. They stand firm even though demons, long-standing habit, malice, pleasure, and countless other vices strive to destroy them.

(3) David also wished to show that these rulers whom Christ put over us would hold sway because men loved them and wanted to have them as rulers. He wished to show that Peter and Paul were not like other rulers—feared, hated, and a burden to their subjects. So he went on to say: "Therefore, nations shall thank you forever,"[3] that is, people will pay to Christ the greatest thanks and gratitude because he gave the nations such men as Peter and Paul to be their rulers.

---

[1] Ps 18(19).4. Rom 10.18 quotes the verse *verbatim* and applies it to those who preach the Gospel.

[2] Cf. Ps 44(45).16 (LXX) or 17 (NAB). The psalm is actually a nuptial ode for the messianic king and his people, but it is traditional to apply this verse to the apostles and their successors. See T. Bird, CCHS 456 and NAB n. to Ps 45.

[3] Cf. Ps 44(45).17 (LXX) or 18 (NAB). NAB reads "praise" for "thank."

(4) The successful spread of the Gospel message all over the world was also predicted. Again, listen to David as he declared this in these words: "Ask of me, and I shall give you nations for your inheritance and the uttermost parts of the earth for your possessions."[4] Another prophet elsewhere expressed again the same thought when he said: "The whole earth will be filled with the knowledge of the Lord, as abundant water covers the seas."[5]

(5) Consider how easy it is for men to heed. For Jeremiah said: "They shall no more teach every man his neighbor, and every man his brother, saying: 'Know the Lord.' For all men will know me from the least of them to the greatest."[6] And Isaiah showed how indestructible the Church would be. "For in the last days the mountain of the Lord will be conspicuous, and the house of the Lord will be on top of the mountains and will be exalted above the hills. And to this mountaintop will come many peoples and many nations."[7]

(6) Not only would the Church be firm, steadfast, and indestructible but it would also gain great peace for the world. Governments and monarchies will be destroyed; there will be but one kingdom put together for all men, and, unlike in times past, its greater part will be at peace. For in the past, all craftsmen and men in public life were trained in warfare and took their place in the ranks. After the coming of Christ, all that was done away with, and wars were confined to widely separated areas. And Isaiah showed that this would be true when he said: "And they shall beat their swords into ploughshares, and their spears into pruning hooks; and nation shall not lift up a sword against nation; nor shall they learn to wage war any more"[8]

(7) Therefore, men used to spend their lives under arms, but now they have forgotten the art of warfare; in fact, most

---

[4] Ps 2.8. The whole psalm refers to the universal reign of the Messiah.
[5] Cf. Is 11.9. The chapter treats of the rule of Immanuel.
[6] Cf. Jer 31.34. Vv. 31–34 are quoted at length in Heb 8.8–12, in part ibid. 33–34, 10.16–17, and Rom 11.27. Chrysostom here quotes the text as given in Heb 8.12.
[7] Cf. Is 2.2. See also Mi 4.1–2. See E. Power, CCHS 543; K. Smyth, ibid. 674; F. Moriarty, JBC 16:9; NAB n. on Is 2.2–4.
[8] Is 2.4 and Mi 4.3.

men have not had even the first taste of weapons. If there should be some, they would be few and they would not be continuously campaigning. They would not be counted in such vast numbers as they were in the beginning, when every nation experienced countless uprisings and revolts.

(8) The prophet also foretold the kinds of people from whom the Church would be established. Not only the meek and the mild and the good would form the Church. The wild, the inhuman, and men whose ways were like those of wolves and lions and bulls would flock together with them and form one Church. Hear how the prophet foretold the diversity of this flock when he said: "Then a wolf shall pasture with a lamb."[9] And by this he showed the simplicity of the way of life the Church's rulers would live.

(9) Since this text [822] did not literally refer to wild beasts, let the Jews say when this actually happened. For a wolf has never pastured with a lamb. If it were to happen that they would pasture together, how would this benefit the human race? The text referred not to wild beasts but to wild men. It referred to Scythians, to Thracians, to Mauretanians, to Indians, to Sarmatians, to Persians. Another prophet made it clear that all these nations would be brought under one yoke when he said: "And they shall serve him under one yoke, and each one shall adore him from his own place."[10] No longer, he said, will men worship him in Jerusalem but everywhere throughout the world. No longer are men bidden to go up to Jerusalem, but each one shall remain in his own home and offer this worship.[11]

---

[9] Is 11.6. Again we have an idyllic picture of the messianic kingdom.
[10] This seems to be a conflation of Zep 3.9 and 2.11. It occurs again in part below in Chap. XVII.7.
[11] See below (XVII.1–7) and FOTC 68.140–44.

CHAPTER VII

The Rejection of the Jews Foretold

(1) Scripture did not pass over in silence the rejection of the Jews. Notice how the prophet Malachi foretold this, too. "Behold, among you the doors will be shut, and a fire will not be kindled on my altar for nothing."[1] He also foretold who would now pay God worship. "From the risings of the sun to its going down my name has been glorified among the nations."[2] And again he said: "And in every place incense is offered to me and a pure sacrifice."[3] Do you see how he made clear the nobility of the worship, how he showed that the new worship had a special honor and differed from the old? Worship will not be confined to a place or a way of sacrifice, nor will it consist in savor or smoke or omens; it will now be a different ritual.

(2) Some one might well ask how the apostles drew to themselves all these people. How did men who spoke only the language of the Jews win over the Scythian, the Indian, the Sarmatian, and the Thracian? Because they received the gift of tongues through the Holy Spirit.[4] Not only did the apostles say this but also the prophets when they made both these facts clear, namely, that the apostles received the gift of tongues and that they failed to win over the Jews. Hear how the prophet showed this when he said: " 'In foreign tongues and

[1] Cf. Mal 1.10. Basically what the text means is that the Lord is displeased with the imperfect sacrifices offered without sincerity by the people of Judah. Cf NAB n. ad loc.
[2] Mal 1.11. The Lord will be pleased with the offerings of the gentile nations throughout the world.
[3] Ibid. This anticipates the universal sacrifice of the Mass. See E. Sutcliffe, CCHS 703. See also FOTC 68.140–44.
[4] Cf. Acts 2.4.

with other lips I shall speak to this people and in this way they shall not hear me,' says the Lord."[5]

(3) What could any man see more clearly than this? The Jews would reject the faith and the gentiles would rush to embrace it. And this, too, had been predicted. Hear how the words of Isaiah made this clear. "I was found by them who sought me not; I became manifest to them who inquired not for me. I said: 'Behold here I am,' to the nation which did not invoke my name."[6] But of Israel he said: "I stretched out my hands all the day long to a disobedient and contradicting people."[7] And again: "As a root in a thirsty soil we have made proclamation to him as to a child."[8] And again: "O Lord, who has believed this report of ours, and to whom has the arm of the Lord been made manifest?"[9] Isaiah did not say: "Who has believed our teaching," but: "Who has believed our report?" In this way he showed that the apostles had spoken nothing of their own but had announced the tidings they had heard from God.

(4) Moses showed clearly that God would prefer our religious ritual to that of the Jews, and that ours far surpasses theirs in honor when he said: "I shall provoke you by what is not a nation, by a foolish nation I will vex you."[10] By calling the Church "what is not a nation," he was speaking of the previous low estate of its people. For it was not considered to be a nation because the people who belonged to the Church were poor, foolish, and lacking in intelligence. But their faith in God produced so great a change that they are now seen to

[5] Cf Is 28.11 where the reference to foreign tongues is actually to the language spoken by armies which will invade Israel for mocking Isaiah. See E. Power, CCHS 558.

[6] Cf Is 65.1. Chrysostom's citation is much closer to that found in Rom 10.20.

[7] Cf. Is 65.2 and see Rom 10.20.

[8] Cf. Is 53.2. The NAB text reads: "He grew up like a sapling before him, like a shoot from the parched earth," where "He" refers to Yahweh's servant. Chrysostom means Israel by "him."

[9] Cf. Is 53.1. See Jn 12.38, which quotes the same text, and Rom 10.16, which gives the first part. See also below Chap. XI.10 and notes.

[10] Cf. Dt 32.21.

stand in much higher honor than the Jews who had been honored above them.

(5) The prophet also made it clear that this would provoke the Jews, and, consequently, they would become better men. For he did not merely say: "I shall honor them before you." At the same time as he made this clear, he also pointed out that, however it would be, some reform and correction would result for them from the provocation. [823] For he said: "I shall provoke you by what is not a nation."[11] It was just as if he were to say: "I shall give them such great blessings that you will exert yourselves, that you will be stung to action."

(6) This certainly did make them better men. These were the men who, by listening to Moses, had seen the waters of the Red Sea divided, who had seen the rocks split, who had seen the air change into a cloud, who had seen such great wonders.[12] But these were also the ones who sacrificed their children,[13] who were initiated into the rites of Baal of Peor,[14] who devoted themselves to the use of many charms and much witchcraft.[15] But after we came and our religion far exceeded theirs in honor, they were so stung by the rivalry and became so much better men, they were so humbled that, out of jealousy for us, they will do the right things which they failed to do when they heard their prophets and saw marvels. Certainly, no Jew now sacrifices his children, no Jew rushes off to idols, no Jew worships a calf.[16]

(7) In the Old Testament the holiness of virginity was not even mentioned, but it would be a source of glory in the New.

---

[11] Cf. ibid.

[12] See Ex 14.21–22 for the dividing of the Red Sea; ibid. 17.5–6 for the splitting of the rock from which water would flow for the Israelites to drink; ibid. 13.21 for the changing of the air into a column of cloud.

[13] The immolation of children to Moloch or Baal is mentioned frequently in the OT. See, e.g., Lv 18.21; Ez 16.20–21; 20.26, 31; 23.37; Wis 14.23; Is 7.34; Jer 7.31; 19.5; 32.35. See also *Adv. Iud.* I.6; VI.2 (FOTC 68.25, 154, 155).

[14] See Nm 25.3 and *Adv. Iud.* VI.2 (FOTC 68.152 and n. 15). Cf. F. Moriarty, JBC 5:48.

[15] See Wis 12.5 and *Adv. Iud.* VIII.7 (FOTC 68.230–32).

[16] See Wis 13.1–15.17 for the folly and shame of idolatry; see Ex 32 for the story of the golden calf.

Yet see how David foretold this when he said: "The virgins in her train shall be introduced to the king. They shall be brought to the temple of the king."[17] Nor was the Old Testament silent on the name of priests—I mean the name of bishops. For Isaiah said: "I shall establish your chiefs in peace and your overseers in righteousness."[18]

[17] Ps 44(45).15–16. The psalm is a nuptial ode of the messianic king.

[18] Cf. Is 60.17. The whole chapter deals with the glory of the new Zion, the Church. Chrysostom seems to understand the Greek word *episcopos* ("overseer") in the ecclesiastical sense of "bishop." Elsewhere he refers to bishops as "fathers."

CHAPTER VIII

The Last Judgment Predicted

(1) Christ will come and demand an accounting of the whole human race and of the Jews along with the others. See how both David and Malachi foretold this. Malachi said: "And he came in like a smelting furnace and like the soap of the fullers, and he will refine and purify the silver and gold,"[1] and Paul's words were: "For the day will declare it since the day is to be revealed in fire."[2] And David said: "God in full manifestation will come."[3] And by this he was again proclaiming Christ's second coming.

(2) The first coming showed great condescension and accommodation to human nature, but the second coming will not. It will be filled with terror and fright from the angels who come rushing before him, from his presence which overtakes all things like a flash of lightning. "For as the lightning comes forth from the east and flashes even to the west, so also will the coming of the Son of Man be."[4] In this way Matthew makes clear how manifestly Christ's second coming will proclaim itself. For it needs no one to herald it. His coming by and of itself will proclaim itself. David also pointed this out when he said: "God in full manifestation will come."[5]

(3) Then David sketched out the judgment to come when he said: "Before him a fire shall blaze, and around him shall

---

[1] Cf. Mal 3.2

[2] 1 Cor 3.13. "The day" usually refers to the day of judgment, as it does here.

[3] Cf. Ps 49(50).3. The whole psalm represents a theophany at which the Lord will be judge.

[4] Mt 24.27. See A. Jones, CCHS 894–95.

[5] Cf. Ps 49(50).3. Chrysostom seems here to be presenting an eschatology which would draw a distinction between *parousia* and last judgment.

be a mighty tempest."[6] He spoke of the punishments and now he speaks of God's splendor. "He will call to the heavens above and to the earth to judge his people,"[7] and by "the earth" he here means the whole human race. Then, counting the Jews along with every other race—for God pays a special heed to them—the prophet went on to say: "Gather together his holy ones to him, those in covenant with him in the matter of sacrifices, and the heavens will declare his righteousness, because God is Judge."[8]

(4) When Christ came, he would reject worship through sacrifices of animals and would refuse to permit such rituals. But he would accept this sacrifice of ours. Hear how the psalmist predicted this: "Sacrifice and oblation you did not desire, but you prepared for me a body."[9] For the new sacrifice would be established through his body and our obedience. This is why he said: "You prepared for me a body." And David declared this in another place when he said: "A people whom I knew not have served me. As soon as they heard, they obeyed me."[10] This means that they obeyed, not because they had seen the Red Sea divided nor the rocks split,[11] but because they listened to my apostles.

(5) Here [824] David says: "You prepared for me a body. Then I said, 'Behold I come; in the volume of the book it is written respecting me.'"[12] Two points become clear from this

---

[6] Cf. Ps 49(50).3.
[7] Cf. ibid. 4.
[8] Cf. ibid. 4–5.
[9] Cf. Ps 39(40).7. This LXX reading is quoted in Heb 10.5. See the following note.
[10] Cf. Ps 17(18).43–44 (LXX) or 44–45 (NAB). There is some similarity between these verses and Ps 39(40).6 (LXX) or 7 (NAB). In 39.6 sacrifice is not desired even from the chosen people; in 17.44 obedience is desired but it is not the chosen people who obey and serve him. The LXX does show a variant reading of "ears" for "a body" in 39.6. The NAB edition (40.7) reads: "Sacrifice or oblation you wished not, but ears open to obedience you gave me." That is, obedience is better than sacrifice. Heb 10.5 gives 39.6 (LXX) as Chrysostom quotes it; it applies the text to Christ, whose sacrifice of perfect obedience surpasses the liturgical sacrifices of the old Law.
[11] See above Chapter VII, n. 12.
[12] Cf. Ps 39(40).6–7 (LXX) or 7–8 (NAB). The Greek text is brief to the point of obscurity. Perhaps Chrysostom is merely contrasting "here" (i.e., Ps 39.6–7) to the psalmist's words in another place (i.e., Ps 17.43–44).

text.[13] First, he is to come after the sacrifices have been rejected. And this happened after the Jewish power passed over to the Roman rule. The second point is that, even before his coming, that coming was predicted.

(6) Where did Scripture foretell that he would come? We already said that Baruch spoke of Christ's coming. "He was seen on earth and moved among men."[14] And Moses said: "The Lord God will raise up to you, from among your brethren, a prophet like me; to him shall you hearken. And it will be that every soul that will not hearken to that prophet shall be destroyed from among his people."[15]

(7) Do you not see that this was fulfilled only in Christ and in no other? Surely many prophets did arise, and men disobeyed them all, but no one suffered for his disobedience. But because the Jews failed to heed Christ, they became vagabonds, lost, refugees who wander the world over in exile. See how they have been shut out of their commonwealth, their ancestral ways and laws, and go about disgraced, dishonored, punished, and avenged. I cannot even tell you what they suffered under Vespasian and Titus, because that tragedy of the Jews surpassed every disaster.[16] But it did fulfill what Moses had said: "Everyone who does not hear that prophet will be utterly destroyed."[17] Since they failed to listen to that prophet, Christ, everything they had was stripped bare and laid waste.

(8) Isaiah made it clear that Christ will raise up all men

---

[13] The difficulty continues because part of Ps 39.6 is omitted. Perhaps all of v. 6 should be in our Greek text, i.e., "whole burnt offerings and sacrifices for sin you did not require" should have been added to "You prepared for me a body." Then the two points Chrysostom mentions do become clear. The "volume of the book" is either the entire OT or the Mosaic Law. See T. Bird, CCHS 455, and W. Leonard, ibid. 1169 (on Heb 10.5). See also FOTC 68.184–85.

[14] Bar 3.38. This text was cited above II.2, where it was attributed to Jeremiah. For a discussion of the text see above, Chap. II, n. 2.

[15] Cf. Dt 18.18–19, but Chrysostom quotes the text almost as cited by Peter in Acts 3.22–23.

[16] For the war in Galilee and the destruction of the Judaean state under Vespasian and Titus see H. Graetz, *History of the Jews* (Philadelphia 1967) 2.272–320 (hereinafter referred to as Graetz).

[17] Cf. Dt 18.19 and Acts 3.23.

when he said: "The dead shall be raised up again, even those in the tombs shall be raised up. For the dew from you is healing for them."[18] That was not all. After his cross, after his slaughter, his glory will shine forth more brightly; after his resurrection, he will advance the message of his Gospel still more.

(9) He was bound, betrayed by an apostle, spat upon, outraged with insults, scourged, nailed to the cross, and, as far as the Jews were concerned, he did not deserve to be buried in a tomb. His executioners divided his garments. They suspected that he aspired to be a king, and he died for it. "For everyone who makes himself king, sets himself against Caesar."[19] They suspected him of blasphemy, and he died for it. "Behold, you have heard his blasphemy."[20]

(10) Even though he would undergo all these torments, he roused up those who would listen, he stirred them to courage by saying: "Do not be afraid because of these things which they did to me. I was crucified, I was scourged, I was outraged and insulted by robbers, I was arrested on suspicion of blasphemy and of being a king. But after my death and resurrection, people will look on my sufferings in such a way that no one will say that they were not filled with abundant value and honor."

(11) Certainly, this did come to pass. And a prophet predicted it long beforehand when he said: "There shall be the root of Jesse, even he who rises up to rule nations. In him nations will put their trust, and his resting place shall be glorious."[21] This kind of death is more glorious than a crown. Certainly, kings have laid aside their crowns and taken up the cross, the symbol of his death. On their purple robes is the cross, on their crowns is the cross, at their public prayers is the

---

[18] Cf. Is 26.19. This text is usually applied to the restoration of Israel in messianic times under the figure of the resurrection of the dead. See Ez 37.1–14; Dn 12.2; Hos 6.2; E. Power, CCHS 557. Chrysostom obviously refers it to the final resurrection.

[19] Jn 19.12.

[20] Mt 26.65.

[21] Is 11.10(LXX). See Rom 15.12 where part of the verse is quoted.

cross, on their weapons is the cross, on the sacred table of
their altar is the cross. Everywhere in the world, the cross
shines forth more brightly than the sun. "And his resting
place shall be glorious."[22]

[22] Cf. Is 11.10.

CHAPTER IX

Christ's Cross a Sign of Glory

(1) In human affairs things do not generally happen that way. Men of distinction [825] flourish while they are alive; after they die, their exploits are reduced to nothing. Anyone could see how true this is not only in the case of the wealthy and rulers but even in the case of the emperor himself. Their laws are abrogated, their images are obscured, people's memory of them is blotted out, their name is forgotten, those who enjoyed their favor are held in scorn. This is the lot even of those emperors who waged wars, of those who, by their nod, changed the conditions of peoples, cities, and affairs, of those who had the power to put men to death, of those who could give a reprieve to men on their way to execution. But all their great powers have perished despite the great honors shown to them while they were alive.

(2) With Christ it is quite the opposite. Before the cross, his situation was one of shame and dejection. Judas betrayed him,[1] Peter denied him,[2] the others fled.[3] He stood alone and was led off in the midst of his foes; many who had believed in him now deserted him. But after he had died on the cross, his situation was not destroyed but became brighter, more glorious, and more sublime. From this you may understand that the crucified one was no mere man.

(3) Before the crucifixion, the prince of the apostles did not endure the threat of a doorkeeper. After such an initiation as he had received, he said that he did not know the man.[4] But

---

[1] See, e.g., Lk 22.3–6; 47–49.
[2] See, e.g., ibid. 54–62.
[3] See Mt 26.56.
[4] See Jn 18.17 who gives the detail that the maid was a portress.

after the crucifixion, he traveled all over the world;[5] as a result of his travels and preaching, countless people died the death of martyrs because they chose to be slain rather than say what the prince of the apostles said when he was frightened by the threat of one doorkeeper who was a mere maidservant.

(4) The result of his travels and preaching was that every land and city, every desert and area where men dwell has joined us in preaching Christ crucified. Now we find on our side emperors and generals, princes and consuls, free men and slaves, private persons, the wise, the unlearned, and the barbarian; among every race of men and in every land over which the sun passes and shines, we hear his name and find him worshipped. From this you may understand what Isaiah meant when he said: "His resting place shall be glorious."[6]

(5) Although the place which received his slain body was very small and narrow, it is more venerable than royal palaces, and the emperors themselves hold his tomb in higher honor. "His resting place shall be glorious."[7] And this is true not only of his tomb but also of the tombs of his apostles. Those men who were dragged from one court of justice to another, who were bound in chains and treated with contempt, those who endured ten thousand torments in their lifetime, now that they have died, are held in higher honor than the emperors themselves.

(6) At Rome, the most imperial of cities, emperors, consuls, and generals put all else aside and hurried to the tombs of the fisherman and the tentmaker.[8] And in Constantinople, those who were crowned with royal diadems did not wish their bodies buried close to the apostles but outside the church, alongside the entrance. In this way, emperors became doorkeepers for the fishermen. Even in death, both the emperors

---

[5] The journeys of Peter, and his residence, martyrdom, and burial in Rome are well known to tradition. See McKenzie, DB 664.

[6] Is 11.10.

[7] Chrysostom has applied the "resting place" of Christ to the cross; now he applies it to his sepulcher (as it is translated in Challoner-Rheims in Is 11.10).

[8] The reference is, of course, to Peter, the fisherman (cf. Mt 4.18), and to Paul, the tentmaker (cf. Acts 18.3). Chrysostom speaks of the tombs of Peter

themselves and their children feel no disgrace in this but even consider it an honor.[9]

(7) As Isaiah said: "His resting place shall be glorious."[10] You will see how great this glory is when you have considered the symbol of his death, a death which was the most cursed and ignominious of all deaths. This kind of death was the only one subject to a curse. Let me give you an example. In ancient times, some malefactors were burned, others were stoned to death, and others ended their lives by some other kind of punishment. But the man who was nailed to a cross and was left hanging on its wood not only endured the harsh punishment to which he had been sentenced but [826] he was also subject to a curse. "Everyone who is hanged on a gibbet is accursed."[11] But that accursed, abominable symbol of the worst of punishments has now become an object of man's desire and love.

The Sign of the Cross Used Often and Everywhere

(8) No royal crown brings such honor to a man's head as does the cross, which is more precious than the entire world. Of old, all men shuddered at the sight of it; now all fight to get a representation of it. So we find these representations of it everywhere: among rulers and ruled, men and women, the married and unmarried, slaves and free. Everyone is constantly making the sign of the cross on the noblest part of his body. Each day people carry around this sign formed on their foreheads as if it were a trophy on a column.

---

and Paul at Rome in *Hom. in Rom.* 32.2 (PG 60.678–79). Quasten, 3.443–44, gives a translation of the passage.

[8] The church at Constantinople here referred to is the Church of the Holy Apostles. The emperors were buried in the portico of this church, which held the relics of Andrew, Luke, and Timothy. See Baur 2.52–53. Montfaucon, in his *Notice* (PG 48.811–12), thinks that Chrysostom here speaks of both Rome and Constantinople as a nonresident would. Hence, he argues that this *Demonstration* must belong to the period before Chrysostom left Antioch.

[10] Is 11.10. Again the "resting place" is the cross.

[11] Dt 21.23. These words are quoted in Gal 3.13 and there applied to Christ who "redeemed us from the curse of the Law, becoming a curse for us." Cf. FOTC 72.171 n.

(9) We see this sign shining forth on the sacred table, at the ordination of priests, and along with the body of Christ at the banquet of the mysteries.[12] Anyone could see a whole chorus of these signs of the cross in houses, in the market places, in the deserts, on the roadsides, on the mountains, in the glades, on the hills, at sea, on ships, on islands, on beds, on garments, on weapons, in bridal chambers, in banquet halls, on vases of gold, on gems, on wall paintings, on the bodies of sick animals, on the bodies of those possessed by demons, in wars, in peace, in the daytime and at night, at worldly festivals, among the groups of those enured to hardships.[13] All men vie in searching out this wondrous gift and this ineffable grace.

(10) No one is ashamed, no one hides his face because he thinks that this is a symbol of an accursed death.[14] Rather, we would all prefer to adorn ourselves with the cross than with crowns, or diadems, or necklaces of countless pearls. The cross is not to be shunned; everyone sees it as something to desire, to love, to seek with all eagerness. It gleams forth on every side, on the walls and roofs of houses, on books, in cities, in villages, in uninhabited places, and in places where men dwell. Now I would gladly ask the pagan how it happens that all men desire and seek with all eagerness this symbol of condemnation and an accursed death. The reason must be the great power of him who was crucified.

---

[12] The sacred table is the altar in the sanctuary which was adorned with the sign of the cross. For the custom of communicants signing their senses with the body and blood of Christ, see Cyril of Jerusalem, *Catechesis* 22.21–22 (PG 33.1124–25) and F. Dölger, "Das Segnen der Sinne mit der Eucharistie," *Antike und Christentum* 3 (1932):231–44. See also ACW 31.229–31.

[13] This may refer to groups of ascetics who practiced such austerities as the stylites, who lived on top of pillars. Simeon Stylites, the most famous of them, lived at Antioch (397?–459).

[14] See above note 11.

CHAPTER X

The Cross Is the Foundation of Many Blessings

(1) If you consider that this sign is nothing, if you still feel ashamed of the cross, if you will not confront the truth, if you are blinded in the face of the light, come and let me show you by another avenue of argument how strong this sign is. What kind of argument shall I now use? Those who pass judgment in court have many forms of punishment at their disposal. They have stocks and pillories, thongs, claws, lead-tipped scourges, instruments to tear the body, and racks to pull limbs from joints.[1]

(2) Who would choose to bring these instruments of torture into his home? Who would let himself touch the hand of the executioners who put these instruments to work? Who would let himself get close enough to look at them? Do not most men loathe these instruments? Do not some men shun them as bad omens and avoid touching them or looking at them? Do they not flee far away from them? Do they not turn away their eyes?

(3) The cross was such an instrument of torture in ancient times; indeed, it was more harsh and cruel than these. As I said before, it was not only the symbol of death; it was the symbol of an accursed death.[2] Tell me this. How is it that, today, all men seek after it so eagerly, find it so desirable, and consider it of greater value than all other things?

---

[1] Chrysostom speaks, in one of his baptismal instructions, of similar instruments of torture used on the martyrs. See ACW 31.111 and G. Racle, "A la source d'un passage de la VIIe catéchèse baptismale de S. Jean Chrysostome," *Vigiliae Christianae* 15 (1961): 46–53. Racle shows that the passage was shaped by Chrysostom's knowledge of the apocryphal 4 Mc.

[2] See above Chap. IX, nn. 11 and 14.

Everybody Seeks Relics of the True Cross

(4) How is it that everyone vies to get the very wood on which they put and nailed Christ's sacred body?[3] How is it that many people, both men and women, take a small piece of that cross, encase it in gold, and adorn themselves by hanging it around their necks? And they do this even though this wood was the symbol of condemnation and punishment. He who does all things [827] and transforms them, he who converted the world from such wicked ways and made a heaven out of earth, he took this thing, which was a sign of the deepest disgrace and the most shameful of deaths, and he raised it to a position higher than the heavens. Isaiah foresaw this and said: "His resting place shall be glorious."[4]

(5) For this symbol of death—and I shall not stop repeating this over and over again—became the foundation of many blessings, a wall to make us secure on every side, a timely trap to catch the devil, a rein to hold in check the demons, a muzzle against the power of our adversaries. This sign has destroyed death, this sign has shattered hell's gates of brass and crushed iron bars. It has destroyed the stronghold of the devil, it has cut the sinews of sin. The cross has rescued the whole world, which was lying under condemnation, and has rid us of the calamity which God was sending down upon our human nature.

(6) Nothing else has done such things. The divided waters of the Red Sea, the rocks which were split and gushed forth water, the air which changed into a column of cloud and a pillar of fire, the manna which was given to so many thousands for forty years, the Law, and the other wonders which were wrought both in the desert and in Palestine did none of these things.[5] But the cross can do them not only in a single nation but in the whole world seen by the sun. The cross had been the symbol of a curse; all men had held it in

---

[3] For the legendary story of how St. Helena, mother of the Emperor Constantine, found the true cross, see Eusebius, *Vita Constantini* 3.41–47 and H. Leclercq, "Hélène Impératrice" in DACL 6.2:2129–31.

[4] Is 11.10.

[5] See above VII.6 and ibid., n. 12.

dread and abomination; it had been the sign of the deepest shame. But after Christ died on it, the cross had the power to accomplish all this and with the greatest ease.

(7) Not only do these things show the strength of the cross but also other events which occurred thereafter. The world had been unproductive of any virtue; its condition was no better than that of a desert with no hope of producing any good. Suddenly the cross changed this desert into a garden and the mother of many children.[6] And the prophet made this clear long beforehand when he said: "Rejoice, you barren woman, who bear no children. Break forth with shouts of joy, you who suffer not the pangs of childbirth; for many more are the children of the desolate than of her who has a husband."[7]

(8) After he made the earth so fruitful, he gave it a Law which was far superior to the Old Law. The prophets did not veil this in silence but foretold it when they said: " 'I will make with them a new covenant, not according to the covenant which I made with their fathers on the day when I took them by the hand to lead them out of Egypt. Because they did not abide by this covenant of mine, I, too, took no care of them,' says the Lord. 'For this is the covenant which I will make with them and I will adapt my laws to their understanding and I shall write them on their hearts.' "[8]

(9) Then, in showing the rapidity of the change and the facility with which they would embrace Christ's teaching, the prophet went on to say: "And they shall no more teach every man his neighbor, and every man his brother, saying, 'Know the Lord' for all will know me from the least of them to the greatest of them."[9]

---

[6] That is, the Church. For the miraculous spread of the Gospel message, see below Chap. XIII.

[7] Is 54.1. Isaiah is referring to Jerusalem as the barren wife who finds herself with many children as the Jews return from exile. Gal 4.27 applies this text, as does Chrysostom, to the Church, the new Zion, the new covenant.

[8] Cf. Jer 31.31–33 (NAB) or 38.31–33 (LXX). This passage is quoted at length in Heb 8.8–12, in part in Heb 10.16–17 and Rom 11.27. See C. Lattey, CCHS 584; McKenzie, DB 423.

[9] Jer 31.34 (NAB) or 38.34 (LXX). See also Is 54.13.

(10) On his coming, Christ would also pardon all men their transgressions and no more remember their sins."[10] What could be clearer than this? By these predictions the prophet revealed the calling of the gentiles, the superiority of the New Law over the Old Law, the ease of access,[11] the grace possessed by those who have believed, and the gift given in baptism.

[10] Jer 31.34 (NAB) or 38.34 (LXX) possibly conflated with v. 33. In the LXX v. 33 reads in part: "For I will be merciful to their iniquities and no more remember their sins." But cf. Heb 8.12, 10.17, and Rom 11.27.
[11] See Rom 5.2; Eph 2.18; 3.12.

CHAPTER XI

Christ Will Judge All Men

(1) The same Christ who did all this will hereafter stand before us as our judge. Certainly the prophets did not pass over this but foretold it. Some [828] saw him in that very form in which he would stand before us; others predicted this only in words. Daniel was in the midst of the barbarians and Babylonians when he saw Christ coming in the clouds. Listen to what he said: "I beheld and lo! One like the Son of Man was coming on the clouds. And he advanced to the Ancient of Days and was presented before him; and to him was given the government and the kingdom, and all the peoples, tribes, and languages will serve him."[1]

(2) And Daniel hinted at God's court and judgment when he said: "The thrones were set and the books were opened. A river of fire rolled before him. Thousands upon thousands ministered to him and myriads waited on him."[2] [Daniel not only revealed that but he also showed the honor that the just

---

[1] Cf. Dn. 7.13–14. The chapter deals with Daniel's vision of the four beasts signifying the Babylonian empire, the kingdom of the Medes, Alexander's empire, and the Selucid dynasty. After the beasts are destroyed, a mysterious man comes from above, not as a successor to any of the heathen rulers, but as a universal sovereign whose power would be everlasting. The Ancient of Days is God, who sits in judgment. Some exegetes take the Son of Man in a collective sense (as each beast was a kingdom) and see in the expression the people of God, who will form his kingdom on earth. Others, along with Chrysostom, see in him the Messiah. This is not contrary to Jewish tradition. In the parables section (esp. chaps. 45–57) of the apocryphal Book of Enoch, there are numerous references to the Son of Man derived from Daniel and applicable to the Messiah alone. For Catholic exegesis the strongest argument for a messianic interpretation is that Christ appropriated to himself both the appellation and the royal prerogatives attributed to the Son of Man by Daniel. See McKenzie, DB 173; P. Saydon, CCHS 634–35; L. Hartman, JBC 26:28; NAB nn. on Dn 7.

[2] Cf. Dn 7.9–10, where it is God who sits as chief judge (the Ancient of Days), the fire symbolizing his judgment. The myriads of angels stand in

would have when he said: "He gave judgment to the holy ones of the Most High, and the holy ones possessed the kingdom."]³

(3) And that judgment will come through fire. Malachi said: "He is coming [like the fire of a refiner's furnace, and] like the soap of the fullers."⁴ And then the just will enjoy great honor. And Daniel was speaking of the resurrection when he said: "Those lying in the dust shall arise."⁵

(4) Do you see how precisely the prophets took up each point and predicted what was going to happen? How, then, do you still have the boldness to refuse to believe, even though you have been given such proofs of his power, even though you hear the words which foretold it so long beforehand, even though you see that events did occur to match the predictions and that everything which they foretold has been fulfilled to the last detail?

(5) These things are not figments of my imagination. As witnesses to prove this I give you the very men who were the first to receive the sacred books and who still preserve them. It is true that these men are our foes and the descendants of those who crucified Christ. But they still preserve these sacred books and guard them even to the present day.⁶ So I offer them to you as my witnesses.

---

attendance ready to execute his orders. Some of these details are also found in Ez 1. See Saydon, CCHS 633–34.

³ Cf. Dn 7.22. Neither the LXX nor the NAB mentions a judgment given to the holy ones, but the idea is quite apposite. The holy ones are those who serve and worship God and participate in his sanctity. Primarily it refers to the Israelites who will be freed from foreign domination, but the expression admits also of a wider application to all who will submit to God's sovereign rule. The LXX reads: "The holy ones of the Most High shall receive the kingdom and hold it forever and ever." See Saydon, ibid. 634. The bracketed words are found in PG 48 but are omitted from McKendrick's text and his basic MSS.

⁴ Cf. Mal 3.2. The same text is quoted somewhat differently above (Chapter VIII.1) but there, too, in a context of judgment. The bracketed words, omitted in McKendrick's text, are given in LXX and seem apposite.

⁵ Cf. Dn 12.2 and NAB n. ad loc. See L. Hartman, JBC 26:34. This text is the earliest clear enunciation of belief in the resurrection of the dead.

⁶ This shows that Chrysostom held all Jews responsible for Christ's death— a position no longer tenable after Vatican II—but that he realized their reverence for the OT since they preserved the sacred books in their synagogues. See *Adv. Iud.* I.5 (FOTC 68.19).

(6) It is a legitimate question to ask how they can have these books but have no faith in what they say. It is for the same reason that their fathers also refused to believe back in the days when Christ worked wonders and marvels for them. So we cannot put the blame on Christ, in whom they refused to believe; we must lay the blame at the doors of those men who refuse to see the truth in the sunlight of high noon.

(7) God put this world right before their eyes; it is an all-harmonious instrument; it lifts its voice on every side and proclaims him who created it. Still, some men say all things arose by themselves; some say the visible world had no creative origin; some ascribe the creation and governance of the universe to demons; others attribute them to fortune and fate, to a horoscope, or to the revolutions of the planets.[7] But this is not an accusation against the Creator; it is a charge against those who still lie sick and will die of their sickness even though there are efficacious drugs at their disposal to cure them.

(8) When a soul has the proper dispositions, it sees what has to be done and has no need of one remedy after the other to help it see. When a soul is ill-disposed and imperceptive, when it is preoccupied with countless calamities, it remains

[7] This is a difficult passage. The preceding paragraph seems aimed directly against contemporary Jews, who are just as blind, according to Chrysostom, as were their ancestors in the days of Christ. The present paragraph appears to have a wider application and to attack anyone who would follow any of what would seem to be three philosophies denying divine creation *ex nihilo*. Those who say that all things arose by themselves (*automata*) or that the visible world had no creative origin (*agennēta*) may well be neoplatonists, perhaps of the school of Plotinus. See P. Pistorius, *Plotinus and Neoplatonism* (Cambridge 1952) 66–71; A. Armstrong, *An Introduction to Ancient Philosophy* (Boston 1965) 195–96. Those who ascribe the creation and care of the universe to demons would probably be gnostics of one stamp or another. For the gnostic cosmogony see G. MacRae, "Gnosticism," NCE 6.525; for the authors and literature see Quasten 1, 254–77. The final group would all subscribe to one or another astral religion or kind of astrology, which was most common in Syria. See F. Grant, "Astral Religion", NCE 1. 985–86; H. Long, "Astrology," ibid. 986–88, and "Horoscopes," ibid. 7.151–52. For fortune and fate in their connection with astrology and magic, see F. Cumont, *Oriental Religions in Roman Paganism* (New York 1956) 195–96 and esp. 179 and 274 (n. 47, which gives sources).

blind to its duty, even though it has any number of teachers to take it by the hand and lead it to the truth. You certainly see that this happens everywhere, not only in this matter but in others as well.

(9) How many men are there who never heard of laws but who lived and died within the law? How many others were reared in these very laws from their earliest youth to extreme old age but never stopped transgressing them? This is what happened in the old days. For the Jews had the advantage of countless signs and marvels but did not become better men. The people of Niniveh heard the voice of one man, were quick to change, and freed themselves from their wickedness.[8] Anyone could see that this happens not only in the case of well-known men but also with the lowly and unknown. Judas had the advantage of all that instruction and still he became a traitor.[9] The thief had the advantage of only a few words of exhortation. Yet, on the cross, he admitted that Christ was God and proclaimed his kingdom.[10]

(10) You must not make your judgments and decisions about the facts by accepting the word of corrupt men. Take the truth of the facts and from that make the proper judgment about those who have resolved [829] to do what was right. The Jews refused to believe; the gentiles did believe. And this was not veiled over in silence. David predicted it when he said: "Strange children have been faithless to me. Strange children became old and limped away from their paths."[11] And Isaiah said: "O Lord, who has believed this report of ours, and to whom has the arm of the Lord been

[8] Cf. Mt 12.41; Lk 11.32. Jonah 3 shows how disposed God is to show love and mercy to all men, Jew and gentile, when they repent of their sins and implore his pardon. Cf. FOTC 72.112, 178.

[9] Cf. e.g., Lk 22.48.

[10] Cf. Lk 23.39–43.

[11] Cf. Ps 17(18) 45–46. Chrysostom obviously applies the psalmist's words to the Jews. But in Ps 17 David thanks God for rescuing him from all his enemies and from the hands of Saul. In vv. 44–46 David thanks God for bestowing on him dominion over many foreign people. The NAB text reads: "The foreigners fawned and cringed before me; they staggered forth from their fortresses." Verse 50 is quoted in Rom 15.9 as foretelling the conversion of the gentiles.

made manifest?"[12] And again: "I was found by them who sought me not; I became manifest to them who inquired not for me."[13]

(11) And at his coming, the Canaanite woman believed in him; the Samaritan woman believed in him.[14] But the priests and rulers waged war on him and plotted against him.[15] They debarred and expelled from the synagogues those who believed in him.[16] However, you must not let this surprise you. The life of us Christians is filled with many examples such as these, both in our day and in times long past. But apart from these examples, even if all the Jews did not believe in him, many did believe in the past and many do believe today. If all have not believed, it is neither strange nor unexpected, because their ingratitude is so great, their power to understand is so blind to reason, and their souls are so overwhelmed by their passions.

(12) I have been speaking about the predictions concerning Christ which the prophets proclaimed so many years ago. Let me now bring forward the prophecies which he gave while he was going about on earth and while he was living among men. And I bring them forward so that you may understand from them how great his power is. He came down to earth and

---

[12] Is 53.1 and see above VII.3 and n. 9. Jn 12.38 quotes the same text and Rom 10.16 gives the first half of the verse. In Isaiah this is a regretful confession that the Jewish contemporaries of the suffering servant neither believed the revelations of Yahweh about his servant nor perceived the manifestations of his power. See E. Power, *CCHS* 567. John cites it as a fulfillment of Isaiah's prediction of the incredulity of the people who witnessed Christ's signs and wonders. In Romans it is applied to those who heard the gospel but refused to believe.

[13] Cf. Is 65.1. Chrysostom inverts the clauses as found in the LXX but cites them as in Rom 10.20, where St. Paul abandons the literal sense and applies the text to the gentiles. In Isaiah, especially as the NAB text reads, it seems to mean that the rebellious Jews neither asked nor sought Yahweh, although he was always ready to help them.

[14] For the story of the Canaanite woman, see Mt 15.21–29; for the Samaritan woman, see Jn 4.6–26. The first incident takes place in the pagan district of Tyre and Sidon and involves a pagan; the second occurs against the background of the strong national hatred between Jews and Samaritans.

[15] Cf. e.g., Mt 16.21; Mk 8.31; Lk 9.22.

[16] Cf. Jn 9.22; 12.42; 16.2.

worked to achieve salvation both for men of his own day and for men of future ages. This he did in different ways. (13) Look at what he did. He worked miracles; he predicted things which would come to pass long afterwards. His miracles guaranteed to men who heard him in his own day that his predictions of what would happen a long time later were true. The fulfillment of his predictions proved to men of future ages that the miracles he worked in his own day were worthy of their belief. And by this double proof, he gave a guarantee that all he had said about his kingdom was true.

CHAPTER XII

Christ's Power Proved by His Own Predictions

(1) His predictions were of two kinds. Some are to be fulfilled in the present life; others will come true after the consummation of the world. But the first kind confirmed the second and gave abundant proof that the prophecies about the world to come are also true. Let me give you an example and, by that example, I shall try to clear up any obscurity in what I mean. When only twelve disciples followed him, neither the reality nor even the name of a Church occurred to anyone. The synagogue was still flourishing. Why, then, did he speak of the Church and predict it at a time when practically the whole world was in the grip of godlessness? "Upon this rock I shall build my Church, and the gates of hell shall not prevail against it."[1]

(2) Put this prediction of Christ to whatever test you wish and you will see that its truth shines brightly forth. For it is a marvel not only that he built the Church throughout the world but that he kept it unconquered even though it was harrassed by so many assaults. The words: "The gates of hell shall not prevail against it," mean the dangers which beget death, the dangers which lead us down to hell.[2]

---

[1] Mt 16.18. "Church" (*ekklēsia* in Greek and the usual LXX rendering of the Hebrew *qāhāl*, i.e., "religious assembly" or "congregation") is the new society of Christ's faithful answering to and supplanting the OT *qāhāl*. The only other place in the gospels where the word *ekklēsia* is found is in Mt 18.17. This society will rest on a rock (as did the house of the wise man of Mt 7.24). Chrysostom does not mention Peter as the rock but, of course, his point here is that Christ predicted the Church and that it will not be destroyed. See A. Jones, CCHS 881; J. McKenzie, JBC 43:114; NAB nn. ad loc.

[2] The NAB note on Mt 16.18 says the gates of hell are the hostile, evil powers whose aggressive force will struggle in vain against the Church. The term *gates* in Hebrew is often used for a fortified city itself (cf., e.g., Gn 22.17; 24.60; Is 14.31). *Hell* means not merely the place of the dead or death itself

(3) Do you not see that this prediction came true? Do you not see the strength of its fulfillment? Do you not see the words shining forth as proved in the light of the facts? Do you not see his invincible power which does all things with ease? Because the words are few—"I will build my Church"—do not simply pass over them. Ponder them in your mind. Think how great a thing it is to fill every land under the sun with so many Churches[3] in so short a time. Think what it means to have converted [830] so many nations, to have won over so many peoples, to have destroyed ancestral customs, to have torn out deep-rooted habits, to have driven out, like dust before the wind, the tyrannous rule of pleasure and the power and strength of evil. People have destroyed their old altars, temples, idols, and rites. They have destroyed their accursed festivals and made the unclean savor of victims disappear like smoke.

(4) They have raised up new altars everywhere, not only in the territory of the Romans but in the lands of the Persians, the Scythians, the Mauretanians, and the Indians. They have even raised up altars beyond the world we live in. The British Isles, which lie beyond this sea and are situated in the ocean itself, have felt the power of these words. For even there churches and altars have been built. That word which Christ spoke in his own day has been planted in the souls of all men and is found on the lips of all. It is just as if land that was filled with thorns has been cleansed and become a cleared field. And this field has received the seeds of godliness.

(5) This is a great thing, truly a great thing. Rather, it surpasses greatness and provides a proof of his divine power. Let us suppose that many men were disposed to work together,

---

(an idea which does not fit the warlike image) but the activity of the forces hostile to the cause of good. Hell is also the dwelling-place of demons. Cf. Rv (Apoc) 1.18; 6.8; 20.13,14. See A. Jones, CCHS 881 but also J. McKenzie, JBC 43:114 ad fin. Cf. above, Chap. IV, n. 35.

[3] No argument can be drawn from the plural "Churches" against the concept of one, holy, catholic, and apostolic Church. Chrysostom refers here to the Churches of Rome, Constantinople, Antioch, and others even beyond the civil jurisdiction of the Roman Empire, as is clear from the following paragraph.

and no one was inclined to oppose them. Even under such ideal circumstances, it would have been a great thing that a world as large as this could suddenly be set free from the wicked ways which had preoccupied it for so long a time; it would have been miraculous that it could change over to another and far more difficult way of life.

(6) For two tyrannical factors opposed this change: habit and pleasure. For many years their fathers, grandfathers, great grandfathers, their ancestors, their philosophers, and public speakers had given them a certain way of life. Yet people were persuaded to reject this, even though it was a difficult thing to do. They were also persuaded to accept a strange and very hard way of life which was introduced to replace their old ways. And this was a still more difficult thing to do.

(7) The new way drove them from luxurious living and led them to fasting; it drove them from the love of money and led them to poverty; it drove them from wanton ways and led them to temperance; it drove them away from anger and led them to mildness; it drove them away from envy and led them to kindliness; it drove them from the broad way and the wide street and led them onto a way which was narrow, strait, and steep, despite the fact that they were used to the wide road.

(8) For the Church did not take a different kind of human being who lived outside this world and its ways. It took those very men who had grown rotten here and who had become softer than mud; it told them to travel on the strait and narrow, the rough road of austerity. And it won them over to this way of life.

(9) How many did the Church win over? Not two, or ten, or twenty, or a hundred, but almost every man living under the sun. With whose help did it win them over? With the help of eleven men. And these men were unlettered, ignorant, ineloquent, undistinguished, and poor. They could not rely on the fame of their homelands, on any abundance of wealth, or strength of body, or glorious reputation, or illustrious ancestry. They were neither forceful nor clever in speech; they could make no parade of knowledge. They were fishermen

and tentmakers,[4] men of a foreign tongue. They did not speak the same language as those whom they won over to the faith. Their speech—I mean Hebrew—was strange and different from all others.[5] But it was with the help of these men that Christ founded this Church which reaches from one end of the world to the other.

[4] Cf. above, Chap IX, n. 8. The reference is at once specific and general. The trades mentioned are lowly ones; most of the eleven were fishermen, while Paul (who was not one of the eleven) was a tentmaker.

[5] This shows how Chrysostom, the rhetorician, can make good use of the argument from silence to strengthen his point that it took a more than human power to bring Christ's prediction to pass. Also, his readers or audience might have had little or no knowledge of the charismatic gift of tongues or, perhaps, would have paid it little credence if they did know. The apostles in all likelihood spoke Aramaic as their mother tongue. Paul, the tentmaker, as the best educated, also spoke Greek.

CHAPTER XIII

The Miraculous Spread of the Gospel Message

(1) And this is not the only wonderful thing. It was also marvellous that these few ignorant, poor, undistinguished, unlettered, worthless men of foreign tongue were entrusted with setting straight the whole world. They were commissioned to lead the world to live a far more difficult life and they did not accomplish this mission [831] at a time of peace but while countless wars were being stirred up against them from every side. And this was the case in every nation and every city.

(2) Did I say every nation and every city? In every home a war was fanned to flame against them. For when their teaching entered a home, many a time it split a son from his father, a bride from her mother-in-law, a brother from his brother, a servant from his master, a subject from his ruler, a man from his wife, a woman from her husband, and a father from his children.[1] For everybody did not all at once accept the faith. Their teaching was harrassed by hatred every day that passed; it stirred up one war after the other and brought death to more men than you could count; it had people avoiding one another as if they were common enemies and foes.

(3) For everybody drove the apostles out. Emperors avoided them, as did lesser rulers, common men, free and slave; whole peoples, entire cities shunned them. Not only did they drive out the apostles but, what is worse, they drove out those who were but newly fixed in their faith, those whom the apostles had instructed. It was one and the same war which

---

[1] Cf. Mt 10.35. See a similar passage in *Adv. Iud.* V.2 (FOTC 68.103).

was waged against the apostles and their disciples, because people saw that their teaching was opposed to the edicts of their emperors and their ancestral ways and customs.

(4) For the apostles exhorted people to keep away from idols, to scorn the altars at which their fathers and all their ancestors had worshipped, to stand aloof from the loathsome dogmas of their forebears, to ridicule their festivals, and to reject their rituals of initiation.[2] And those people used to think these pagan practices worthy of their deepest awe and fear. They would have laid down their lives for them rather than accept what the apostles said and believe in Mary's son, the Crucified. After all, had he not stood at the governor's tribunal, was he not covered with spittle, did he not suffer ten thousand torments, did he not endure an accursed death, was he not buried before he rose again?

(5) The strange and unexpected thing is that everybody knew about his sufferings: the scourging, the thorns driven into his temples, the outrage done to his person by those who spat on him, the blows with which they struck his face, the cross, the many men who scoffed at him, the comic drama staged for every eye, the tomb given to him only out of kindness. Everybody saw his sufferings, but this was not the case with the risen Christ. After he rose again, he appeared only to the disciples.

(6) Even though the apostles told so harsh a story, they still won people over to believe. This is how they built up the Church. How did they do it and by what means? They did it through the power of him who had commanded them to do it. He made ready the way; he made all the hard things easy. If it were not the power of God which accomplished this, the Church would not have had a preface, much less a beginning. How could all this be done?

---

[2] Chrysostom speaks of all these things as gone once the Church spread over the world. See below Chap. XV. But in apostolic times all these presented grave dangers. The first Council of Jerusalem sent a letter to the gentile brethren in Antioch, Syria, and Cilicia bidding them abstain from things sacrificed to idols (cf. Acts 15.23–29). Paul found Athens wholly given to idolatry (Acts 17.16) and had occasion to chide Romans (Rom 1.18–32),

(7) It was God who said: "Let there be heaven," and showed forth his work; it was God who said: "Let the earth be founded," and he produced its substance; it was God who said: "Let the sun shine," and he showed forth the star;[3] it was God who caused all things to be. And it was the same God who planted these Churches. And that word: "I will build my Church"[4] is what produced all this. For this is the power of the words of God. They create works which are wondrous beyond our expectation.

(8) God said: "Let the earth produce the grassy plant,"[5] and suddenly everything was a garden, everything became a meadow; the earth heard his command and plumed itself with plants beyond number. In the same way he later said: "I will build my Church,"[6] and this was done with the greatest ease.

(9) It is true that rulers armed themselves against the Church, soldiers wielded their weapons on it, whole peoples raged against it with a rage more violent than a conflagration. The Church had to face in battle the ranks of long-established customs; the public speakers, the teachers, the rich, the private citizens, the rulers all opposed it. But the word of God went forth more violently than a conflagration to consume the thorns; it cleansed and cleared the fields; it sowed the seed of the gospel message.

(10) It is also true that, from the ranks of those who be-

Corinthians (1 Cor 5.10–11; 8.1–13; 10.14; 19–21; 2 Cor 6.16), Galatians (Gal 5.19–21), Ephesians (Eph 5.5), and Colossians (Col 3.5) for idolatrous practices. He praised the Thessalonians for turning to God from idols (1 Thes 1.9).

[3] The *star* par excellence is the sun and is so used by Pindar, *Olympian Odes* 1,16 and in a spurious work attributed to Plato, *Definitiones* 411 b. Notice that Chrysostom is paraphrasing the creation account of Gn 1.1–8; 14–18.

[4] Mt 16.18. Christ, the Word, is identified with the Father in his creative word which produces wondrous works.

[5] Gn 1.11. Notice that implicit in the creation account is the repudiation of all polytheistic creeds. All God created was good and he made it beautiful even if man would mar this beauty by his wicked ways.

[6] Mt 16.18 Christ's creative word not only produces the Church but restores beauty to the earth, despite the wickedness of man, by clearing from its fields the thorns of evil.

lieved, some were imprisoned, some exiled, some had their possessions confiscated, some [832] were taken away and cut to pieces, some were given over to the flames, some were drowned in the sea. They endured every form of punishment, they were dishonored, they were driven off, they were hunted out on every side, as if they were common enemies.

(11) But it is also the truth that others came forward in greater numbers. And these were just as ready to suffer despite what the others had undergone. In fact, they were all the more eager and even rushed to meet those who were out to capture them; they saw their arrest as a noble thing. So they were not caught in the nets because they were forced or carried off by violence; they ran into the nets and were grateful to those who were hunting them. When they saw the blood gushing in streams from those who had already embraced the faith, they became themselves more courageous and fervent for the faith.

(12) And this was true not only of the apostles and of their disciples. Some were shackled, some were driven into exile, some were scourged, some were subjected to countless other torments. But other disciples came forward in greater numbers and with a deeper fervor. It was Paul who exclaimed: "So that the greater number of the brethren in the Lord, gaining courage from my chains, have dared to speak the word more freely and without fear."[7]

(13) Again, in another place, Paul said: "For you have become imitators of the churches of God which are in Judaea, in that you also have suffered the same things from your countrymen as they have from the Jews,[8] who both killed the Lord and hinder us from speaking to the gentiles, that they may be saved."[9] In writing to the Hebrews, he again had this to say:

[7] Cf. Phil 1.14. Paul's sufferings, as did the martyrs', increased the courage of the majority of Christians. The blood of martyrs is the seed and strength of Christians.

[8] Cf. Acts 17.5–9. The Judaean persecutions may be those referred to in Acts 8.1–3; 9.1–2; 12.1. See B. Orchard, CCHS 1139.

[9] Cf. 1 Thes 2.14–16. This outburst against the Jews, paralleled nowhere else in Paul, may have been evoked by their earlier opposition to his work at

"But call to mind the days gone by, in which, after you had been enlightened, you endured a great conflict of sufferings, knowing that you have a better possession in heaven, and a lasting one."[10]

(14) Do you see the surpassing power of Christ who effected these results? The Hebrews were undergoing great sufferings but they did not lose heart nor were they distressed. They were even rejoicing and jumping for joy. Paul spoke these words to his disciples because they had joyfully accepted the confiscation of their property.[11] In the book of Acts, Luke was speaking about the apostles who taught the Hebrews when he said: "They came away from the presence of the Sanhedrin rejoicing that they had been counted worthy to suffer disgrace for the name of Christ."[12]

(15) Again, Paul was speaking of himself when he said: "I rejoice now in my sufferings; and what is lacking in the sufferings of Christ I fill up in my flesh."[13] And why do you wonder that he rejoiced in his sufferings when he not only rejoiced as he was on his way to endure death but even called upon his disciples to share his joy? And this was the mark of an exceedingly joyous soul. For he said: "I am glad and re-

---

Thessalonica (cf. Acts 17.1–9) and Beroea (ibid. 13–14) which prevented him from preaching salvation to the pagan world.

[10] Cf. Heb 10.32,34.

[11] Cf. ibid. 34. Strangely Chrysostom omitted from his quotation of this verse words which would have been most apposite to his present point, viz.: "For you both have had compassion on those in prison and have joyfully accepted the plundering of your own goods."

[12] Cf. Acts 5.41. The apostles were Peter and John.

[13] Cf. Col 1.24. Again the point is joy in suffering, but the text itself is difficult. The sufferings are either those which Christ endured or those of his Mystical Body, the Church. Not even Paul could add to the first, which are infinite, although the application of Christ's merits to individual souls involves a toll of suffering, especially on the part of Christ's chosen ministers (cf. 1 Cor 3.9). Since Paul's sufferings are in union with Christ's, they convey Christ's merits to men and thus bring an external completeness to his passion (cf. 2 Cor 1.5; 4.10; Phil 3.10). If the sufferings are those of his Mystical Body, the passion of Christ is continued in the members of his Body, the Church. Both interpretations have defenders. The latter fits in with the concept that the Church is, in a real though mystical sense, Christ himself. See D. Leahy, CCHS 1135; J. Grassi, JBC 55:19.

joice with all of you. And in the same way do you also be glad and rejoice with me."[14] And what happened, tell me, to fill him with such great joy? "As for me, I am already being poured out in sacrifice, and the time of my deliverance is at hand."[15]

[14] Cf. Phil 2.17–18.

[15] 2 Tm 4.6. "Poured out," i.e., as a libation. Cf. Phil 2.17 (first part of verse) which reads: "But even if I am made the libation for the sacrifice and service of your faith," where the Philippians are the priests, their faith is the animal to be sacrificed on the altar, and Paul's life blood is poured out as a libation. In 2 Tm 4.6 Paul, in prison and abandoned by almost all his companions, is reflecting on his approaching martyrdom and the reward it will bring (v. 8.).

CHAPTER XIV

Christ's Power Worked Through His Disciples

(1) It was in this way that they founded the Church throughout the world. But no man could have built a single wall if he were stopped or driven away while he was trying to put together a structure of stone or stucco. Yet these men founded so many churches all over the world at the same time that they and their disciples were being slain, imprisoned, hunted down, exiled, and plundered of their property. Their persecutors scourged them, cut their throats, burned them, or drowned them in the sea.

(2) And they did a far more difficult thing than build a church from stones. They built all these churches out of souls and principles, and not with stones. They took souls which demons had driven to frenzy for many years. They won those souls over to free themselves of the demons, to stand aloof from that madness, and to come over to a life of great temperance. And this is a far greater thing than putting together a wall from stones.

(3) And they were still able to do this although they went about the whole world poorly clad, without shoes, having only a single garment. For [833] they had as their ally to assist them in the fight the invincible power of him who said: "Upon this rock I will build my Church, and the gates of hell shall not prevail against it."[1] Count up how many rulers from that time drew up their lines of battle against the Church; count up how many persecutions they started and how severe these persecutions were. Consider the situation of the faith during all that time when it was newly planted and when the minds of men were all too weak.

[1] Mt 16.18.

CHAPTER XV

All the Emperors Vainly Persecuted the Christians

(1) The emperors were pagans. Augustus, Tiberius, Gaius, Nero, Vespasian, Titus and all his successors were pagans, down to the time of the blessed Emperor Constantine. All the pagan emperors waged war against the Church. Some were less harsh, others were more severe, but all waged their wars against it.

(2) Some emperors, it seemed, did leave the Church undisturbed. But they were emperors and obviously pagans and ungodly men. These very facts caused a constant threat of war since other men would ingratiate themselves with the emperors and prove their loyalty by a war against the Church. Yes, men did plot against the Church. But all their plots and assaults were torn asunder more easily than a spider's web, they were dispersed more swiftly than smoke, they passed over with no more strength than a cloud of dust. Still, these plots did produce many martyrs. But they left the Church treasures that will never perish, columns that will always stand, towers that no force can take by storm. In death as in life, these martyrs have become a source of strength and assistance to those of a later age.

(3) Do you see the power of his prediction? "And the gates of hell shall not prevail against it."[1] Let these words give you faith for the future. Believe that no one will ever get the upper hand over the Church. There was a time when it consisted of only a few men, when it seemed to be an innovation and a novelty. There was a time when the seed of its teaching was newly planted, when there were so many wars and such great battles burst into flame from every side. But these conflicts could do nothing nor did they get the upper hand.

[1] Ibid. See above, Chap. XII, nn. 1 and 2.

(4) This is all the more true now that the Church has spread over the entire world, every place, mountain, glade, and hill. It has made itself master over land and sea and every nation under the sun. Even if ungodliness still holds sway among a few people, the altars, the temples, the idols, and all such pagan things are gone. Gone, too, are the festivals, the rituals of initiation, the smoke, the savor, and the accursed assemblies.[2]

(5) The Church is great and has spread over the world. Since there were so many obstacles to hinder its progress, how did it have such a glorious outcome, an outcome which bears testimony to its truth? Only through the divine and invincible power of him who foretold these things and then brought them to accomplishment. No one would contradict this unless he be crazy, out of his senses, and deprived of the right use of his reason.

(6) These are not his only predictions; there are other things which he also foretold. And all of these things proclaim his invincible power. For he truly foretold things which would come to pass and then he did bring them to accomplishment. It is impossible that any word he spoke should fail to come true. It is easier for heaven and earth to pass away than for any of his words or predictions to be proved false. He made this very fact clear, even before the events came to their outcome, and he spoke very clearly about his own words when he said: "Heaven and earth will pass away but my words will not pass away."[3]

(7) And this was very reasonable. For his words are not mere words; they are the words of God, and such words create works. This is the way God made the heavens, this is the way God made the earth, this is the way he made the sea,

---

[2] See above, Chap. XIII, n. 2.

[3] Mt 24.35. Chrysostom is making a point of the power and necessity of Christ's words. The text itself may mean that the old order will pass and yield to the new messianic era (cf. Mt 19.28–29). Possibly 24.35 (like 5.18) is parenthetical and has no reference to the reward symbolized in 19.28 but points out that Christ's words (i.e. his doctrine in general) are more stable than the physical universe. See A. Jones, CCHS 861 (on 5.18); 886 (on 19.28–29); 896 (on 24.35).

this is the way he made the sun, this is the way he made the choirs of angels, this is the way he made the other invisible powers. And the prophet made this clear when he said: "He spoke and they were produced; he commanded and they were created."[4]

(8) And the psalmist was speaking about all creation together. He spoke of the creation above and below, of the creation perceived by the senses and by the mind, of bodily creatures and those without bodies. As I said before, Christ's prediction about the Church [834] showed forth the greatness, the scope, and the loftiness of his truth, of his providence, of his goodness, and of his solicitude.

[4] Cf. Ps 148.5 (LXX). Cf. also NAB n. on Ps 148.

CHAPTER XVI

Christ's Prediction on the Temple

(1) Come, now, and let me deal with another prophetic utterance which shines forth more clearly than the sun and which is brighter than its rays. It is a prophecy which lies before every man's eyes and extends, as did the last, to generations yet to come. This is the case with most of the things he foretold. They are not limited to a short time nor do they come to fulfillment in a single generation. They are for all men—for those now alive, for those who will soon come to birth, for those who will follow them. Just as did the previous prediction, these prophecies offer the power of their own truth to all men right up to the consummation of the world.

(2) For certainly the previous prediction has stood and will stand firm and unshaken from the day it was spoken until the day when the world will end. It has flourished, shone forth, grown, and become stronger with each passing day. It led men to greater power and provided those who would live from that time until the day when Christ will come again with the opportunity to enjoy the greatest blessings and to benefit from an aid beyond description.

(3) For men of the age before ours, and those before them, and those of a still earlier time knew the power of this prediction. They saw the wars which came upon the Church, they saw the troubles, the tumults, the waves, and the storms. But they saw that the Church was not drowned in the sea, it was not conquered, it was not vanquished, nor was it consumed by fire. Rather, they saw that the Church flourished and raised itself to greater heights. And the prediction of which I am now going to tell you is such that it will also prove the power and truth of his words.

(4) What is this prediction? One day he entered the Jewish temple area, which at that time was flourishing. On every side

its magnificent structures shone with gold and beauty. No
expense had been spared on its workmanship or materials.
His disciples were amazed. But what did he say to them? "Do
you see all these things? Amen I say to you, there will not be
left here one stone upon another."[1] He was revealing the future destruction of the temple, the utter ruin, the desolation,
the wreckage which now exists in Jerusalem. For all those
glorious and splendid buildings are now in ruins.

(5) Do you see in both these things his great power and how
it defies description? First, he built up and exalted those who
paid him worship. Then, he humiliated, destroyed, and uprooted those who had offended him. Never before had the
temple been so famous and glorious; never did it enjoy such
ceremonies and worship. In those old days, Jews living all
over the world and at the very ends of the earth used to come
there. They brought their gifts, their sacrifices, their offerings, their firstfruits, and many other contributions. They
beautified the temple with the wealth of the world. Jewish
converts streamed in there from every land. The fame of the
temple was great and well-known to the ends of the earth.

(6) But a single word from the lips of Christ destroyed this
temple, obliterated it, swept it from sight like so much dust.
Not all Jews could enter its sanctuary, nor even all the priests.
Only the high priest could enter it, and he could do this only
once a year while wearing the sanctuary robe, tiara, the mi-
ter, and the rest of the vestments.[2] Now, anybody can walk in,
whether the person be a whore-chaser, an effeminate, a harlot, or an adulterer. And there is no one to stop him. For when

---

[1] Mt 24.2. Not only would the temple be abandoned by God but it would be
completely destroyed. Actually this was the temple started under Zerubbabel
in 537 B.C., but Herod had begun to remodel and enlarge it in 20 B.C., and
the work would not be completed until A.D. 64. But even at the time of
Christ's prediction it must have been a magnificent spectacle. See Mk 13.1–2;
Lk 21.5–6; Graetz 2.109–111. This temple was destroyed in 70 A.D. The
whole chapter in Mt is difficult because it superimposes several themes: the
ruin of the temple, the destruction of Jerusalem, the end of the Judaic age
and ritual, the *parousia*, and the end of the world. See A. Jones, CCHS 893–
94; NAB note on Mk 13; J. McKenzie, JBC 43: 164–72. Chrysostom's interest
here, however, is in the power of Christ's prediction.

[2] For the sanctuary, priests, vestments, etc., see FOTC 68.158–69; J. Hues-
man, JBC 3: 69–86; R. Faley, ibid. 4:5–22; E. Power, CCHS 225–26.

Christ uttered that word, it destroyed and obliterated the whole temple. Only enough of the temple remains to show where it once stood.

The Jews Could Not Restore the Temple

(7) Consider how great is the power to which this points. This was a nation of men who were once strong enough to win out over other [835] nations and kings, who often carried the day without shedding a drop of blood, men who set up new and wonderful trophies beyond number to mark their triumphs.[3] Yet from that day to this, these people could not build a single temple, even though there were so many emperors who were ready to help them, even though there were so many fellow Jews scattered all over the world, and even though such financial resources were available to them.

(8) But do you see how no one has destroyed what Christ built and how no one has rebuilt what Christ has destroyed? For Christ built the Church, and no one could destroy it; Christ destroyed the temple, and no one has been able to raise it up again, even over so long a period of time. Many have tried to destroy the Church but they did not have the power to do so. Even though many were eager and tried to raise up the temple again, they could not do so.

Julian the Apostate Tried but Failed to Rebuild the Temple

(9) But God let them try so that no one could ever say that, if they had tried, they could have rebuilt it. Look how they did try and how they could do nothing! In our own generation, the emperor who surpassed all emperors in godlessness, during his reign, authorized the rebuilding of the temple.[4] But

---

[3] Many such exploits are told in the historical books of the OT. For one of these incidents see *Adv. Iud.* VI.3 (FOTC 68.157–58) and DB 357–59, s.v., "Hezekiah;" 786, s.v., "Sennacherib."

[4] Julian was emperor from 361 to 363. For his relationship with the Jews see J. Bidez, *La vie de l'empereur Julien* (Paris 1930) 305–309. On the attempted rebuilding of the temple see *Adv. Iud.* V.11 (FOTC 68.136–40). For an account from the Jewish point of view see Graetz 2.597–601. Cf. also Wilken, 131–32; 134–41; 153–58.

little progress could be made on its construction because flames came leaping forth from the foundation stones and drove all the workmen away.[5]

(10) The foundation stones lie bare to this day and provide proof that the Jews wanted to rebuild the temple. You see where they tried to dig the trench for the foundation. But they could not raise the structure because Christ's prophecy was working against them. Yet that temple had once before been destroyed and, when they returned from the seventy years' exile, it was immediately rebuilt.[6] The new temple shone forth with greater glory than the old. And the prophets had said this and foretold it before it came to pass.[7] But four hundred years have now passed,[8] and there is no thought, no expectation, no hope that anyone will ever see the temple again.

(11) And yet what was to stop the Jews from rebuilding it if the divine power was not at work resisting their efforts? Did they not have a great abundance of wealth? Did not the patriarch[9] collect tribute from Jews all over the world? Did he not possess limitless treasure? Were the Jews not a reckless nation? Were they not a shameless, contentious, rash, and rebellious people? Were there not large numbers of them in Palestine, in Phoenicia, everywhere?

[5] Graetz 2.600, gives a natural explanation for this phenomenon. Gases, long compressed in subterranean passages beneath the old temple, were suddenly released, came into contact with the air above, ignited, and caused repeated explosions and fires, which drove the workmen away. Cf. FOTC 68.139.

[6] The rebuilding after the captivity in Babylon was started in 537 B.C., under the leadership of Zerubbabel, and the work was completed in 515 B.C. See Graetz 1.356–59; E. Power, CCHS 93–94.

[7] Ezechiel (chaps. 40–47) describes (in a vision) the new temple. Zec. 6.11–12 (in the NAB text) even mentions that it will be rebuilt under Zerubbabel. See NAB n. ad loc.

[8] Chrysostom's chronology is faulty; he overestimates the interval by more than a century. Titus had destroyed the temple in A.D. 70. Some fifty years later Hadrian gave permission for a new temple on a different site, but the Jews saw this as temporizing on Hadrian's part and refused to rebuild. See Graetz, 2.401–403. For the failure to rebuild the temple under Julian see ibid. 597–601 and above, n. 4. Graetz, ibid. further maintains that the Jews were not interested in rebuilding it and expected the restoration of their former magnificence only at the appearance of their Messiah.

[9] Under the Emperor Severus Alexander (A.D. 222–35) the Patriarch

(12) How is it, then, that they could not build a single temple, especially since they saw that, with no temple, Jews were shackled and constrained from their worship all over the world? Did they not see that their customary ritual had disappeared? Did they not see that their sacrifices, offerings, and other religious rites which the Law prescribed had been destroyed and ceased to exist? For the Jews were not permitted to erect an altar, nor offer sacrifice, nor pour libations, nor immolate the sacrificial lamb, nor offer incense, nor read the Law, nor celebrate any festival, nor do any other thing connected with their ritual and worship unless they were within the precincts of the temple.[10]

Judah II began the practice of drawing revenues (called the Patriarch's tax) from the Jewish communities. See Graetz, ibid. 486–87. Emperor Julian called the Patriarch Hillel his venerable friend and assured him of his help and good-will in an autograph letter, although in another letter addressed to the Jewish congregation, he said he had asked Hillel to stop the Patriarch's tax. See Graetz, ibid. 597–98; Downey, *History of Antioch* 382, says that the authenticity of Julian's letter to the Jews is disputed. Graetz, ibid. 599, says that later Christian reports (which he calls "purely fictitious") told how women sold their jewelry, and distant communities forwarded sums of money to restore the temple, but that none of this was necessary since Julian had amply provided both materials and workmen.

[10] Chrysostom will explain the importance of the temple for the Jewish ritual in the next chapter. Actually there was another temple, built by the high priest Onias IV (154–52 B.C.) near Heliopolis in Egypt. Sacrifices were offered, perhaps illegally, in this temple, which was closed by Vespasian about the same time that Titus destroyed the temple in Jerusalem, thus taking from the Jews both focal points for worship. See Graetz, 2.318. Graetz, 1.508–510, discusses the temple of Onias and says that if Judaea had at that time been enjoying peace and prosperity, this innovation would have been resented and an interdict would have been laid upon Onias's temple, as had been done upon the temple on Mount Gerizim in Samaria (ibid. 2.8). The Egyptian-Judaean congregation would have been excluded from the community, as were the Samaritans. Later, when the divine service had been restored in Jerusalem, the Jews of the mother country regretted the existence of a temple in a foreign land, and the uncompromisingly pious party "never could forget that its existence was in violation of the Law." But by that time the Egyptian temple had become firmly established.

CHAPTER XVII

The Temple Could Not Be Rebuilt

(1) Even when they were exiles in Babylon, and their captors were trying to force them to sing a sacred hymn, they neither yielded nor obeyed, even though they were captives and slaves to the masters who had conquered them. They had been driven from their homeland and had lost their freedom. They risked their very lives since they were caught, as it were, in the net of their captors' grip.

(2) Yet, when they were ordered to play their harps and sing a sacred [836] canticle, they said: "By the rivers of Babylon[1] there we sat down and wept. For they who had captured us asked of us the words of a song, and they who had carried us away asked for a hymn. 'Sing for us one of the songs of Zion.' How can we sing the song of the Lord in a strange country?"[2] And no one can say they refused to sing because they had no harps. They made their reason for refusing quite clear when they said: "How can we sing the song of the Lord in a strange country?" Furthermore, they did have their harps with them. In the same psalm David said: "Upon the willows in the midst of them we hung up our harps."[3]

(3) And they could not observe the fast. The prophet made this clear when he said: "'Did you keep a fast for me for seventy years?' said the Lord."[4] Nor could they offer sacrifice

---

[1] The rivers are the Tigris and the Euphrates and the numerous irrigation canals which branched off from them.
[2] Cf. Ps 136 (137).1,3,4. This is the only psalm which unmistakably speaks of the Babylonian captivity.
[3] Cf. ibid. v.2.
[4] Cf. Zec 7.5. The context in Zec 7 is that the question was raised whether, now that the temple was being rebuilt (after the Babylonian captivity), one must still observe the day of mourning over its destruction. The prophet's

or pour libations. Listen to the three boys when they said: "We have no prince, prophet, or leader, no place to offer firstfruits in your sight and find mercy."[5] The prophet did not say: "We have no priest," because there were priests among the captives. But to make you understand that the whole matter was a question of the place and that the whole code of laws was bound up with that place, he said: "We have no place."

(4) And why do I speak of offering sacrifice and libations? They were not even allowed to read the Law. Another prophet charged them with doing this at one time when he said: "They read the Law in a foreign land and called for a profession of faith."[6] They could not celebrate the Pasch, Pentecost, the feast of Tabernacles, or any other festival of their nation.[7] They knew that the desolation of the place shut them off from all these observances. They knew that they

---

answer, quoting the Lord, is in the form of a question which asks whether they had observed the prescribed fasts for God while in Babylon. A negative answer was expected, as is clear from the next verse: "And though you ate and drank, did you not eat and drink for yourselves?" Therefore, they had not kept the fasts during the captivity, but this is not to say that they should not have done so. Chrysostom uses this same text in Adv. Iud. IV.5 (FOTC 68.85) and there, too, he implies that the Jews were forbidden to fast during the captivity in Babylon.

[5] Dn 3.38. Again the same text is used in the same way in Adv. Iud. IV.5 (FOTC 68.85) to show the importance of Jerusalem and the temple to Jewish ritual. The whole section of Dn 3.24–90 (which treats of the deliverance of Shadrach, Meshach, and Abednego) is not in the Massoretic text (see McKenzie, DB 880) but is found in the LXX, the Greek translation from a Hebrew or Aramaic original now lost. The Church has always regarded this section as an inspired part of the canonical Scripture. Vv. 37–40 describe the miserable condition of the exiles. They had none to govern them, no prophets, no temple, no liturgical service to propitiate God. They hoped their offering of a contrite heart would have the same propitiatory effect as the Levitical sacrifices. See P. Saydon, CCHS 628; L. Hartman, JBC 26:8.

[6] Cf. Am 4.5. The Greek exō has been translated "in a foreign land" (which seems to be Chrysostom's sense) but could also mean "publicly." The LXX reading is quite different from the NAB edition and the Jerusalem Bible. All three, however, are clearly ironical in tone and call the Jews to task for thinking that the Lord will overlook their evil lives if they do not fail in the sedulous performance of ritual—which is quite far from Chrysostom's use of the text. See M. Leahy, CCHS 662; NAB n. on 4.4.

[7] For the Pasch or Passover, see McKenzie, DB 643–44; for Pentecost (fifty

could never attempt to practice any of the rites without violating the Law, without paying the penalty for trying to offer worship in the wrong place.[8]

(5) Despite all this, they still could not raise up a temple and restore the place in which they would be allowed to observe all these rituals according to the Law. For the power of Christ, the power which founded the Church, has also destroyed that place. The prophet foretold that Christ would come and that he would do these things, even though he would not come until after the captivity.

(6) Listen to what the prophet said: "By you the doors will be shut and a fire will not be kindled on my altar for nothing. I have no pleasure in you. For from the risings of the sun to its goings down my name has been glorified among the nations, and in every place incense is offered to me, and a pure sacrifice."[9] Do you see how clear it is that God has rejected Judaism? Do you see how clear it is that God has made known the shining glory of Christianity and has revealed how it would reach to the ends of the earth?

(7) Another prophet again made clear the way God would be worshipped. "They shall each adore him in his own place and serve him under one yoke."[10] And again another prophet said: "The virgin of Israel has fallen. Never more shall she rise."[11] And Daniel explained clearly that everything would be destroyed—the sacrifice, the libation, the anointing, the judg-

---

days after Passover), a harvest festival which also marked the giving of the Law to Moses, see ibid. 657–58; for the feast of Tabernacles, ibid. 863–64.

[8] For the importance of the place see *Adv. Iud.* IV.4 (FOTC 68.82–84).

[9] Cf. Mal 1.10,11. The imperfect sacrifices insincerely offered by the people of Judah are displeasing to God. The word *for* shows that the universal and pure sacrifice is to replace the existing Jewish sacrifices. God will rather take pleasure in the offerings of the gentile nations throughout the world which anticipate the pure offering in messianic times, the universal sacrifice of the Mass. See E. Sutcliffe, CCHS 703; C. Stuhlmueller, JBC 23:63; FOTC 68.141.

[10] Cf. Zep 3.9 conflated with 2.11. See above VI.9 and n. 10.

[11] Cf. Am 5.2. Amos, in prophecy, utters a dirge over fallen Israel as if it were already ruined. See M. Leahy, CCHS 662; P. King, JBC 14:17.

ment.[12] When I shall speak against the Jews, I will give a clearer and fuller explanation of these things.[13]

(8) Meanwhile let me keep to the path I have set for myself and correct the stubborn and senseless pagans. I did not speak to you of the dead who were brought back to life or of the lepers who were made clean. Why? So that you will not say: "Those are lies, empty boasts, fairy tales. Who saw these things? Who heard them?" The very same ones who reported that he was crucified by the Jews, that he was spat upon, that he was scourged, that he was struck on the head with blows. These are the same ones who told about men restored to life and cleansed of their leprosy.

(9) Why, then, do you consider them as trustworthy witnesses of Christ's passion and death but, in the matter of miracles, why do you regard them as imposters who reported those events although [837] they never happened? Certainly, if their purpose in writing about the miracles were to make idle and empty boasts for their master's sake, they would have remained silent about the gloomy side and the events which the majority of men would think of as shameful and ignominious. But they wanted to prove that his miracles were true. This is why they spent so much time describing his sufferings and death. Their account of these was lengthy and accurate; they passed over no detail, great or small. But they

---

[12] The reference is probably to Dn 9.25–27 which is discussed in *Adv. Iud.* V. 10 (FOTC 68.132–35). These verses present many difficulties. The Vulgate gives a translation based on an interpretation by St. Jerome which is followed in Challoner-Rheims; the NAB text differs considerably from Challoner-Rheims and the Jerusalem Bible. All differ from the LXX, and Chrysostom quotes this inaccurately in *Adv. Iud.* The point here, however, is clear: the Jewish priesthood, ritual, and temple are to be destroyed and disappear. See P. Saydon, CCHS 637–39; L. Hartman, JBC 26:30–31.

[13] This statement presents another grave problem. Is this promise fulfilled? Williams (135–36) says it is not and that this probably explains the incompleteness and abrupt ending of the *Demonstration* as we have it. Montfaucon, in his *Notice* to *Adv. Iud.* (PG 48.839), not only quotes this promise but goes on to say that Chrysostom kept his promise when he proved at length that the Jewish ritual had been rejected and destroyed in *Adv. Iud.* IV–VIII (FOTC 68.71–241) the argument from Daniel's prophecy is especially pursued, he says, in the fifth discourse.

did omit most of the details connected with the signs and wonders. All the evangelists spent time on his sufferings; all the things which people regarded as shameful they accurately reported.

(10) And I had nothing to say about these signs and wonders so that I might stop up every shameless mouth. I took what you see today, what lies before your very eyes, what is clearer than sunlight, what has spread over the whole world and taken root in every land. I took a success which far surpasses any merely human power, a success which could only be the work of God, and I brought this forward as my proof. What do you say now? Did he not bring the dead back to life?

(11) Can you say there are no churches throughout the world? Can you say that no one ever plotted war and destruction against them? Can you say that these Christians have not prevailed and conquered their foes? Of course you cannot say these things. To deny them is just like denying that the sun exists.

(12) And what [838] about this? Do you not see the desolation of the Jewish temple which lies before the eyes of the entire world? Why do you not reason this way with yourself? If Christ were not God, if he were not a mighty God, how could those who worship him have grown to such great numbers despite such suffering and persecution? And how could those who beat him and crucified him have been so humbled that they were driven out of their whole commonwealth and way of life? Now they go about as vagabonds, wanderers, and exiles. And no length of time has changed the status of either the Christians or the Jews.

(13) And yet these very people—I mean the Jews—took upon themselves to wage war against the Roman Empire. They continued their resistance to Rome for a long time, won some battles, and caused no small trouble for the emperors of those times. Yes, the power of the Jews was considerable. These Jews resisted many emperors in battles, they possessed strength in manpower and weapons, they harrassed many generals, but they could not rebuild a single temple. They did

build synagogues in many cities. But there was only one place which had given them the security of their own commonwealth and way of life, one place where they were accustomed to observe their rituals and ceremonies, one place which welded Judaism together. And this one place they could not rebuild.[14]

[14] Notice the abrupt ending which argues strongly to the incompleteness of the *Demonstration*. See above, Introduction, paragraphs 5, 57, 59, 62.

INDICES

GENERAL INDEX TO DISCOURSE ON BLESSED BABYLAS AND AGAINST THE GREEKS

INDEX OF HOLY SCRIPTURE TO
DISCOURSE ON BLESSED BABYLAS
AND AGAINST THE GREEKS

The numbers to the right of chapter and verse citations refer to pages of Bab.
*Numbers in italics indicate Scriptural
allusions. Numbers in roman type indicate Scriptural quotations.*

GENERAL INDEX TO DEMONSTRATION
AGAINST THE PAGANS
THAT CHRIST IS GOD

INDEX OF HOLY SCRIPTURE TO DEMONSTRATION AGAINST THE PAGANS THAT CHRIST IS GOD